1991

Gender
and Genius

Gender and Genius

Towards a Feminist Aesthetics

Christine Battersby

INDIANA UNIVERSITY PRESS

Bloomington and Indianapolis

First published by The Women's Press Limited, London, 1989

The paper used in this publication meets the minimum requirements of
American Standard for Information Sciences—Permanence of
Paper for Printed Library Materials, ANSI Z39.48-1984. $\otimes$™

Manufactured in the United States of America.

Library of Congress Cataloging-in-Publication Data

Battersby, Christine
    Gender and genius : towards a new feminist aesthetics / Christine
Battersby.
      p.   m.
    "First published by the Women's Press Limited, London, 1989"—T.p.
verso.
    Includes bibliographical references.
    ISBN 0-253-31126-8 (alk. paper). — ISBN 0-253-20578-6 (pbk. :
alk. paper)
    1. Creation (Literary, artistic, etc.) 2. Genius. 3. Feminism—
Philosophy. 4. Aesthetics, Modern. 5. Romanticism. I. Title.
BH301.C84B37   1990
111'.85'082—dc20   89–46346
                                                      CIP

Contents

Acknowledgments

It was during 1984 that I wrote a first draft of roughly half this book. After I returned to my job teaching Philosophy at the University of Warwick, it was two and a half years before I could obtain the additional study-leave that I required to complete the project. During this interim period – aware that my subject-matter had forced me to venture outside my field of competence – I used friends, colleagues, students, and a variety of societies and conferences, as a testing-ground for these chapters. I would like to thank here all those whose criticisms and arguments helped transform that early manuscript. I received so much feedback that I can thank by name only those who made the most extensive contributions: John Fletcher for his methodological queries; Cyril Barrett for his translation of medieval Latin and his comments on Christian history; Barbara Caine for her acute, perceptive and always encouraging criticisms.

It was Barbara Caine also who helped me restructure the second draft of the manuscript. That was during 1988 when – feeling satisfied with a text that, I supposed, required only minor revisions – I had to face up to the fact that the book had not worked. I still do not understand how she managed to make utterly devastating objections function as constructive suggestions. My debt to her is immense, as it is to Ruth Kimber, my editor at The Women's Press, who also helped me to see how to put things right . . . and who offered unflagging support as I worked through the third version of this text. I would also like to thank Paulina Palmer, who acted as an additional reader at this stage. She was an ideal critic: sympathetic, but picking out key political and critical details that I had glossed over too lightly. Obviously, the mistakes that remain – and there will be mistakes in a work of this scope – are entirely my responsibility.

I took my initial manuscript to a feminist – rather than to an academic – publishing house, because I wanted to force myself to take risks. I knew that my conclusions would be important for *all* creative women . . . not merely for those working inside the academies. I also knew that I could easily lose confidence in my ability to synthesise facts into conclusions if I thought of my audience as a collection of over-scholarly readers. I would, therefore, also like to thank Ros de Lanerolle at The Women's Press for sharing the risk . . . and for believing that I would (eventually) find a way of making abstruse metaphysical and aesthetic theories accessible to a non-specialist audience. I hope the difficulties that I have experienced in writing this book translate into ease of reading it. Thanks are also due to Deborah Sugg of the National Art Library,

viii   Victoria and Albert Museum, for her invaluable help with the artist
Hannah Höch; to those who attended the Saturday meetings of the
Women's Studies Group, 1600–1825, and whose own interests helped
me to keep up the momentum; to the University of Warwick for my
paid and unpaid leave; to friends not mentioned above, especially
Eliani, and Dick and Jaki Smith, who provided hospitality and humour.

Finally, I would like to thank the feminist historians, literary and art
critics, philosophers, anthropologists and theologians, whose combined
endeavours over the last twenty years have made this book possible. If I
do not always make my own allegiances clear in the body of the text, this
is because I see feminist scholarship as a *collective* venture in which even
false paths can lead to a ground-breaking advance. Thus, my criticisms
of other feminist theorists should not be read as implying that there is
no merit in their alternative positions. Nor should my comments be
construed as pessimism about the current state of feminist inquiry. On
the contrary, I find it remarkable that in two short decades we should
have progressed so far in the task of re-thinking the role that women
can and have played in Western culture.

In order to keep the text as readable as possible, I have used a
minimum of footnotes. Where the date of the first appearance, or of
the first relevant edition, of a work is enclosed within square brackets,
full details of my source can be found in the Bibliography.

Acknowledgments

1
Starting Out

It was by accident that I first got involved in researching the subject of genius. As an undergraduate studying both Philosophy and Literature, I had read theories about what it is that makes an author a genius. When I enrolled as a graduate student, however, I had no intention of studying this question in any direct way. I had wanted to concentrate on the German Romantic philosophers. The notion of genius was deeply embedded in their writings, so I knew that I could not avoid the topic entirely. What I didn't know was that I would end up studying not the Romantics themselves, but 'genius'. Nor could I have guessed how central this research would come to be in my own life . . . or that it would be nearly fifteen years before I could start to write about it. It took me that long to see that the muddle I had got into as a graduate student required a feminist solution.

My undergraduate degree had left me fascinated by the influence of Immanuel Kant (1724–1804) on Romantic philosophers and literary theorists. After I graduated I spent a year fruitlessly studying Kant in Germany, and an even more pointless period working in London on Arts Administration. It was only then that I decided to return to a British university to sign up for an MA, which I hoped to turn into a Ph.D. What I wanted was a degree course that would enable me to keep up both my philosophical and literary interests. Needless to say, at that time no such course existed. As a compromise I decided to opt for something then called grandly and pretentiously 'History of Ideas'. And I picked a university that offered a course on the nineteenth-century German Romantics.

Imagine how let down I felt when I rolled up at the university in the first week to discover that this particular course was not going to be on offer! I debated transferring back to Philosophy, but remembered (after a few classes) why this was a bad idea. Back I went to the History of Ideas programme to try and salvage a coherent set of courses from the ones on offer. I was persuaded that a course on the eighteenth century would be a suitable prelude to the Romantics. And 'History of Taste' seemed vaguely relevant to the topics in aesthetic theory that I wanted to work on. I then looked round for a Ph.D. topic that linked the four fields: Kant, Romanticism, taste, and the eighteenth century. Given the Romantics' obsession with the problem of 'genius', and the hundreds of eighteenth-century texts that bandied the term around, this seemed an obvious choice. Of course, what I overlooked was that thousands of scholars before me seemed to have reached the same conclusion.

2   Thus it was that I came to spend the early years of the 1970s living in the eighteenth century. After about five years there I gave up the project, deciding that there was nothing interesting to say on the subject that had not already been said. I eventually wrote my Ph.D., quite quickly, on a very different eighteenth-century topic. Looking back, I wonder how I could have been so blind. The way that generations of scholars, creative writers and critics have given a male gender to genius is a field still almost entirely unexplored – then it was quite unmuddied by scholars' footsteps. Yet the amount of material requiring research is so enormous, and so central to our culture's conception of the 'female' and the 'feminine', that it is not possible for any one person to exhaust it. Even if I had restricted my study to the eighteenth century (as I intended at the time), there was more than enough there for a Ph.D. thesis. Now, writing this book, I am only too aware of the mass of material I haven't got the space, time or (sometimes) the expertise even to touch upon. Yet, when I looked as a graduate student, I could see nothing. How could this have happened?

In the 1970s I read an enormous amount of material in an attempt to narrow down the topic for research. Most of it was eighteenth century; but I also dabbled in nineteenth- and twentieth-century texts in order to think about influences and to clarify my own confused ideas. The eighteenth century has been called 'The Age of Reason'. But this is to misunderstand that secular century. The dominant concern of the age was to discover the *limits* of reason. As the Christian Church declined in authority, old truths about man were undermined. Thinkers started to doubt that man had been created in the image of God in order to rule the Universe through the exercise of his reason. Or, rather, they started to look around for naturalistic explanations for the superiority of man over the animals. And, as information about other cultures and other peoples started to trickle through, writers started to speculate about whether or not European man *was* at the pinnacle of all natural development. The eighteenth-century man of letters was obsessed with discovering what made a civilised man different from – better than – an animal or a savage.

By the end of the eighteenth century, reason was looking pretty sick. Aristotle had defined man as 'a rational animal', and that view had been incorporated into Christian teaching. But by 1800 there was a general agreement that it was not reason – at least not reason alone – that made a man more than an animal. Man was special in that he had feelings, imagination, sensibility and 'genius'. 'Genius' was an ambiguous word. At the start of the eighteenth century it meant the special and unique talents that all (or most) individuals possess. By the end of the century, it had come to be closely linked to human creativity. It was creativity, not reason or talent, that made man resemble a god . . . made him more than an animal, and made some men superhuman and superior to others. This special spark of divinity was confined to *some few* individuals. The élitist way of talking about genius became a commonplace of the nineteenth century, and was dominant up to the Second World War.

Gender and Genius

It was genius that was evoked to explain the difference between civilised man and both animals and savages. It was genius that was supposed to make the 'Art' (with a capital 'A') that European civilisation produced different from the 'crafts' (with a small 'c') produced by primitives and other lesser human types. It was genius that made Poetry different from verse; Science different from industry or technology; Music more than mere tune, harmony and rhythm. Genius was the bedrock of European culture. Even great political leaders and military men were credited with genius. Napoleon (and later Bismarck) came to embody genius by symbolising the dream of a Europe constructed across the boundaries of smaller states and countries. Genius was the flame of divine omnipotence that inspired European man and European culture. Through their reverence for genius, even those thinkers who rejected God kept the essentials of the old Christian framework. Inside the human frame Christians had hidden an immortal 'soul'; now 'genius' was concealed within the chest of European man.

But what does 'man' mean in that last sentence? Does it, or does it not, include woman? Because many of the qualities praised by the advocates of genius included stereotypically 'feminine' characteristics (intuition, emotion, imagination, etc.), I failed to notice a new rhetoric of exclusion that developed in the eighteenth century, and which gradually grew louder as the nineteenth century progressed. This rhetoric praised 'feminine' qualities in male creators . . . but claimed females could not – or should not – create. To buttress the man/animal, civilised/savage division, the category of genius had to work by a process of exclusion. The non-genius was always described as lacking some quality or qualities: a lack that made his or her output valueless. The descriptions of these deficiencies contradicted each other, but were used to explain the differences between civilised European man and animals, primitives, children . . . and women. The genius was *like* an animal, a primitive, a child or a woman; but, of course, this likeness was deceptive.

The genius's instinct, emotion, sensibility, intuition, imagination – even his madnesses – were different from those of ordinary mortals. The psychology of woman was used as a foil to genius: to show what merely apes genius. Biological femaleness mimics the psychological femininity of the true genius. Romanticism, which started out by opening a window of opportunity for creative women, developed a phraseology of cultural apartheid . . . with women amongst the categories counted as not-fully-human. The genius was a male – full of 'virile' energy – who *transcended* his biology: if the male genius was 'feminine' this merely proved his cultural superiority. Creativity was displaced *male* procreativity: male sexuality made sublime. Females, however, were represented either as lacking sexual drive, or as incapable of resisting their sexuality. The creative woman was an anomaly that simply introduced complications into the patterns of exclusion. A woman who created was faced with a double bind: either to surrender her sexuality (becoming not *masculine*, but a surrogate *male*), or to be *feminine* and *female*, and hence to fail to count as a genius. This is the logic behind Goncourt's epigram, quoted so approvingly by Cesare Lombroso in *The Man of Genius* [1863]:

Starting Out

4   'there are no women of genius; the women of genius are men' [p. 138].

As a graduate student I noticed none of this. Or, rather, I *did* notice it, but didn't register it. It seems extraordinary now; but neither did any of the other scholars whose works I looked at whilst working for my Ph.D. In all that reading (literally hundreds of books), I can remember no single study that critically explored the gendering of genius. Even books profoundly hostile to the 'ideology', the 'élitism' or the 'cultural bias' of genius ignored the sexual bias. Of course, I might have found it easier to see that bias had the standard accounts of the origin of the word explained that the term 'genius' derived from the worship of the most sacred aspects of male procreativity amongst the ancient Romans. But nobody made this clear. The textbooks suggested that the history of the *word* 'genius' was not really relevant to the history of our present notion of genius. In any case, potted histories of the term told me that the Romans believed that a *genius* was a guardian spirit that watched over every man from birth to death. Some of the texts mentioned the splitting of the *genius* in two: into a good *genius* and an evil *genius*. Some also mentioned that worship of the *genius* originated in family cults that invoked household spirits or gods. Further than that the texts rarely went. That 'every man' meant only 'every male' was utterly obscured. Years later I was astonished to discover this limitation.

But, of course, I noticed (subliminally) the sexual prejudices inherent in the eighteenth- and nineteenth-century comments on genius. I remember reading out loud and laughing with a friend about the way that geniuses were standardly described as 'sublime', and then the sublime was linked to male power, to size, to strength . . . even sometimes quite explicitly to the sexuality of males. I also remember an afternoon spent reading Schopenhauer's essay 'On Women' [1851] to the most beautiful and imaginative woman that I knew, and being astonished when she said she agreed with him. (This was only partly to be explained by the fact that she misheard me. She thought he had called woman 'the anaesthetic sex', instead of 'the unaesthetic sex'. We laughed ourselves silly over that, too!) I can't plead ignorance – either of the material or of feminism. The latter splattered into my life towards the end of 1968 when a group of German women disrupted the starry-eyed unity of the German Left in a hail of tomatoes and eggs. Although this (sticky) beginning left me at first confused rather than committed, I was still interested enough a few years later to go to the first British Feminist Conference at Ruskin. And that was during the time I was doing my graduate research into genius.

I knew the score. But I couldn't read the figures written so clearly on the pages in my hands. Why not? What excuse have I got? It is true that the eighteenth century was by no means as hostile to women of genius as the nineteenth. But that does not mean that misogyny was absent from the texts I was looking at. I decided to focus my thesis around the Scottish aestheticians, including William Duff whose *Essay on Original Genius* [1767] and *Critical Observations* [1770] made genius a matter of strong imagination and lively passions. In terms of previous stereotypes

Gender and Genius

of woman's nature, genius was, consequently, quintessentially 'feminine'. I never even guessed at the existence of Duff's *Letters on the Intellectual and Moral Character of Women* [1807], in which he quite explicitly argued that women can't be great geniuses. Significantly, none of the (quite extensive) secondary literature on Duff's aesthetics hinted at the importance of this book.

As a graduate student I overlooked the gendering of genius out of a comfortable (and unexamined) optimism. I believed that what was written about women two hundred years ago should not occupy me unduly. Hadn't the situation for creative women improved since then in a slow, but steady way? . . . It had not . . . Obviously, there has been progress. But it has been neither constant nor consistent. The nineteenth-century rhetoric of genius fed upon (and gave new life to) an earlier tradition of writing about sex difference that condemned women to cultural and biological inferiority. The genius view of art acted as a deterrent to female ambition in the arts, and in some ways even caused a deterioration in the position of creative women. Because we still operate within the broad framework of Romantic assumptions about creativity, feminists do not always see how damaging Romanticism was for women. In 'Double Focus' (1983), for example, Sigrid Weigel argues that Romanticism helped increase the number of female authors by encouraging poetic expressiveness. Romanticism, it seems, enabled women to develop a female language of experience [in Ecker, 1985, pp.67–8]. But did Romanticism help women? My account of history will suggest that this view of the past is far too simple.

Social and ideological changes certainly enabled many hundreds of women to take up the pen or the paintbrush. But these statistical improvements started before Romanticism became the dominant European aesthetics, and were already well under way in the eighteenth century. We often overlook this. When we read that the eighteenth-century novel was a 'female' genre, we suppose that this was because it was mainly women who were novel-readers. They were. But they were authors, too. Indeed, it has been estimated that by the second half of that century the majority of novels published in England were by women [Halsband, 1976, p.55]. We can't know how accurate this calculation is, since male Grub-Street writers sometimes signed their work 'By a Lady', or published under female pseudonyms. But such disguises prove that, within certain restricted fields, being a woman was becoming the norm for an author.

As women started to compete with the men for artistic recognition, two things began to happen. Firstly, institutional doors were slammed in women's faces. Angelica Kauffman and Mary Moser had been amongst the founder members of the Royal Academy of Arts in England in 1768. Both were respected and celebrated painters: Moser mainly of flowers and decorative pieces, and Kauffman of historical and allegorical subjects. They were barred from life-classes for painting the nude, and excluded by implication from the audience of 'gentlemen' addressed by Sir Joshua Reynolds' inaugural lectures. Nevertheless, two

Starting Out

eighteenth-century women were honoured by the establishment for their artistic achievements. After their deaths, however, it was not until 1922 that women were again admitted as members of the Royal Academy. In Scotland it was 1952 before a woman was elected to the Royal Scottish Academy.

Despite its praise for 'feminine' aspects of creativity, the aesthetics of Romanticism was of little help in re-opening such institutional doors. For, indeed, the second thing that happened amongst the nineteenth-century artistic, literary and musical fraternities was that the rhetoric that debarred women from culture became more prevalent. Genius, apparently, required a penis. Indeed, the more psychically feminine genius appeared, the louder the shout that went up: 'It's a boy!' Women, it was maintained, had procreative and domestic duties that would take all their (limited) energy. I had thought that the misogyny of some prominent Romantics was no more than a historical accident. But I was wrong. Romanticism relies on a logic of exclusion. For the Romantics the figure of the genius was used to distinguish between the work of Art (appreciated by an élite group of critics) and works produced for popular consumption by the masses. In the nineteenth century the masses and popular culture were given a female gender; high culture was envisaged as the culture of males [Huyssen, 1986]. This meant a continual blotting out of the contributions of women artists. Romanticism turned the artist into a demi-god: the genius. Woman, by contrast, became simply 'Other'. The occasional female creator could be countenanced; but being a creator and a truly feminine female were deemed to be in conflict.

None of this interested me as a graduate student. I did not recognise how closely intertwined were the vocabularies of aesthetic praise and those of sexual difference. One of the things I *did* notice, however, was that an unusually large number of twentieth-century scholars and academics who had written on the subject of genius were women. Although I would guess that many of these sensed that there is something very fishy about the language of genius – something elusively wrong, that requires historical analysis – none of them managed to bring the sexual apartheid into focus. Until feminist theory began to disentangle the category of the 'female' (the biologically given) from the 'feminine' (the culturally moulded), the gendering of genius remained unexplored. I know that being part of a crowd is no real excuse; but it does indicate how intractable this material is for any woman who examines it.

Like most other scholarly women in our culture, I had grown used to blanking out questions of gender while reading books. My childhood addiction to novels fostered a type of reading that involved a complete identification of myself with the main character in the story. But very few of the books I most admired – even books by female novelists – sketched women that seemed to be at all like me, either in terms of moods or experience. I found many of the male characters, on the other hand, quite compelling. A woman who reads a lot has to learn a

Gender and Genius

process of not noticing sexual difference. When gender became so intrusive that noticing it was unavoidable, I would laugh – and by laughing refuse to confront the issue head on. By the time I was a Ph.D. student I treated myself not as a woman-academic; but as *either* an academic *or* a woman, as *either* a neutered reader *or* a woman. Never both at once. No wonder I looked away (or simply giggled) when I noticed that the writers wrote of the typical genius in terms appropriate to the typical male.

None of this excuses my failure to realise the signficance of what I was seeing, noticing, and even recording. But perhaps, at least, it starts to explain it. What was needed was a Gestalt-shift. And this did not come until many years later. The change only came when, in my head, I abandoned the academic persona that always stood between me and the texts I read, and which made me simply laugh at male (and female) absurdities about sex. It was like suddenly seeing through a new pair of glasses. The material I had painstakingly assembled years before, and put aside, suddenly fell into a distressingly consistent shape. Like the shadow of some giant penis of truly eighteenth-century proportions.

In the last few years feminist art and literary critics have helped to pick out that shadowy shape. But the full story of gender bias in the concept of genius will have to be told by many different voices. The rhetoric of genius operates to exclude women on so many different and contradic-tory levels that it is hard for any one woman to synthesise what she finds. It is hard to think through the implications of the fact that 'feminine' – generally used as a sneer-word in reference to art-works by *women* – takes on much more positive connotations when applied to *males*. The myth of the bisexual androgyne might have been integral to the Romantics' account of true genius; but – as Virginia Woolf noted in *A Room of One's Own* [1929, p.102] – when a writer like Coleridge insisted that the mind of the great artist is androgynous, he certainly did not mean that such a mind has any special sympathy with women. Nor did he mean that a great creative artist is female. His advice to young authors (with their wives and sisters) in Chapter 11 of *Biographia Literaria* [1817] makes that abundantly clear. The Romantics' andro-gyne has male genital organs; it is only his soul that is 'feminine'.

As Jung's comments on creativity illustrate, talk of the 'femininity' and 'androgyny' of creative genius often serves to exclude the biologically female:

Just as a man brings forth his work as a complete creation out of his inner feminine nature, so the inner masculine side of a woman brings forth creative seeds which have the power to fertilize the feminine side of the man. [Jung, 1945, §336, p.207; emphasis added]

The great artist is a *feminine male*. Although Jung allows women an inner 'masculine' self – bound up with what he calls the *'logos spermatikos'* ('the spermatic word') – he insists that a woman's creativity reaches only as far as *inspiring* a man to productive activity (loc. cit.). This is because her masculine self (a woman's 'animus') is but 'a quasi-intellectual factor

8   best described by the word "prejudice" . . . an inferior Logos, a caricature of the differentiated masculine mind'. [1957, §60, p.41]. Thus, the
mind of a male *benefits* from the emotion, the moodiness and love that
Jung associated with his inner femininity. By contrast, the masculine
woman merely *parodies* the male Logos: a term that Jung glosses as
'knowledge', 'clarifying light', 'discrimination', 'detachment' – with that
which makes a human being a sublime and god-like creator (loc. cit.).

In this book I offer a history of the concept and the word 'genius',
showing the explicit and implicit gender bias in both. Starting from the
persistence of sexual prejudice in art and literary criticism today, I
move back in time to explore the way that our modern notions of
creativity are modelled on notions of a male God creating the universe,
and the devious tricks used to represent all creative and procreative
power as the attribute of males. I give the origins of the term *genius* in
ancient Rome, show its connections with the ancient Stoic doctrine of
the *logos spermatikos*, and explore the evolution of these notions in the
Middle Ages, together with classical (Aristotelian) accounts of sex difference. The Romantics' exclusion of women from culture is revealed
as a re-working of older forms of sexual apartheid. Romanticism re-
cycled a number of ancient myths that portrayed woman as outside
culture, as alien and 'Other' . . . despite the fact that Aristotelian
explanations of what it was that made females inferior to males had
broken down during the opening years of the Industrial Revolution.

Woman's inferiority had been rationalised by the writers in the Aristotelian tradition as a deficiency in judgement, wit, reason, skill, talent
and psychic (and bodily) heat. Women had been blamed for an excess
of passion, imagination, sexual needs and for vapour-inspired delusion
and irrationality. But if we look at the aesthetic literature of the late
eighteenth century, we will see that the greatest *males* (the natural
'geniuses') were being praised for qualities of mind that seem *prima facie*
identical with Aristotelian femininity. I discuss the new qualitative
distinctions that were developed, that used different types of passion,
imagination, frenzy and irrationality to account for the difference
between geniuses and females. A man with genius was *like a woman* . . .
but was *not a woman*.

The distinction between *ordinary* males and females continued to be
represented in broadly Aristotelian terms – as a type of superior
rationality. But the revalued 'feminine' qualities of mind were appropriated for a *supermale* sex. The resulting confusion between the categories of 'male', 'female', 'masculine' and 'feminine' still affects the way
that we think now about sexual difference and about cultural achievement. I will indicate how psychoanalytic theory continued to bind
culture and civilisation to the sexual energies of males. And, since
Freud and Lacan are current influences on feminist theory, I also argue
that feminist criticism of the arts has been adversely affected by the
slippage between 'femininity' and 'femaleness'. It has not been generally recognised that it was 'femaleness' – and not 'femininity' – that was
consistently downgraded in our culture. As a consequence, some

Gender and Genius

feminists are now arguing for a kind of psychic bisexuality that favours *males* in the history of culture. Other feminists are insisting that the coincidence of the 'feminine' and the 'female' implies that there is no possibility of a positive *female* aesthetic. I hope this book will reveal why both these positions are wrong.

In *Old Mistresses* [1981] – a book to which I am enormously indebted, despite my criticisms – Rozsika Parker and Griselda Pollock show quite conclusively that the paradigm genius is male; but they also write as if genius is always non-feminine. They confuse the categories of 'female' and 'feminine' when they write:

It thus becomes clear why there is not a female equivalent to the reverential term 'Old Master'. The term artist not only had become equated with masculinity and masculine social roles – the Bohemian, for instance – but notions of greatness – 'genius' – too had become the exclusive attribute of the male sex . . . The phrase 'woman artist' does not describe an artist of the female sex, but a kind of artist that is distinct and clearly different from the great artist. The term 'woman', superficially a label for one of two sexes, becomes synonymous with the social and psychological structures of 'femininity'. [p.114]

Parker and Pollock have fallen prey to the extraordinary difficulties that women face when confronted with a rhetoric that praises 'femininity' in *males*.[1]

Although my account of history seems to make the difficulties facing women creators more extreme even than those revealed by *Old Mistresses*, my approach is more fundamentally optimistic than the one presented there. Parker and Pollock push the concepts of 'woman' and of 'femininity' together, and then argue that . . .

Women's sense of self, their subjectivity, is not to be understood as a matter of social conditioning, for it is determined by the structures of the unconscious. These are based on the impact of sexual difference, the meanings attributed to sexual difference in our culture, and the way in which the lack of the phallus is represented to women. [p.132]

They go on to put forward a basically Lacanian theory which represents woman as Other and as a kind of cultural absence. 'Feminine' means merely 'not masculine': it has no positive significance, and merely indicates a psychic lack. Consequently, 'within the present organisation of sexual difference which underpins patriarchal culture, there is no possibility of simply conjuring up and asserting a positive and alternative set of meanings for women.' [pp.132–3]

For Parker and Pollock there is thus no distinctively female perspective on art: a feminist aesthetics has to accept the values of a patriarchal society, and merely deconstruct these standards from within. This is a task of limited effectiveness, since woman is ruled by her unconscious which has been moulded by a patriarchal value-system that represents a woman as a deficient man. There are a number of puzzles, however, with Parker and Pollock's version of their own feminist aims. For one thing, they claim that there is no positive female way of reading symbolic significances, but in practice their own analyses of women's paintings

Starting Out

and sculptures help establish just such a positive alternative. Similarly, although Pollock dismisses the whole ideology of genius as 'élitist', and as therefore hostile to the 'democratic impulse of the Women's Movement', she contributes to the establishment of an alternative canon of great, individual female artists [1987, p.84]. If we disentangle issues of femininity from issues of being biologically female, we can begin to provide a rationale for such practices.

What follows from my insistence that femininity has only been represented as bad in inferior human types? Why does it matter that, whereas ordinary males have been blamed for effeminacy, in (male) geniuses femininity has been transformed into a virtue? I hope this book will make clear how women have been presented with contradictory evaluative norms against which to measure their attainments. The logical (and illogical) tensions between the different ideals of maleness, masculinity and femininity mean that women are not always fated (via the culturally determined unconscious) to have a uniform vision of themselves as lacking. Women adopt a double perspective on themselves . . . and on males. From one of these perspectives it is males who are lacking (or excessive), and women who provide the norm and perfection. Women will always have to manipulate our society's presentation of themselves as Other; but they are not continuously trapped by that perspective into seeing themselves as Other. Nor are they the cultural non-entities that the equation of genius with maleness would suggest. A feminist aesthetics is one that exposes the prejudice that represents the female as lacking, seeks to show how we can escape it . . . and then goes on to trace matrilineal traditions of cultural achievement. A feminist aesthetics interests itself in *female*, not feminine, genius.

The Romantics supposed that to call somebody a genius is to *describe* a type of creative personality. But this was to dress up *evaluation* as description. A genius is judged valuable in terms of what s/he added to the traditions of art and to the history of culture. But until very recently we used male standards – in fact the standards of Romanticism – to decide what is and is not culturally valuable. The traditions of great art or great literature were constituted out of a series of individuals who were judged to have succeeded. As Gombrich put it in the first two sentences of his popular *The Story of Art:* 'There really is no such thing as Art. There are only artists' [1950, p.4]. This notion of art might be simplistic, but it remains the dominant view. And as long as this remains the case, feminist art and literary historians have to make sure that the great women artists and authors are recognised as such – something that Gombrich's own *Story* fails spectacularly to do.

Feminist art and literary criticism has already shown that there are other standards by which we can judge the past, and in terms of which we can recognise the greatness of past women creators. The perspective of woman's Otherness helps obscure the women artists hidden in history by treating them as not-fully-individual. The work of women writers and artists has to be constructed into individual *oeuvres* and situated in traditions of female creativity. These traditions will be different from the traditions of male achievement, because males did not have to confront the rhetoric of sexual exclusion each time they tried to create. In calling a woman a 'genius', feminist critics (collectively) reconstruct history from the point of view of their own value scheme. The process is already well under way, although it has a long way to go yet. This book thus uses cultural history to validate a feminist aesthetics that renders visible, interprets and also evaluates the achievements of great, individual women artists.

Starting Out

2
Amongst the Ghosts

Over Christmas 1986 the BBC broadcast a radio series called *Wives of the Great Composers*. The assumption underlying these supposedly humourous talks was that the great composers had lives that mattered, and wives (and mistresses) who also mattered – but only to the extent that they helped the great geniuses of music father their timeless progeny. Clara Schumann featured; but it was her husband's music that was played, not her own. George Sand appeared as an adjunct to Chopin; but she was barely recognisable as a great and influential novelist. Instead she wore the conventional nineteenth-century disguise of a 'masculine' woman. And the treatment of Cosima Wagner made it puzzling that either Richard Wagner or Nietzsche should have found this termagant so compelling. The eccentricities of the male geniuses were excused; but not those of their partners. The latter were treated favourably only in so far as they fitted comfortably into a narrow range of sexual roles: as love-objects, muses, scribes, or housekeepers to the class of great musicians. One woman was particularly inspiring. Her composer-husband, Carlo Gesualdo (*c.* 1560–1615), murdered her and re-lived that act again and again in strange and original melodies which were ahead of his time.

As I listened to these programmes (turning off from time to time in real anger and impatience), I thought about the ghosts that Virginia Woolf writes about, the ones that disturb all creative women:

Outwardly, what is simpler than to write books? Outwardly, what obstacles are there for a woman rather than for a man? Inwardly, I think, the case is very different; she has still many ghosts to fight, many prejudices to overcome. [Virginia Woolf, 1931, p.62]

I kept seeing myself, aged about sixteen, reading in the library at grammar school. Whenever I could find the time I would gravitate towards two shelves by the window, one above the other. On the upper shelf were books of biographies of great artists – mostly composers, but including painters, and some men of letters. I can remember no books about women on this shelf. On the lower shelf was a curious selection of books (some very old) on rules of conduct for women. Some of these books were lavishly illustrated with pictures of stays and other even more extraordinary contraptions. Amongst these books I can remember no books of critical commentary; nothing ironic; nothing that distanced itself from the conventional etiquette described. When I should have been doing other things, I enjoyed getting out these books

Gender and Genius

and having a good laugh over them. The lives of women then seemed so distant from my own life I found it hard even to imagine the connections.

Of the two sets of books the ones I read most obsessively were the artistic biographies. The ones on the lives of the great composers were, I think, my favourite. It was these that I supplemented with similar books from the public library, and which I devoured along with survey books on music and modern art. I can now barely reconstruct what I thought of these texts. But I know they were important to me. My most secret fantasy was to be a singer, but since I knew I would be useless at it I never even tried. Being a composer would have been much more realistic. (I learnt poems and quotations for A level by making up tunes. I think I set the whole of *King Lear* to music.) But this was not a career that ever occurred to me. Just as there was nothing in the ladies' etiquette books that seemed to impinge on my own life, so there was nothing in the books of biographies of composers. At least some singers were women! It was only later I discovered the blues, and the way women blues singers combined performance and invention. But it wouldn't have helped much. I was the wrong colour. And by that time the fantasies about what I could do had turned into a tendency to fall in love with certain kinds of creative men.

The ghosts from my past that confronted me as I listened to *Wives of the Great Composers* were ones that came to me from my schooldays. Long before I decided to study the Romantics as a graduate student, I had acquired their admiration for 'originality' and 'creativity'. Romanticism valued artists for their capacity to express their own feelings and imaginings in their works. Authenticity and sincerity became the most important kinds of truth: more important by far than faithfully mirroring Nature, Beauty or Goodness. The originality of the art-work was not seen as a reflection of the external world, but of the mind and the personality that brought that work into existence. Consequently, the uniqueness and individuality of the artist's own character also became aesthetically significant. From Byron and William Blake to Nietzsche and Van Gogh, the typical genius was atypical: in one way or another, an Outsider, misunderstood by society and at odds with it. The history of art was represented as the history of the achievements of isolated individuals at war with the Establishment. But Romanticism always represented that extreme form of individualism in terms of male social roles and male power.

In *On Heroes and Hero-Worship* [1840], Thomas Carlyle made sincerity, originality and inspiration necessary characteristics of '"genius", the heroic quality we have no good name for' [p.209].

The most precious gift that Heaven can give to the Earth; a man of 'genius' as we call it; the Soul of a Man actually sent down from the skies, with a God's-message to us . . .

. . . A messenger he, sent from the Infinite Unknown with tidings to us. We may call him Poet, Prophet, God; – in one way or other, we all feel that the words he utters are as no other man's words. Direct from the Inner Fact of things; – he

Amongst the Ghosts

14   *lives, and has to live, in daily communion with that. [pp.58,62]*

The genius is born, not made. He is inspired by God and is, in fact, a kind of god himself, with Protean powers to take on different forms and roles in the various ages and stages of historical development:

[T]he Hero can be Poet, Prophet, King, Priest or what you will, according to the kind of world he finds himself born into. I confess, I have no notion of a truly great man that could not be all sorts of men. The Poet who could merely sit on a chair, and compose stanzas, would never make a stanza worth much. He could not sing the Heroic warrior, unless he himself were at least a Heroic warrior too. I fancy there is in him the Politician, the Thinker, Legislator, Philosopher; – in one or the other degree, he could have been, he is all these. [p.106]

The genius can be *all* sorts of men; but he is always a 'Hero', and never a heroine. He cannot be a woman. Nor are his social duties consistent with those of fulfilling mundane domestic and reproductive tasks, nor of living a life of enforced, upper-class ease. The genius is male (however capable of empathising with, or even impersonating, female psychology). Carlyle's pseudo-religious language makes clear the pretensions of the genius theory: the genius's power is modelled on that of God the Father: the King and patriarchal Ruler of the Christian universe. God the Father is the Author of Nature; human authors, artists and composers mimic divine creativity. The artist constructs a mini-world by imposing meaning and significance on formless matter: what his work means is a function of what he intended it to mean, and of the strength of his will in bending words, images and sounds to his design. Like God, the author possesses authority. Power, energy and divine inspiration are revealed in all facets of the artist's production. The better the artist, the more nearly he approaches omnipotence: his hand is omnipresent in the work of art, and detectable in even the most insignificant details.

But the artist, unlike the Christian God, is supposed neither omniscient, nor necessarily good. The work of art is created by the self, but in the dark part of the mind – amongst the emotional intensities of the male unconscious. The artist's self is divided; the universe of art that he creates is Manichean. In the theology of art criticism the devil has creative powers as well as God. And the devil is generally located amongst the driving forces of male lust. The sexual antics of the male genius are thought of as causally related to his art. They are also, therefore, redeemed by that art. Whether the great artist visits brothels, is homosexual, murders his wife, or is simply promiscuous, he can still be celebrated as a great and god-like human being. Much contemporary biography of geniuses reads like hagiography: these are the new saints (devil-driven saints) whose sayings and sufferings must be recorded. The genius is unconventional, bohemian, unique – often, like Byron himself, 'mad, bad and dangerous to know'. This caricature of genius has even spilled over from the arts on to the figure of the Mad but Brilliant Scientist . . . another variation on the theme of male genius.[1]

Gender and Genius

Programmes like *Wives of the Great Composers* implicitly gender the notion of artistic greatness in the same ways that I did whilst still at school. I couldn't be a Real Artist (I supposed), because the kind of authentic, self-centred and bohemian life that an Artist lived was not (remotely) like my own. Nor could this be a realistic ideal for a young girl growing up in the suburbs – however much she hated them. But without that kind of life and personality, I considered it impossible to be interesting enough to have a fully-developed self worth expressing. I'm not complaining about the upbringing that produced these misconceptions. I feel sufficiently remote from my teenage self not to feel angry on my own account. But I still do feel rage as I listen to programmes of this type. I also feel sad when year after year I see eighteen-year-old students entering university with the same preconceptions about creative gender roles that I had. I offered a paper on 'Women and Genius' to a student society. After the posters had gone up I received reports of male students in the Philosophy common-room discussing the advertised topic with genuine puzzlement. 'What could the argument be? After all, not all geniuses had wives or girlfriends!' The posters themselves were also covered with revealing graffiti, some of which suggested that I would only be able to talk for ten minutes on such a subject. None of my other posters have ever attracted graffiti.

Professional art critics and academics like to pretend that Romanticism is a disease that has been cured by the hygiene of history. Not for the 1980s the mythology of artist as hero, creating in a state of ecstasy that often crosses the boundaries into clinical madness. Post-structuralists assure us that the author is dead, adding their voices to previous generations of Marxist critics who have undermined the authority and isolation of the lone author. But in popular culture we find the old vocabulary, and the figure of the artist as hero, as alive and well as ever. Which pictures are bought, which books are read, which plays performed, which films are shown in art centres is largely a product of an aesthetics that assumes the centrality of the author to the work of art. Indeed, it is because of this that a feminist aesthetic cannot simply join the post-structuralists and their allies in deploring the individualism and the élitism of an aesthetics that builds on individually great artists. The concept of genius is too deeply embedded in our conceptual scheme for us to solve our aesthetic problems by simply amputating all talk of genius, or by refusing to evaluate individual authors and artists. Before we can fundamentally revalue the old aesthetic values, the concept of genius has to be appropriated by feminists, and made to work for us.

The new formalist aesthetics of post-structuralism would like to replace the author with the text; the painter with the canvas; the composer with the score, or even the musical performance. But this new aesthetics is self-defeating. Given the nature of modern art, there seems no way to define a work of art except in terms of that which is produced by an artist. But who is 'the artist'? How can he be distinguished from the man in the street, or from the bohemians and poseurs who aspire to this title? Because the new aestheticians don't try to re-describe the figure of

Amongst the Ghosts

the artist, but instead set out to deprive him of all authority, they actually help the old Romantic aesthetics to thrive in the world outside specialist journals and outside university walls.

An extramural course on Michelangelo and Van Gogh offered by my university to the inhabitants of a local town advertises itself with the following two-sentence summary: 'Illustrated comparison of two artists of genius who suffered greatly. Their lives, words and works will be contrasted.' Thus, precisely at the boundary that separates specialist academics from those with a general interest in the arts, we still find courses structured round the old Romantic concept of the genius. Indeed, once one starts listening and watching out for the word 'genius', it is soon noticeable how much work this word still does in the description and evaluation of cultural achievement. Even those academics who have given up using the word often still cling to the old assumptions about genius in the way that they talk, write and think about human creativity. This was proved to me in 1987 by a conference on *Genius: The History of an Idea* that was organised by one of the interdisciplinary groupings within my home university.

The setting up of the conference had been nothing to do with me. In fact, I had been startled to read the circular that came around about it over twelve months before. The organisers were no doubt equally surprised (and, I suspect, rather embarrassed) when they discovered that they had picked a topic which coincided with the book I had already started to write. When the overlap was pointed out, I was asked if I would be willing to give a paper to the conference on the topic of 'Women and Genius'. I agreed, of course, and began to put together fifty minutes of thoughts on the gendered origins of the modern concept of genius in the eighteenth century. Some time later it was my turn to be embarrassed. Talking to one of the representatives of a publishing company, I gathered he expected my paper to be included in the book of conference papers that his firm would issue. I was puzzled, and mumbled some excuse about my material perhaps being published elsewhere. Nobody had said anything to me about publishing my piece.

I waited for some time to see if I would receive an invitation to publish from the editors of the volume. Nothing happened. So eventually, with some awkwardness, I telephoned to try and find out what was proposed. I was told that the idea was to publish only some of the papers, to invite some extra papers from academics unable to attend, and that my paper was not deemed relevant to the overall enterprise which was centred round the 'classical' concept and tradition of genius. This rationale seemed to me to be mildly eccentric, but not altogether implausible. The conference had already been advertised, and I did not wish to be rude or pushy, so I made no fuss about it. It was only when I got to the conference and heard the other papers, and also realised that (as far as I could tell) I was the only speaker being excluded from the proposed volume that I began to feel angry.

Practically every speaker used William Duff – but none apparently

Gender and Genius

knew of the existence of his book on women. The comments of other authors, such as Coleridge, were treated as if they applied equally to all human beings, regardless of sex. For the two days that the conference lasted I felt as if I were stuck in a kind of time-warp. Here I was back in exactly the same scholarly world that I had abandoned nearly fifteen years before. I had expected to detect heavily ironic quotation marks around the word 'genius'. But they were not much in evidence. I found myself listening to quite lengthy (and solemn) discussions about whether or not there has ever been a genius who was sane. As Newton's biography was inspected for the signs of insanity that are associated with genius, it was I who felt mad. Despite the (very occasional) use of the pronouns 'she' and 'her', gender was not an issue. One man asked why I so obsessively focussed my questions on this topic.

Footnotes were being added to the traditions of scholarship with which I was familiar; but the framework of assumptions was undisturbed. The only thing that was different this time around was that the first paper of the conference went out of its way to stress that the history of the concept 'genius' and the history of the word 'genius' were unconnected. This, I supposed, was a response to the attack that I, as a feminist, was expected to mount. But this new defensiveness indicated no real change in attitude. In the time-honoured way the terms 'man' and 'male' were muddled by the speaker. My own paper was positioned right at the end of the proceedings. That, and my exclusion from the volume, made it feel as if the issue of gender is only a footnote to 'real' academic scholarship on the question of genius, instead of being positioned (as it should be) at its heart.

Feminist academics will know exactly how I felt. They are all too used to being pushed to the margins of an academic enterprise, or hearing their arguments speedily dismissed by too quick an appeal to 'authorities' and 'traditional' scholarship. Because sympathetic criticism is so rare, and because ideological objections nearly always masquerade as purely 'objective' criticisms, we never know where we are, which voices are sincere and which are dishonest. We are always made to feel that our words are being left unpublished because we are mediocre bores with bees in our bonnets. Others might squirm as our bees enter their bonnets and sting . . . but they rarely let on. Feminist academics waste a lot of time speculating about the underlying reasons for some particular response. Perhaps there was an entirely innocent explanation? . . . How can we be sure? We anxiously (or angrily) inspect the words used, looking for clues in the language.

A senior colleague came into my office to complain (in the mid-1980s!) that I had listed 'Philosophy of Woman' amongst my research interests. 'There's no such subject,' he said. 'Yes,' he agreed, '"Philosophy of Man" is a subject. No,' he insisted, '"Philosophy of Woman" is not. You might as well say you're interested in "Philosophy of Dog", or "Philosophy of Door-knob".' Similes are often the only clue. But it is not often that the language is as blatant as this. Sometimes I feel a kind of nostalgia for the (relatively) honest misogyny of pre-feminist days.

Amongst the Ghosts

18   Cultural prejudice against women has, to some extent, gone under-
      ground. These days it is the fake friends of feminism who are our more
      dangerous enemies. This is not because their arguments are any more
      valid, but because time has to be wasted exposing the inner pig before
      they can be refuted. It is also, of course, because somebody who
      deceives himself about his motives for objecting will never back down.
      An alternative specious objection will simply be adopted.

      When tackled about their attitudes to the creative capacity of women,
      most modern males would deny that they retain elements of misogyny.
      But the long list of responses that I collected to early (spoken or written)
      versions of this book suggest that many have fooled themselves by the
      false teeth that smile out of their mirrors. The first phrase was usually
      something like, 'I agree with every word you say.' Then comes a 'BUT',
      and a rider. Some of the more startling of these were:

      *'I'm not convinced that women are capable of great achievement in . . . (a variety
      of subject areas, most commonly mathematics, music, metaphysics and other
      disciplines described as "abstract").'*

      'Great female artists are virile,' or '. . . have masculine sexual energy.'

      'Women don't suffer the kinds of psychological disorder conducive to genius.'

      *'It is a proved psychological fact that all really creative men (he means "males")
      are feminine.'*

      *'All great painters have produced pornographic drawings, and have a strong
      male sex drive.'*

      Really, I prefer the response of the colleague who said, 'What you are
      doing is exciting and very important. But I do wish you'd take the
      feminism out!' The others missed the point of my arguments in as
      radical a way. At least with this last reply I knew exactly where I stood.

      All these responses involve preconceptions about creative gender-roles
      that have been conditioned by the way genius has been portrayed
      during the past two hundred years. All take maleness as the norm for
      artistic or creative achievement, however 'feminine' that male might be.
      Great artists and scientists have *male* sexual drives, whether or not they
      are biologically female. Males can *transcend* their sexuality; females are
      limited by theirs – or, if not, must themselves have *male* sexual energy.
      These comments from 'sophisticated' academics reveal a kind of tunnel-
      vision that makes female creativity a puzzling exception to the norm of
      male capacities.

      The way that creativity is still gendered today reveals itself in a variety
      of hidden (and no so hidden) ways. Cultural misogynists have learnt to
      disguise themselves, and hide their sexual prejudices behind innuendo,
      omissions, or even behind claims that they are really women's allies. In
      'Grunts from a Sexist Pig', for example, Anthony Burgess pretends
      ignorance of the reasons that have in the past led to his award of a pink
      marzipan pig from the Female Publishers of Great Britain [1986, p.1].
      He presents himself as fair and open-minded: 'I believe that the sex an
      author is irrelevant, because any good writer contains both sexes'

Gender and Genius

[p.3]. He listens to, and agrees with, feminists, using the musicians Thea Musgrave and Ethel Smyth – 'a great feminist herself ' – to dismiss as 'nonsense' the claims of other feminists that there will be one day a great woman composer 'when women have learned to create like *women* composers, a thing men have prevented their doing in the past.' [p.4]

Burgess must suppose all women to be simple-minded if he expects us to believe that the humorous title he gives his piece does not describe it exactly. Feminists have become used to reading articles like his backwards, and watching for the mess round the beast's rear end. And there it is, sure enough: 'I believe that artistic creativity is a male surrogate for biological creativity . . .' [p.4]. Well, fancy that! How then are we to explain all those great women writers? Mr Burgess has thought of an answer to this, too: 'if women do so well in literature it may be that literature is, as Mary McCarthy said, closer to gossip than to art'. Did McCarthy really say this? I haven't the patience to find out. In any case, quoting what somebody else says does not make that statement true. This type of pseudo-logical reasoning is called an 'argument from authority', and is one of the oldest tricks in the textbooks of rhetoric.

'But no one will be happier than I to see women produce the greatest art of all time, so long as women themselves recognize that the art is more important than the artist' [p.4]. If only this were the case, and creative women did not have to continually fight to be recognised by those who demand male lusts of artists. Burgess pretends not to see how such practices discriminate against female artists: 'Take music, for instance. Women have never been denied professional musical instruction – indeed, they used to be encouraged to have it – but they have not yet produced a Mozart or a Beethoven' [pp.3–4]. This from a man who claims knowledge of the writings of Ethel Smyth! In *Female Pipings from Eden* (1933), this British composer charted in detail the reasons why

to-day it is absolutely impossible in this country for a woman composer to get and to keep her head above water; to go from strength to strength, and develop such powers as she may possess. [Extract in Neuls-Bates, 1982, p.280]

Is it good news or bad news for women that Burgess's type of concealed misogyny is now more common than the open variety amongst writers on culture? I suppose we should be relieved that we now have to hunt (though not very hard) for the likes of Paul Ableman. In *The Doomed Rebellion* [1983], he argues in a much more frank way than Burgess that the male's sexual drive ensures that the arts 'were originally, and remain essentially, expressions of male consciousness' [p.61]. Ableman refuses to allow that the differential success of male and female creators has been produced by social pressures – or by the type of sexual stereotyping that he himself indulges in. It is much 'more likely that the host of relatively minor female writers and thinkers had, in fact, reached the limits of their capacity' – a capacity determined by biological difference [p.59]. Because a man cannot be 'biologically creative' (i.e. become pregnant), he is

driven to fulfill his creativity 'out there' . . . . A woman may go 'out there' but part

Amongst the Ghosts

of her is always tempted back towards her womb and the future, and the divided impulse, which blunts her culturally creative drive, is undoubtedly the reason why so few women ever produce major cultural contributions. [pp.59–60]

Ableman had previously explained this notion of the 'out there': 'A man's empire begins at the tip of his penis . . . A woman's empire is within' [p.42]. It is her womb . . . and its physical container her body.

Ableman argues for this thesis by setting up a contrast between male sexuality – 'a surface phenomenon', given that 'the male penis and testicles are both on the surface, or beyond the surface, of his body' – and the 'incomparably richer' female sexuality. Since the womb is located deep within the body, it is argued that a reproductive drive is 'integral' to female consciousness [p.19]. That a male has hormonal urges is not seen as a limiting factor on his autonomy or rationality: they are 'marginal' to his mind . . . and 'male sexuality can almost be considered ancillary to his masculinity' [pp.23,19]. But woman is Other: she is not-fully-individual and not-fully-human. Designed by Nature solely for the purpose of perpetuating the species, women's 'biological, and hence psychological, mission remains child-bearing and home-building and, sooner or later, it will assert itself ' [p.31]. Like a fish or a bird, a woman is genetically programmed into obeying the demands of instinct . . . into becoming pregnant, 'a bulky egg on legs' [p.21]!

Via such simple-minded dichotomies – and a series of apparently wilful self-deceptions – Ableman rehearses the kinds of arguments that have been commonly employed to represent female genius as somehow 'against nature'. Although, in excusing rape, men have been anxious to excuse their acts by reference to their overwhelming sexual urges, when it comes to cultural creation, the rhetoric is different. Males, it seems, can transcend their animal nature to produce culture; females cannot. The openness of Ableman's cultural misogyny is now unusual. Some of the underlying sentiments, I fear, are not. Old prejudices re-surface as established truths. According to these stale preconceptions, a woman can't participate in the creative process without becoming unsexed. As Andrew Gemant explains in *The Nature of the Genius* [1961],

. . . nearly always highly gifted women, approaching in some degree the nature of a genius, are masculine. In certain instances we have proof of that masculinity, as in George Sand. Eminent women scientists are nearly always plain or have definitely masculine features. They are actually half men, physically and mentally, their primary sexual organs happening to be female. [pp.114–15]

This same author (a scientist) earnestly explains why men are more likely to be creative when in love and before 'intimacy':

With the chemistry of the matter partly well established, there is every evidence for a hormonal activity of the testes, a positive activation of the brain. This influence is general, found in every individual; in a genius, it is of greater importance, since the activity it promotes is at an incomparably higher level than in others. [p.87]

What is supposed to be common to all men and all 'individuals' turns out to apply only to males. Women, obviously, can't be fully individual.

Gender and Genius

Furthermore, women who approach genius also approach maleness. For Gemant, George Sand typifies the great female writers (and scientists). She *almost* has genius; she *does* have male sex hormones – all she lacks is balls!

Mental energy is secreted by male glands. Consequently, Gemant treats the sexuality of great male and female achievers in quite different ways. Although he describes intellectually talented women as 'masculine', what he really means is that they are 'pseudo-males': 'Nature is playing here on borderline fields, producing unusual types, unusual in two ways' [p.115]. Thus, it is an 'abnormality' of *brain* and *body chemistry* that turns a woman into a great – probably homosexual – artist or scientist. By contrast, male homosexuality (usually so despised in our culture) is not viewed as 'a pathological sex deviation' – and is even condoned – in the case of equivalent males.

For a man of exceptional mental powers it may be that women are not adequate spiritual company . . . [A] true genius may find it difficult to exchange his ideas with a woman and to receive the expected impetus for further work from a conversation with her . . .

There may be other causes. The Greek sculptors maintained that the male body was superior in beauty to the female. No wonder then that a genius in whom the mental concept of beauty dominates over the natural instincts is led to choose a partner of ideal beauty in preference to one of second rate. [pp.90–91]

Gemant's book – dedicated to his wife – was still in print as I started to write this book! In it we find many of the clichés of the most debased forms of Romanticism. 'Hermaphrodite': a being with the sexual organs of *both* sexes. 'Androgyne': a being with clearly defined sexual organs, but with *psychic* bisexuality. These two categories have been applied differently to women and men ever since the Romantics re-valued 'feminine' characteristics of mind . . . and housed them in the bodies of *male* geniuses. Although a Renaissance woman was credited with a too wayward and too fanciful imagination, it is Gemant's *woman* who is unable to cope with 'anything fantastic and imaginary' [p.113]. Gemant's idealised woman – an 'eminently practical' housewife and mother – contrasts markedly with the passive and narcissistic creature described by Ableman, but the rationale for excluding women from culture is exactly the same. Women, it seems, are involved in a primary way in the processes of reproduction; whilst the males' role is merely 'secondary'. Women's 'chief destination' is the 'perpetuation of the human species', and that is why they have evolved as down-to-earth creatures with minds that tend 'to the concrete, the easily visualizable' [p.113]. '[T]he genius's pursuit is essentially "idle", hence the true woman, the true mother has a mentality incompatible with such kind of creative activity' [pp.113–14].

Gemant's use of George Sand to epitomise the problem of female genius – and to prove all talented women unnatural freaks – could (apart from the scientific jargon) have been written over a century before. As one of the critics writing in the *London Review* of 1864 put it:

Amongst the Ghosts

The greatest female author living is certainly George Sand. How much has George Sand given up to gain her literary crown. She has simply abandoned the distinctive characteristics, not to say the distinctive mission, of her sex. She has gratified her genius by immolating to it her instincts and her nature.' [Helsinger, 1983, p.21]

The more Sand's genius and art were admired, the more *male* she became:

She is boyish, an artist, she is great-hearted, generous, devout, and chaste; *she has the main characteristics of a man;* ergo *she is not a woman. [Balzac, quoted Barry, 1979, p.xv]*

Balzac's emphasis on Sand's chastity in this last sentence is unusual. In general, commentators magnified her one (unsubstantiated) lesbian relationship. They even used her sexual relationships with younger men to prove her own *male* lusts. For it was not just her sexual habits – nor even her mannish garb – that proved her a man. It was her 'genius'. It was obviously this kind of logic that led Elizabeth Barrett Browning to write her sonnet 'To George Sand: A Recognition' [1844]. It opens with the words, 'True genius, but true woman', and goes on to stress Sand's 'woman's hair' which 'all unshorn/Floats back dishevelled strength in agony'. Although Sand 'burnest in a poet-fire', her 'woman-heart beat evermore/Through the large flame'. Sand might have cut off her hair, and worn men's clothes. She might also (possibly) have been bisexual. But, as her English contemporary indicates, she is still a *woman* with *female* passions and sexual energies. To pretend otherwise is, as we will see, to recycle the mythology that was used to confine females within the domestic and reproductive space that men had marked out for them.

3
The Clouded Mirror

The progress of women in the arts has been like the slow, sideways progress of a crab towards the sea: a crab that keeps being picked up by malicious pranksters and placed back somewhere high on the beach. This book is an effort to help women advance by showing the enemies that still remain. What I am arguing is that the Romantic conception of genius is peculiarly harmful to women. Our present criteria for artistic excellence have their origins in theories that specifically and explicitly denied women genius. We still associate the great artist with certain (male) personality-types, certain (male) social roles, and certain kinds of (male) energies. And, since getting one's creative output to be taken seriously involves (in part) becoming accepted as a serious artist, the consequences of this bias towards male creators are profound. Women who want to create must still manipulate aesthetic concepts taken from a mythology and biology that were profoundly anti-female. Similarly, the achievements of women who have managed to create are obscured by an ideology that associates cultural achievement with the activities of males.

Although I am arguing that the particular problems that creative women face *now* are ones that derive from a Romantic inheritance, it is not part of my thesis that there was no previous history of linguistic harassment of women in the arts. What the nineteenth century did was re-work and amplify an older rhetoric of sexual exclusion that has its roots in Renaissance theories of art and of sexual difference. And, since the Renaissance writers themselves explicitly re-cycled theories taken from the ancient Greeks and Romans, nineteenth-century cultural misogyny turns out to have a very ancient pedigree indeed. What gives the Romantic contribution to the anti-female traditions a distinctively new feel is that women continued to be represented as artistic inferiors . . . even though qualities previously downgraded as 'feminine' had become valuable as a consequence of radical changes in aesthetic taste and aesthetic theory. What I will be exploring in this book is the way that cultural misogyny remained (and even intensified) despite a reversal in attitudes towards emotionality, sensitivity and imaginative self-expression. But, before I can do this, I must explore the older traditions of cultural misogyny that Romanticism assimilated and transmuted. Consequently, this chapter starts by contrasting Romantic and pre-Romantic notions of artistic value, and then explains why, in terms of the earlier aesthetics, women were considered artistic inferiors.

'[P]oetry is the spontaneous overflow of powerful feelings: it takes its

The Clouded Mirror

origin from emotion recollected in tranquillity': Wordsworth's words typify the Romantic attitude to all the arts [1800, p.26]. The Romantic artist feels strongly and lives intensely: the authentic work of art captures the special character of his experience. Although Wordsworth has been much criticised for suggesting that the artist must always feel the emotions that he conveys in his work, we still think of art as expressing, communicating or representing emotion. Much modern criticism of the arts, literature and music seems, on the surface, purely formalistic. But technical analyses of particular brush strokes, colours, sounds or uses of language often dissolve into comments about what is, or is not, 'appropriate' to the 'atmosphere' or the 'effect' of the work of art as a whole. And that involves making a judgement about what is, or is not, emotionally warranted. Modernists have insisted, with T. S. Eliot, that 'the more perfect the artist, the more completely separate in him will be the man who suffers and the mind which creates' [1919, p.74]. But, with Eliot, these critics have carried on valuing 'objective correlatives' for emotion: images, sounds, colours or situations that are supposed to serve as analogues and concentrations of human feelings within the work of art. The old Romantic values of expressiveness, experiential uniqueness, originality, spontaneity and authenticity have not disappeared, but have merely been transformed.

Indeed, we take the Romantics' view of the importance of self-expression so much for granted that we can only really see around it by contrasting it with alien views of artistic worth. Some years ago I went to visit a Tibetan painter who was working in exile in a monastery in Scotland. He could not speak much English, so it was hard to understand him. But he gave the impression of being an archetypal artist figure with his slightly long hair, his eccentric meat-eating (the community was vegetarian), and a routine of painting constructed round candles and natural light. Interestingly, however, he seemed to share the perspective of the other Tibetan monks. A painting was good if it was an accurate representation of the divine traditions. A more perfect painting contained more detail, more ornament, more gold paint – as long as these additions were in the places allotted by the authority of his particular sect. His long years of training and religious preparation had shaped his aspirations . . . to be a supreme copyist.

A similar view of artistic excellence dominated Europe throughout the classical and medieval periods, and really only finally died out round about 1800. European conceptions of the artist's task were inherited from the ancient Greeks, who did not even have a term that meant 'creation' in our sense. How could something come from nothing? The Greek gods shaped pre-existent matter in the manner of an architect (Plato), or by the processes of giving birth. The artist's only task was to imitate nature as it had been patterned by the gods. The Greeks lacked the words for concepts that we now take for granted in discussing the arts: 'originality', 'inspiration', 'genius', 'create', 'creative'. Although some scholars think they can find rough verbal equivalents to our modern vocabulary of art, these are at best approximations. Most of the supposed parallels are to be found in early discussions of poets and

Gender and Genius

poetry. But, as Tatarkiewicz explains, the ancient Greeks did not think of poetry as an art [1980, pp.83ff.]. Instead the poet was seen as a kind of prophet, a rhapsodic bard who delivered messages from the gods. In *Phaedrus* [*c*.370 BC] Plato even suggested that writing the messages down spoilt their effect. The poet was not the creator of a timeless work of art, but something more like a shaman, or even a medicine-man.

When the Greeks judged painting and sculpture what they were looking for was beauty of form and truthfulness to nature. Once the perfect form had been discovered (not invented), it was to be repeated without any deviation. Progress in the arts was a matter of increased accuracy in mimicking the beauty shaped by the gods [Tatarkiewicz, pp.92ff.]. Art on this model was essentially *mimetic*: nothing more than imitation. And that was how art remained throughout the Middle Ages. Within the monasteries the artist's task was to reproduce divine truth and Christian teaching as faithfully as possible. Authenticity, individuality or self-expression were values alien to the didacticism of the medieval artist. Received wisdom and orthodoxy had to be absorbed, and then passed on to others. Artists conveyed the universal through the medium of the particular work of art, rather than representing an individual's particular experience in a manner that made it universally accessible. The medieval artist was like the contemporary Tibetan painter. In a way that made the medieval artists very different from the Greeks, even perfection of form was supposed to be subsidiary to the exact replication of the religious message.

Unlike the Greeks, the men of the Middle Ages had a word for creation out of nothing. But they insisted that it was solely an attribute of God [ibid., p.252]. The artist was not god-like; he did not create the new; he was an imitator who reproduces what is visible to the eye of faith. Originality was not a virtue. Creativity was a theological and not an aesthetic concept. Thus we often do not even know the names of many of those who produced icons, illuminated manuscripts and other artefacts. *Who* was the workman mattered hardly at all; *what* was produced was the important thing. Although the term 'masterpiece' comes to us from the arts of that time, it has nothing at all to do with genius, creativity or early Christian art theory. Its origins are instead in the medieval craft traditions.

The Latin word *magister* (master) was a legal term meaning 'one who possesses authority over others' [Cahn, 1979, pp.7ff]. The word 'masterpiece' was first used by the medieval craft guilds to denote the piece of work produced by an apprentice which showed sufficient skill or competence to permit admission to the privileges of the guild. Then, in the twelfth century, the term *magister* became used as part of the title of the elected head of a craft guild. The 'master' was a kind of trade-union leader. As feminist scholarship is beginning to show, women were active in these guilds – despite the need to prove their merit with a 'masterpiece'. Hostility towards women in the arts only increased when the status of the artist began to be distinguished from that of the craftsman, and the arts in general represented as activities suitable for only the most perfect (male) specimens of humanity.

This change in the status of the arts and the artist started during the Renaissance. Private and court patronage meant that wealth and power were beginning to flow into their hands. Painting and sculpture began to be occupations for well-bred men, instead of manual crafts. Their practitioners began to puff up the status of these arts, by talking about them in a way previously reserved for music and poetry. Patronage also meant that art could begin to free itself from the domination of the Church. Theorists emerged who tried to explain the role of the artist by invoking Plato's account of the relationship between man and the gods, but in a way that mixed Greek ideas of art and the gods with Christian notions of creation (out of nothing). Instead of merely reflecting religious dogma, the artist mirrored Nature – improved, and made more perfect, as God Himself had created it. Departures from orthodoxy (or the painting out of blemishes) were justified by the claim that this knowledge of what God intended came to them through divine inspiration. Thus, the stage was being set for the Romantic portrayal of the artist – as being, in Byron's words, 'half dust, half deity'.

In the Renaissance, however, art was still seen as *mimetic*. The artist was an *imitator* . . . whether of previous art-works, or the most perfect and most universal natural forms. For the neoplatonist art theorists these 'forms' or 'types' were *Ideas* which existed in the artist's mind. But they did not exist solely in the artist's mind. His task remained that of mirroring Truth, Beauty and Goodness, not creating an alternative reality. Not even the greatest of all artists was an inventor in our modern sense of the word. His task was not to express his feelings, nor his own individuality – only to copy. 'Originality' began to be valued. But there was no contradiction in talking about an 'original imitation' – which might be a more perfect version of some historical event or person, or even a re-working of an old story, myth or piece of art.

We can see a lot of this in Vasari's *Lives of the Artists* [1550 and 1568] which records the ever-increasing esteem, power and social position allocated to individual artists during the Renaissance period. Giotto (1266/7–1337) was the son of a peasant; Michelangelo (1475–1564) was said to be 'related to the most noble and ancient family of the counts of Canossa' [p.326]. Vasari's *Lives* is often credited with having invented the modern concept of genius, celebrating as it does the lives and powers of individual artists. But although the term 'genius' is sprinkled liberally through modern English translations of Vasari's text, I have been unable to locate the Italian term *genio* in corresponding passages in the original. The English 'genius' translates a number of Italian phrases, most commonly including the Italian word *ingegno* – perhaps best rendered as 'ingeniousness'.

Italian, like Latin, had two terms, the history of which has been thoroughly confused. The Italian *genio* was like the Latin *genius* in starting out as a word referring to the divine forces associated with, and protective of, male fertility. *Ingegno*, like the Latin *ingenium*, was associated with good judgement and knowledge; but also with talent, and with the

Gender and Genius

dexterity and facility essential to the great artist working in the mimetic traditions. Without such skills an artist might conceive perfect beauty, but he would be unable to reproduce it. Being able to execute one's design without sweating over it became one of the qualities most valued in an artist. It harmonised well with the class pretensions of the new group of painters and sculptors, who were anxious to play down the manual work involved in their professions. Similar values spread to the literary arts.

The terms 'ingenious', 'ingeniousness' and (later) 'ingenuity' were used in English, too, and involved the executive power of reason, judgement and what used to be called 'wit'. Ingeniousness was not associated with creativity, imagination, originality, emotion or self-expression. It was primarily a matter of skill, talent, good judgement, and the ability to adapt means to ends with 'ease' and 'facility' — aesthetic virtues that lasted until the end of the eighteenth century. The Renaissance term 'genius' meant something quite different — even in English. When Shakespeare's Macbeth lamented 'My genius is rebuk'd', he was bewailing the fact that he had been given a 'barren sceptre' and that his rival had been hailed 'father to a line of kings' (Macbeth, III, i). Thus, the English term 'genius' was as associated with male sexual and generative powers as the Latin genius, which originally meant 'the begetting spirit of the family embodied in the paterfamilias' [Nitzsche, 1975, p.4]. In fact, as we shall see in Chapter 6, the Roman genius involved the divine aspects of male procreativity which ensured the continuance of property belonging to the gens or male clan. It involved the fertility of the land, as well as the fertility of the man. Here we find the roots of the second sense of 'genius' during the Renaissance. 'Genii' were male protective spirits and divinities attached to places, people and natural objects.

This is the sense of the word that we find illustrated in the most important dictionary of symbolic meaning of the seventeenth century. In his Iconologia, Cesare Ripa represents 'Genius' ('Genio') by a small, naked, smiling child wearing a garland of poppies, and carrying in his hands corn and grapes [1709 trans. of 1602 text, fig. 135]. The symbols of the fertility of the harvest (poppies, corn and grapes) were themselves metaphors for the father's seed. To us this seems extremely odd. Although we carry on using the term 'Genius' in the sense of a spirit-Genius, we certainly wouldn't think of symbolising genius as a chubby little boy. But Ripa was not being simply eccentric. Modern dictionaries of the 'lost' language of symbolic meaning point out that in Renaissance art often what we take to be little cupids were little genii [Tervarent, 1958]. In Ripa's dictionary of symbols it was 'Ingenuity' ('Ingegno') that was represented by a winged male youth 'of a vehement, daring Aspect' wearing a helmet with an eagle's crest on it, and carrying in his hand a bow and arrow [fig. 161]. His unageing intellect, his strength, vigour, generosity, loftiness, inquisitiveness and acuteness were qualities that later were all transferred from 'ingenuity' to 'genius' itself.

The senses and symbols of genius have changed dramatically. This was

The Clouded Mirror

a process that started when, sometime during the seventeenth century, the two different words 'genius' and 'ingenuity' (Latin *ingenium*; Italian *ingegno*) collapsed into each other. It is not easy to put an exact date on the blending of the two concepts since modern histories of ideas also conflate the two terms. But certainly by the start of the eighteenth century the two Latin words and the two corresponding English words were no longer sharply distinguished. And other European languages (French, German, Italian, Spanish) seemed to have undergone the same transition. It is only in the eighteenth century that the term 'genius' begins to be in general use in anything like its modern sense. It is only when the two Latin terms *genius* and *ingenium* merge that our modern concept of genius emerges.

The Renaissance artist was great not in so far as he possessed great *genius*, but in so far as he had a superior *ingenium*. In the Renaissance our modern concept of the genius simply did not exist. Of course, when Vasari wrote his *Lives* he often wrote in a way that seems to prefigure our modern conception of artistic creativity. After all, the painters and sculptors he is describing often seem like the Tibetan artist I visited. The personality of the Tibetan seemed to be in conflict with his consciously held beliefs and his stated opinions. Vasari's *Lives* reveals the direction that art criticism and theory would move in. He presented Michelangelo and Raphael as sublime heroes and, as such, it is tempting to read into Vasari our modern understanding of genius. But, during the Renaissance period, the artist possessed *genius* only in so far as he was a fertile male in a patrilineal culture, and in so far as his goods, lands and powers were watched over (and guided) by spirit-genii.

Renaissance women lacked *genius*. But it was not this, as such, which was supposed to make them artistic inferiors. This was put down to a deficiency in *ingenium*: those inherited mental and physical talents that helped an artist conceive and execute his projects. Women, apparently, were fated to lack wit, judgement and skill simply by virtue of the fact that they were born female. Hence, unsurprisingly, cultural inferiority became linked with a lack of *genius* as such . . . a lack of that aspect of maleness that made men divine. We can see why the concepts of *genius* and *ingenium* should eventually have collapsed into each other to form that of the modern (male) genius. Even in the Renaissance what made a human being great was what made him distinctively *not-female*. There is nothing accidental about the way that the Romantic concept of genius is gendered: the term was forged at the point where two modes of misogyny meet . . . the creative and the procreative.

Why was a woman supposed to have a feeble *ingenium*? We can see some of the most common rationalisations in Juan Huarte's *Examen de Ingenios* [1575], which was translated into English in 1594 as *The Examination of Mens Wits*. What Huarte claimed to have 'proved' was that all the 'differences of mens wits' can be explained by reference to three qualities: 'hot, moist, and drie' [see Huarte, ch. 5]. What Huarte is doing here is drawing on the authority of Aristotle (384–322 BC) who claimed that males are hot and dry; females cold and wet. Aristotle had argued

Gender and Genius

that the superiority of males can be seen in their larger size, and in the fact that the reproductive organs have grown outwards, instead of remaining undeveloped inside the body. Heat, Aristotle supposed, is necessary for growth. For Aristotle a woman is a lesser man: a kind of monster or abnormality who, through lack of heat during the period of conception, fails to develop her full (= male) potential. In perfect conditions there would be only male children.

According to Aristotle, women can't even be said to procreate: they are the sterile sex. Only the male seed contains the formative principle that allows the parent to be reproduced in the next generation. Aristotle adopted what feminists have dubbed the 'flower-pot' theory of reproduction. Woman provides the soil, the container and the environmental conditions in which the seed grows to embryo, to foetus, and emerges as a baby. But it is only the male semen (seed) which is active, and has the power to form the matter or material provided by the female into a human. The woman reveals her lack of formative force through the unshaped matter which is expelled each month as blood. Since she has insufficient heat to allow semen (sperm) to develop, this 'unconcocted' blood means that she is wet, as well as cold. Wetness, however, is supposed to affect the proper operation of her mind. A woman is treated as a cultural, as well as a biological, flower-pot. She lacks the potentiality of an individual male, and cannot represent the essence of humanity. The role of the woman within the society is like the role of her womb: she provides a suitable environment within which the best individuals (free Greek males) can flourish and perfect human civilisation.

Huarte differed from Aristotle in one respect: he allowed that women as well as men have 'seed'. This was an idea Huarte took from Galen (AD 131–201), the most influential of the Greco-Roman medical writers. Galen modified Aristotle's views slightly, in order to bring them into line with his own medical observations. But neither Galen (nor Huarte after him) ever suggested that women are men's reproductive equals. Galen still described a woman as 'imperfect, and, as it were, *mutilated*' [quoted in Allen, 1985, p.189]. The seed of a female was inferior to that of a male. As Huarte put it: 'And the man who is shaped of the woman's seed, cannot be wittie, nor partake abilitie through the much cold and moist of that sex' [Huarte, p.317]. The cleverest and the most able human beings are always the hottest and driest; but women are, constitutionally, cold and wet.

For Huarte, a female is an underdeveloped male (as she was for Aristotle). A male turns into a female because of lack of heat at the moment of conception, during the nine months in the womb, and even on odd (very odd!) occasions after the birth. Extra heat reverses the processes, and turns girl embryos and children into boys. Huarte spelt out the implications of this misogynistic theory of procreation. He used Adam and Eve, Solomon, and the Bible generally, to conclude, 'Therefore we are to shun this sex, and to procure that the child be borne male: for in such only resteth a wit capable of learning' [p.287]. In an

The Clouded Mirror

orthodoxy that now seems much more eccentric than Laurence Sterne's lampoon on it in *Tristram Shandy* (1759), Huarte provided recipes for procreating talented offspring. The detail included such things as what food to eat to make suitable sperm; how to select a suitable female with the right degree of coldness and wetness; what positions to adopt during intercourse – and even the ideal weather conditions for intercourse. These recipes were all also, quite explicitly, ones for producing male children.

Huarte's Spanish text was translated into seven languages, and was important throughout the seventeenth century. Indeed, it was still being used as late as the nineteenth century when, for example, we find Schopenhauer referring to it in his essay 'On Women' in support of his claim that women lack all higher mental faculties [1851, p.108]. Schopenhauer's appeal to Huarte's authority is bizarre, given that Huarte explained female deficiencies in terms of an utterly discredited physiology. But Schopenhauer's use of Huarte is an interesting demonstration of the way that the Romantics dressed the old cultural misogyny in new clothes. Another aspect of this Romantic re-working of the old Renaissance artistic biases can be seen in the way that they excused, or sometimes even glorified, the craziness of an élite group of males . . . whilst, often at the same time, downgrading female madness. How often do we meet the figure of the melancholy poet in nineteenth-century texts? How little do we realise how this figure draws on a tradition that makes melancholy a kind of madness that benefits *male* artists – and harms *female* pretenders to artistic excellence?

This is an important point, because it is fast becoming feminist orthodoxy that 'the differentiation' between male and female madness 'began at the end of the eighteenth century' at the time 'that the dialectic of reason and unreason took on specifically sexual meanings' [Showalter, 1987, p.8]. Showalter is right to point to important changes that took place round about this time in attitudes to irrationality. The Romantics admired the eccentric and bizarre imaginings of the mad male genius in a way that was quite alien to the Renaissance admiration for the man of great *ingenium*. But she is wrong to suggest that the Romantics did not revivify a Renaissance discourse that also gendered madness: a discourse that (as we shall see in Chapter 9) persisted throughout the so-called 'Age of Reason'.

The great *ingenium* of the Renaissance period was primarily associated with 'masculine' *sanity*: with judgement, reason, wit and the like. But the Renaissance writers on the arts turned to the Greek and Latin sources for information about what it is that provides some human beings with access to the Ideas in the mind of God. And what they found was Plato's shamanistic view of the poet: not, for Plato, an artist at all (he didn't think much of artists), but a kind of medium. In *Phaedrus* Plato had claimed:

If any man come to the gates of poetry without the madness of the Muses, persuaded that skill alone will make him a good poet, then shall he and his works of sanity with him be brought to naught by the poetry of madness . . . [§245A]

Gender and Genius

The neoplatonist art-theorists of the Renaissance extended this view to *all* artistic activity, whilst (paradoxically) retaining their admiration for reason, universal truths, judgement and masculine rationality. What was suggested was that although *most* human beings cannot transcend these reasonable virtues, a man of truly great *ingenium* (who is very hot and dry, and hence necessarily male) could be led to a kind of vision of the truth by a form of madness.

Seneca's claim that a man of great *ingenium* has a touch of madness was much quoted. There was also a lengthy debate about some comments in a work then supposed to be by Aristotle, which seemed to suggest that the madness which afflicted the gifted man was melancholy [Wittkower and Wittkower, 1963, pp.98ff.]. In terms of the Renaissance theory of the humours, melancholy was a common personality-type, which could be quite normal and healthy, but which also involved a tendency to particular diseases. These illnesses could be brought on by a number of organic and non-organic factors, such as a disordered spleen, eating the wrong kind of food, feeling passions that were too strong, or even studying for too long. According to this physiological theory, what happened in all these cases was that the fluids in the body were raised to too high a temperature. Some of the liquid boiled off and left behind a residue of semi-solid black bile which interfered with the patterns of fluids coursing round the human body and produced symptoms of physical sickness. The vapours sent up by the boiling process also interfered with the correct functioning of the brain, and produced disturbances there [Babb, 1951].

To the disadvantage of women, physiological theories made the amount of heat available in a body a matter of the greatest importance. The liver was likened to a fire that warmed the contents of the belly. From this process of 'concoction' came the four humours out of which all fluids in the body were supposed to be composed: blood, phlegm, yellow bile and black bile. These four humours circulated through the body, and were themselves heated by the heart to form 'vital spirits', which were seen as the vehicle of life itself. In the brain this rarefied fluid was refined even further into 'animal spirits', which were then supposed to flow back down through the nerves to act as the link between mind and body and to form semen. In normal human beings any disturbance to this process of heating bodily fluids was held to be damaging. Melancholy was a dangerous and vicious disease which interfered with virility and fertility, as well producing a large range of dramatic mental aberrations (including becoming, literally, slow-witted, and suffering hallucinations and fits). It was, however, claimed that the man with a great *ingenium* benefited from melancholic vapours rising to his brain. The man of great *ingenium* had enough natural heat to counteract the coldness and dryness of the residual bile.

Melancholy was not a gender-specific illness. But if a person's *ingenium* was suitably great, he could *use* his melancholy to produce great art, great philosophy and the like. The visions caused by the vapours rising to his brain were not then delusions, but inspired ideas that helped him

The Clouded Mirror

to recreate truth [Babb, pp.58ff.]. This, of course, was bad news for a woman, whose *ingenium* was supposed to be too cold and wet to be great. Women could *suffer* the pathological disease of melancholy, but were unlikely to experience its more glorious side-effects. Sometimes the delusions of witches were explained in these terms, as were the delusions of lovesick women.[1] Occasionally female powers for religious prophecy were also linked with melancholy. By a special grace from God women could become Sibyls. But although *Dame* Melancholy was a common allegorical figure, the benign form of melancholic madness that was associated with great *ingenium* was always a problem for flesh and blood women.

It is thus surely no coincidence that it was a woman writer, Hildegard of Bingen (1098–1179), who was the first to try and work out in detail how melancholy and the other humours affected males and females in different ways [see Allen, 1985]. This musician, poet and painter projected herself in her theological and autobiographical writings as subject to melancholic visions. In her medical texts she redescribed female physiology in a way that would have made it quite normal for melancholic females to be true visionaries. Women's bodies, she claimed, are more porous than men's – especially during menstruation, when a gap opens up between the top of their brains and their skulls and serves to vent the cold, wet vapours that were supposed to interfere with female understanding. Women 'are like windows through which the wind blows' [quoted in Newman, 1987, p.129 and see 126ff.]. Hildegard even went so far as to deny that women are in all respects colder and wetter than males. Her own gender led her to confront head-on an orthodoxy that made women cold, wet and inferior. Her radicalism was well known in her day, but seems to have been largely forgotten by the fifteenth century – by which time the idea that the man of great talent is a male of great melancholy had gained considerable currency.

A tendency towards melancholy came to be associated with the influence of the planet Saturn on a man. In the Middle Ages men of intellectual ability were standardly described as being born under Mercury, the youthful and bisexual messenger of the gods. But Renaissance artists, philosophers and poets boasted that Saturn was in the ascendant at the hour of their births. The astrological significances were explained in terms of the Roman and Greek gods. Saturn (Kronos) was the father of Jove (Jupiter, Zeus) and was the embodiment of male insanity – an autocratic and castrating tyrant – and also, as spiritual father of the gods, of sublime male reason. In terms of the Christian allegories which overlaid the astrological theories, sometimes Saturn was Satanic, and sometimes another God the Father. By allying himself with Saturn, the Renaissance artist emphasised once again the distinctively male aspirations of the man of great artistic *ingenium*. Women and feeble men suffered by being born under Saturn – and were tormented by melancholy. The man of great *ingenium* was ennobled by his fate. His madness was a gift of the gods. That cliché of pulp fiction was born – the saturnine hero [Klibansky *et al.*, 1964].

Gender and Genius

The neoplatonists often wrote about women in ways that apparently conflicted with the misogyny of medical orthodoxy [Maclean, 1980, pp.24ff.; 28ff.]. They suggested that female physical beauty reflects inner goodness; that the soul of a pure woman (usually a virgin) could separate itself from her body and communicate directly with God and the angels – acting as a medium between the male who loves her and the divine. But this did not, of course, imply that flesh-and-blood women had the physiology or psychology to become great artists. A woman's face might mirror aspects of the divine (and even refract God's image to male minds); but a woman's own mind was clouded with vapours that rose up from her womb and prevented her from perceiving Truth, Beauty and Goodness with the same clarity as could a man. A woman could be a Muse – but was physiologically unsuited to be a great artist.

Dryden might have written, 'Great wits are sure to madness near alli'd'; but women were denied great wits. Lunacy in a woman was unlikely to be perceived favourably. In most cases female madness was put down not to melancholy, but to 'hysteria': a disease that both superficially resembled melancholy, and symbolised the supposed inferiority of the female intellect. Like melancholy, hysteria was also supposed to involve vapours rising to invade the lungs and brain. But in hysteria the source of the fumes was not the spleen, but the womb – *hystera* means 'womb' in Greek – that classical container of cold, wet menstrual blood, and cold, wet female semen [Veith, 1965]. In hysteria (almost by definition) there was insufficient heat for the vapours to boil off to produce the rarefied atmosphere that inspired the élite male melancholics. The wits of a sane woman were decreed sluggish (because of her womb); but, out of her wits, a female fared no better. She was declared hysterical: able to experience only those phantasms created by her own self, not the universal Truths of the mad male visionaries. Long before Freud, the womb was (literally) the female *sub*conscious: the vapours rising up from it were thought to interfere with her consciousness, and produce delusions and illusions of a perverted type. The hysterical woman was a shadowy (cold, wet and vaporous) imitation of the fiery melancholic male.

This sounds so like some of the things that were to be said about women in the post-Romantic period, that it is important to stress here that we are still in a world where art is *mimetic*. Women were artistic inferiors because they lacked *ingenium*: judgement, skill, and the ability to see and faithfully to mirror pre-existent and universal truths. The modern concept of genius did not exist; and the ideals of artistic self-expression, sincerity, authenticity and originality were still centuries away. Emotion was not valued; and imagination was only useful in so far as it involved a literal *imaging* of a truth that was there independently of the person perceiving it. Women's wombs made them liable to emotions and fantasies of a delusory type; they invented fictions, instead of perceiving truths. Women had access only to their own individual psychologies, not to universal truths. In our terms, women were thought of as *too* creative, *too* original, with much *too* much subjectivity. In Renaissance terms, none of these were artistic virtues, and women lacked the fires of

The Clouded Mirror

34   male physiology that could burn out an image of the truth. They were trapped in the cloud of unknowing.

4
The Male Gift

The Renaissance artist had aimed to *mirror* a universal truth that existed independently of his own self, and subjectivity was therefore a barrier rather than an aid to artistic invention. But for the Romantics individuality and particularity were no longer handicaps to artistic production. The artist offered his own inner landscape as one of the poles against which others could align the compasses of their own minds. Coleridge theorised the new aesthetics in *Biographia Literaria* [1817]; but the changes in taste that embraced artistic idiosyncrasy pre-dated him, and occurred during the closing years of the eighteenth century. Thus Jean-Jacques Rousseau's autobiographical *Confessions* [1781] opens with a boast that a Renaissance author or artist would have scorned to make:

I have resolved on an enterprise which has no precedent, and which, once complete, will have no imitator. My purpose is to display to my kind a portrait in every way true to nature, and the man I shall portray will be myself.

Simply myself. I know my own heart and understand my fellow man. But I am made unlike anyone I have ever met; I will even venture to say that I am like no one in the whole world. I may be no better, but at least I am different.

These words of Rousseau's symbolise the new attitudes to the self: as an author he is proud of his uniqueness; he preens himself on his originality. His aim is to 'tell the truth' – sincerely, if not always accurately – by faithfully portraying his own (very individual) soul, and the desires and needs of his own (very inadequate) body. Rousseau paints himself as a naïve, vain, impetuous, obsessive, fickle, fanciful, childlike creature – swayed more by strong emotions and sympathies than by reason. He is a charming monster: sometimes bafflingly pure, but with a tendency to disease and madness. Rousseau projects himself, in other words, in very much the way that the Renaissance caricatured woman: as locked into his own very subjective and sexually disturbed psyche. Later, for the nineteenth-century Romantics, Rousseau's defence of the common man – his attack on the institutional privileges of property, Church and urban society – came to symbolise the (lost) potential of revolutionary France . . . when all men had been declared equals and brothers in freedom. But Rousseau also symbolises the way that Romanticism made women Others rather than brothers. The free, imperfect man whose abasement and unique individuality was glorified remained a *hero* . . . heroines had, at best, a supportive role.

The 'feminine' Rousseau was anti-female . . . at least, anti-educated and creative females. In his *Letter to Mr d'Alembert* (1758), women are even denied the appropriate feelings to *appreciate* art properly, let alone *produce* it:

Women, in general, possess no artistic sensibility . . . nor genius. They can acquire a knowledge . . . of anything through hard work. But the celestial fire that emblazens and ignites the soul, the inspiration that consumes and devours . . . , these sublime ecstasies that reside in the depths of the heart are always lacking in women's writings. These creations are as cold and pretty as women; they have an abundance of spirit but lack soul; they are a hundred times more reasoned than impassioned. [Quoted and trans. Citron, 1986, p.225]

In the Renaissance, it was males who possessed judgement and *ingenium* . . . and women who had too much in the way of feelings, too little in the way of reason to be real artists. For Rousseau the equations are reversed: woman has too much judgement, too little emotion. In the older tradition, fire was a physiological reality that was essentially bound up with the vital forces of male sexuality . . . and women were, in general, too cold to be great artists. By the time that Rousseau was writing, this physiology was out of date. But Rousseau's woman remains cold: still lacking the fires of sublime ecstasy and of divine inspiration. The accounts of maleness and femaleness have changed; but the old misogynistic vocabulary remains – reinterpreted in such a way as to represent women as metaphorically frigid and hence as creatively sterile.

Rousseau was by no means alone in maintaining this link between creative power and the psychic 'heat' of the heroic male. One of the most famous eighteenth-century descriptions of poetic genius was that of Shaftesbury: 'a poet is indeed a second *Maker*; a just Prometheus under Jove' [1711, i, p.136]. The idea that the genius is a Prometheus, who has stolen fire from the gods and brought it to earth as a gift to male-kind, is one that we find in many Romantic writings. In Percy Bysshe Shelley's 'Prometheus Unbound' (1820), for example, speech, civilisation and poetry are all gifts of Prometheus to mankind. Prometheus allies himself with Saturn – said by Shelley to be the true god of energy and power – rebels against Jupiter (Saturn's upstart son) and, through his heroic daring and extreme suffering, produces a revolution that makes all men (= males) quasi-divine.

When Shelley wrote about Prometheus, he did not go on to spell out the misogynistic implications of a mythology that made Woman (Pandora) part of the punishment meted out to male-kind for Prometheus's presumption in stealing fire from the gods. In a way appropriate to Mary Wollstonecraft's son-in-law, Shelley (quite consciously) tried to distance himself from the gender-stereotyping of his time – and especially of his great hero, Rousseau. Shelley was revolutionary enough to dream of extending freedom and equality to women. But, as McNiece remarks – thinking that this proves Shelley makes men and women 'transcendently equal' – for Shelley the heroine is always 'the beloved counterpart, shadow, other self, and ideal support of the hero' [1969, p.180]. She has instinctive knowledge of the truth . . . and her beauty (of spirit, as well as body) inspires the poetic hero to effective action. It is, however, always a *male* task to shape this truth into verse and, by so doing, to act as a charismatic leader of mankind.

As in the Galenic account of procreation, females could provide the matter – and assist the males in a kind of subsidiary way with the processes of (re)production – but it was a primarily *male* task to form that matter into art. The Romantics' muddling of the old categories of 'female', 'feminine' and 'male' did not fundamentally disturb the old sexual hierarchies – and produced, at best, a male ambivalence towards female authorship. On a personal level, for example, Shelley encouraged Mary Wollstonecraft Shelley to write . . . but also (apparently) found her writing threatening. We can see this in the original 'Preface' to *Frankenstein* [1818] which Percy wrote himself, assuming his wife's voice to explain the story's genesis in an informal competition set up in 1816 between Byron, himself and Mary (still, at that time, his wife-to-be). The idea, it seems, was to emulate the German ghost-stories that the three friends read to each other during wet evenings spent round Byron's Swiss fireside.

Percy's 'Preface' places the two male authors centre-stage – and not in the manner implied by the novel itself, as the models for Frankenstein's dream of divine omnipotence . . . and consequent monstrosity. Instead, Percy's voice presents Byron and himself as Mary's authorial rivals: they, too, had supernatural stories to recount. 'The weather, however, suddenly became serene', and the two men set off on a comradely trek through the Alps, where they 'lost, in the magnificent scenes . . . all memory of their ghostly visions'. The sun-lit visions of the males in the mountains were so vivid that they effaced the fictions of the fire-lit darkness. Percy's 'Preface' implicitly ranks the natural sublimities of the two men's day-time world (which produced poetry) above the hallucinations of Mary (a 'most humble novelist') [pp.58, 57]. The men transcend the enclosed space – and the horrors of domesticity – which trap the woman in a world of shadows. In the Myth of the Cave in Plato's *Republic* (one of Percy's favourite texts), sunlight represents Truth, whilst firelight only creates a ghostly imitation of reality for those imprisoned down below, inside the Cave of Illusion. Appropriating Plato's imagery and the voice of female modesty, Percy puts Mary in her authorial place. Ghost stories are for women; Poetic Truth for men.

Shelley's anxieties about female authorship are further illustrated by one of his own 'ghostly visions' during the weeks when Frankenstein was born. We know from Byron's mistress and doctor – also full (writing) members of the Gothic house-party, despite Shelley's version of events – that during one of the recitations, Percy retired, screaming . . . traumatised by a vision of Mary's body with nipples transformed to eyes. Medical expertise was required before the poet could recover his equilibrium.[1] Since the Romantic author creates the world anew in the way that it presents itself to his own, unique angle of view, Shelley's 'fit of phantasy' is symptomatic of a general male unease. As Gilbert and Gubar show in the brilliant opening chapter of *The Madwoman in the Attic* [1979], throughout the nineteenth century – and even today – the

The Male Gift

pen has been represented as a metaphorical penis. The writer's watching eyes belong with penises. . . not with female breasts.

In a letter to R. W. Dixon dated 1886, Gerard Manley Hopkins pithily summarises this phallic view of art. For him the artist's 'most essential quality' is

masterly execution, which is a kind of male gift, and especially marks off men from women, the begetting of one's thoughts on paper, on verse, or whatever the matter is . . . [T]he mastery I speak of is not so much in the mind as a puberty in the life of that quality. The male quality is the creative gift. [Madwoman, p.3]

The Jesuit poet has dressed in Victorian majesty the rather bathetic view of Timon, one of Rochester's characters: 'I . . . never Rhym'd, but for my Pintle's [penis's] sake' [quoted ibid., p.6]. The sexually chaste nineteenth-century Christian and the notorious seventeenth-century rake unite in making the poet's pen an extension of the male sexual organ.

We can find a similar perspective in twentieth-century poetics, after Romanticism has merged into Modernism. In 'The Figure of the Youth as Virile Poet' [1943], for example, Wallace Stevens remarked that 'The centuries have a way of being male', and says that this maleness comes 'in part, from their philosophers and poets' [p.52]. For Stevens this is appropriate, since 'There can be no poetry without the personality of the poet', and the definition of poetry has to start with character-sketches [p.46]. The sketch he offers us is that of 'the genius, or, rather, the youth as virile poet' [p.66]. Stevens even denies that the Muse is female:

No longer do I believe that there is a mystic muse, sister of the Minotaur. This is another of the monsters I had for nurse, whom I have wasted. I am myself a part of what is real, and it is my own speech and the strength of it, this only, that I hear or ever shall. [p.60, original in italics]

All the poet's energies come from his own strong self, and that self is necessarily male. The poet, he claims, should write a poetry that 'satisfies both the reason and the imagination' [p.42].

With the Muse (the imagination) incorporated within the male body, the poet remains male, virile and powerful. But

if, for the poet, the imagination is paramount, and if he dwells apart in his imagination, as the philosopher dwells in his reason, and as the priest dwells in his belief, the masculine nature that we propose for one that must be the master of our lives will be lost as, for example, in the folds of the garments of the ghost or ghosts of Aristotle. [pp.66–67]

Stevens's poet is a male androgyne. Imagination is the feminine side of his mind; this is the Muse that must be incorporated into his virile male body. Stevens denies woman reason – and creativity. The final evocation of the ghost of Aristotle seems to suggest that he is aware of the sources of his beliefs. But whatever the metaphysical wrappings of this masculine poetics, Stevens seems to be agreeing with the anonymous eighteenth-century objector to Aphra Behn, who wrote in 1702:

Gender and Genius

What a Pox have the Women to do with the Muses? I grant you the Poets call the Nine Muses by the Names of Women, but why so? not because the Sex had any thing to do with Poetry, but because in that Sex they're much fitter for prostitution. [Lock, 1976, p.26]

The paintbrush and sculptor's chisel are also phallic signifiers. Renoir, for example, is alleged to have said 'that he painted his paintings with his prick' [quoted *Madwoman*, p.6]. He most certainly wrote that

women are monsters who are authors, lawyers and politicians, like George Sand, Madame Adam, and other bores who are nothing more than five-legged beasts. The woman who is an artist is merely ridiculous, but I feel that it is acceptable for a woman to be a singer or a dancer. In Antiquity and among simple people, women sing and dance and they do not therefore become less feminine. Gracefulness is a woman's domain and even her duty. [White, 1972, p.171]

This is a common form of artistic misogyny. But in the fine arts there is another logic of sexual exclusion that is more prevalent than Renoir's . . . or even that underlying Ruskin's pronouncements about male and female roles in *Sesame and Lilies* (1867):

Now their separate characters are these. The man's power is active, progressive and defensive. He is eminently the doer, the creator, the discoverer. His intellect is for invention and speculation. But the woman's intellect is not for invention or creation but sweet ordering, arrangement and decision. Her great function is praise. [Parker and Pollock, 1981, p.9]

For Renoir, woman's status as a beautiful object confines her to social roles that involve artistic *display*, rather than artistic *invention*. By contrast, Ruskin's woman is a born housekeeper. She tidies the house of art while man exercises his inventive muscles, and she applauds when he brings home the creative bacon. But many of the examples provided by Parker and Pollock in *Old Mistresses* [1981] provide a further position in the pornographic gymnastics of sexualised art criticism. Writing in 1871, John Jackson Jarves provides an illustration. He divides 'feminine' from non-feminine fields of art, suggesting that women '*Naturally*' pick artistic fields that involve 'the least expenditure of mental capital'. Crafts that appeal to women's 'nice feeling for form, quick perceptions' and 'mobile fancy' are allocated to the 'feminine'. He gives clay-modelling as his example, but adds that when women venture into the more masculine genre of sculpture, 'women by *nature* are likewise prompted . . . to motives of fancy and sentiment rather than realistic portraiture or absolute creative imagination' [ibid., p.10, Parker and Pollock's emphases].

Male cultural supremacy is secured by such territorial divisions. Unlike Renoir and Ruskin, Jarves allows women inventive capacities – but only of inferior kinds. Absolute creative imagination is limited to certain subsections of subject-matter in certain privileged genres: such as realistic sculptures, oil paintings of (nude) human beings, group portraits or history paintings. Since women were deemed 'unsexed' by skill in these exclusively male fields of art, there could be no temptations to the truly 'feminine' psyche. Thus, although the 'feminine' is not consistently

The Male Gift

downgraded in phallic criticism, in these modes of *territorial* apartheid, 'feminine' and 'masculine' are synonymous with 'female' and 'male', and 'genius' becomes a kind of psychic beard – a secondary sexual characteristic of mature (European) males. In the words of Léon Legrange (1860):

Male genius has nothing to fear from female taste. Let men of genius conceive of great architectural projects, monumental sculpture, and elevated forms of painting. In a word, let men busy themselves with all that has to do with great art. Let women occupy themselves with those types of art they have always preferred, such as pastels, portraits or miniatures. Or the painting of flowers, those prodigies of grace and freshness which alone can compete with the grace and freshness of women themselves. [Trans. from French and quoted ibid., p.13]

Such gendering of creative territories is much more common in the fine arts than in literature. But there are, of course, examples in literary criticism, too. Indeed, we saw Shelley implicitly gendering the ghost-story as female. And in Chapter 2 we observed Anthony Burgess employing similar devices to downgrade female novelists. Burgess (a novelist himself) is supercilious about novel-writing: this female genre does not represent True Art. It is an inferior form of literature . . . and literature itself is inferior to musical composition . . . an activity, apparently, that requires *male* sexuality. Significantly, in *The Independent* of 23 May 1988 Anthony Burgess reveals that he thinks of himself as 'primarily a composer' . . . which explains why he can use music as a truss to protect his own creative balls. But, of course, few male novelists view themselves as essentially musicians, and as such have had to opt for more subtle means of guarding their manhood. Historically, the novel has been less easy to marginalise from High Art than flower-painting, clay-modelling, watercolour landscapes and other 'crafts'. Male novelists have had to find ways of reassuring themselves of their virility whilst still recognising that 'feminine' qualities such as sensitivity, passivity, emotionality and introspective self-consciousness are also expected of them.

The Virility School of Creativity seems to have been particularly important in the middle years of this century. Its sires include Picasso, Jackson Pollock, and in literature Hemingway, Henry Miller and Mailer. It was by no means a cohesive school . . . but rather a variety of gut reactions to an ideology that credited a creator with a male sexual drive but a feminine psyche. It encompasses a variety of machismo stances. Jackson Pollock and Henry Miller, for example, stressed their maleness precisely in order to compensate for the essentially intuitive and passive nature of their own working methods. Pollock's famous 'drip' paintings started by liquid simply falling on to the huge unstretched canvases laid out on floors or walls: and then (he claimed) the paintings 'contacted' him as he walked round and 'in' them, and revealed to him the shapes that he must form [O'Hara, 1959, p.32]. Scale, size, aggression – and picture-titles drawn from the mythologies of patriarchal power – were employed to masculinise these 'drip' techniques into 'Action Painting'. Analogously, Henry Miller idealised auth-

Gender and Genius

ors as radio 'antennae', picking up currents and ideas from the pervading atmosphere [Plimpton, 1963, pp.172–3]. But Miller's prose is frantically insistent that the author is *not-female*: hence the excessively violent (and monotonous) details of sexual exploits with the Otherness of cunts.

The typical Hemingway hero, on the other hand, was very different: full of machismo, but sexually impotent. As Peter Schwenger notes in his analysis of a group of these Virile Novelists, in every case 'Beneath the blatant *machismo* one finds considerable ambivalence towards the traditional masculine role' [1984, p.14]. In his subsequent chapters, Schwenger expresses his puzzlement in reconciling feminist theory (with its analysis of the way the pen has been represented as a penis) with his own observations that the buddies of the Virility School are only too aware that it is 'sissy' to write novels. Like the feminist critics whose writings he cites, Schwenger fails to make a clear distinction between the 'feminine' and the 'female'. Indeed, the novelists he examines also seem confused. Their texts stress maleness to counterbalance the effeminacy expected from members of their profession.

A kind of vulgar Freudianism was used to portray all creative activity as sublimated sexual libido . . . as Freud himself indicated that only males could be really said to have libidos, Freudianism was very reassuring [see Chapter 14, below]. Via Freud the figure of the talented male melancholic (who transcends his melancholic madness) was transposed into that of the virile but neurotic artist (who sublimates his neurosis). Metaphors of male lust and male sexual sickness are thus scattered liberally through George Plimpton's third compilation of Paris Review Interviews, *Writers at Work* [1967]. There James Jones talks about the writer's 'desire for self-exposure'. The writer wants to 'impose [his] personality upon the world', and the simile that follows excludes the woman writer. The author is 'like one of those guys who has a compulsion to take his thing out and show it on the street' [p.250].

Cocteau, by contrast, seems to have male masturbation in mind when he asks, 'This sickness, to express oneself. What is it?' The query follows on from a remark that seems to resemble Rousseau's in excluding women from having even good taste in art. 'Appreciation of art is a moral erection; otherwise mere dilettantism. I believe sexuality is the basis of all friendship' [ibid., p.81]. For Norman Mailer, on the other hand, his own act of writing is like the desire of a man 'to perform the sexual act under every kind of condition, emotion, and mood available to him' [ibid., p.275]. The sexual performance fantasised must surely be that of a sexual bully . . . not the raped or sexually degraded victim! But just how mentally sick *is* Mailer? He would feel happier – more male – if he could persuade us that he is potentially very sick indeed, but has redirected his sickness into literature instead of deeds. As he famously brags elsewhere, 'a good novelist can do with everything but the remnant of his balls' [1961, p.387].

Even contemporary male novelists who present themselves as sympath-

The Male Gift

etic to feminism, like John Fowles, find themselves trapped within the spiritual pornography of the School of Virility. And I am not just thinking here of *Mantissa* [1982], Fowles 'comic' excursus into soft porn. This parody of male fantasies about women functions as just one more male fantasy, in which (between acting dirty) the male narrator talks dirty with a (sometimes feminist) Muse [Woodcock, 1984]. Fowles caricatures feminism; but he has not simply grown more conservative with age. Throughout his fiction, his alliance with the 'feminine' always co-existed with a double *male* perspective on women. On the one hand, his heroines are cyphers objectified by male desire. On the other hand, they are represented as having wants and needs which must be respected: otherwise female allure will be lost [*The Collector*, 1963]; male happiness and the fabric of a patriarchal society will be threatened [*The French Lieutenant's Woman*, 1969]; and men will be trapped in delusory fantasies about muses, goddesses and love [*The Magus*, 1966].

Fowles recognises that there never was a time in which males could simply treat women as objects, and that this is a superficial conception of a male utopia. He tries to maintain authorial distance from the fetish that makes 'MOUSE' the signifier for Woman – 'the letter M and then, after a space' (in which 'an O-shaped vulva' is inserted) 'the letters U, S, E' [1974, pp.81–2]. But what gives Fowles's fiction its power is his own attraction towards that zero: that mysterious O(therness) that completes the male creator and the male procreator. Like the narrator of 'The Ebony Tower' [1974], Fowles feels nostalgia for the old aesthetics of virility, that made great art emerge from '"Balls. Spunk. Any spunk. Even Hitler's spunk. Or nothing"', and which consigns the abstraction and intellectualisation of modern art to the '"Triumph of the bloody eunuch"'. What is needed instead is '"Cock. Not fundamentals. Fundaments . . . Pair of tits and a cunt. All that goes with them. That's reality"' [pp.45–46]. Although in Fowles's story there is a female creator (nicknamed 'Mouse') – and self-conscious echoes of Gwen John (and Rodin) – the woman's creativity emerges out of sexual perversion: 'the real repression must be of a normal sexuality, a femaleness that cried out for . . .' [p.93]. Fowles clings to the tradition that makes great creators male.[2] L Like the other members of the Virility School, he makes art *dis*placed male sexuality . . . but *mis*placed female sexuality.

5
The Great 'I am'

'I am the author.' 'I am male.' 'I am God.' Romantic and modernist art binds these three sentences together into an unholy trinity. Post-structuralist fashion pretends that a post-modernist artist has no authority, and is far from god-like. But the convention that makes the artist a god was, as John Fowles notes in *The French Lieutenant's Woman* [1969], 'universally accepted' in the nineteenth century, and as long as we retain Romantic notions of artistic creativity, we retain the author as a pseudo-god.

The novelist is still a god, since he creates (and not even the most aleatory avant-garde modern novel has managed to extirpate its author completely); what has changed is that we are no longer the gods of the Victorian image, omniscient and decreeing; but in the new theological image, with freedom our first principle, not authority. [Fowles, 1969, p.86]

The twentieth century has re-defined God, and turned Him from an authoritarian and all-knowing Victorian patriarch into 'the freedom that allows other freedoms to exist' [p.86]. As a consequence, the 'once full, patriarchal beard' of the watching, modernist narrator-god 'has been trimmed down to something rather foppish and Frenchified' – as befits a God who is a respecter of existentialist freedoms [p.394]. But the author is still a god. He also still sports a beard. The new God of modernism is still (implicitly) male.

Romantic aesthetics built its theory of artistic creativity on epistemological foundations laid by the eighteenth-century German philosopher, Immanuel Kant. According to Kant, there are three levels of reality: the world of appearances (which includes everything we see, hear, smell or otherwise sense); the world of the noumena, or things-in-themselves, which are always unknowable and ungraspable by all men during their life on earth; and the world of transcendental objects and subjects, which is the world in which we live. Kantian man is, as it were, stuck behind spatio-temporal sunglasses that he can never remove from his head. Just as pink sunglasses make everything look pink, so these spatio-temporal sunglasses make everything appear to us in three-dimensional space and one-dimensional time. We can never remove them: so we can never see what things-in-themselves are really like. The only reality we have is one strung together out of perceptions by means of the imagination. And the first thing we construct for ourselves is a stable self (the transcendental ego) which constructs itself and a stable world (of transcendental objects) at the same time. We live our lives in a fiction constructed by the imagination.

Copernicus placed the sun, instead of the earth, at the centre of the universe. Kant thought of himself as equally revolutionary: locating the individual human being at the fulcrum of the knowable universe. The 'I am' of the Kantian self brings the world into existence. My 'I am' creates the world I (and you) live in. It's a pretty grandiose conception of the power of the imagination! And Kant modelled it on his Christian pietistic beliefs about the way that God created matter. Kant here was entirely inconsistent. He had said we can only know what we can string together out of sense experiences. On his account, therefore, we should not be able to know anything about whether God exists, or about how He might operate if, indeed, He does exist. But somehow Kant can guess this. He talks about beings with 'intellectual intuition' who don't just bring the world as it appears to be into existence, but also bring things-in-themselves into existence.

Kant seems to have in mind here the obscure verse from the Bible, Exodus 3:14, 'And God said unto Moses, I AM THAT I AM . . .' Kant is envisaging a Being who can literally think himself into existence, unlike a human being who can only think into existence the self he appears to himself to have. This is the metaphysical model that the Romantic theorists appropriated for art. In Coleridge's *Biographia Literaria*, for example, an author stands in the same relation to his work as does the Kantian self to the world of appearances . . . and God to the world of things-in-themselves. Coleridge's artist creates by means of the secondary imagination:

The Imagination then I consider either as primary, or secondary. The primary Imagination I hold to be the living power and prime agent of all human perception, and as a repetition in the finite mind of the eternal act of creation in the infinite I AM. The secondary Imagination I consider as an echo of the former . . . differing only in degree, and in the mode of its operation. [1817, p.159]

For the Romantics, then, art grows out of individuality. The Christian God is the great 'I am'; and the artist is the lesser 'I am' – God's son, who booms out 'I am' in a definitely male voice. As Anaïs Nin observes in her *Journals* for August 1937:

As to all that nonsense Henry [Miller] and Larry [Durrell] talked about, the necessity of 'I am God' in order to create (I suppose they mean 'I am God, I am not a woman') . . . But what neither Larry nor Henry understands is that woman's creation far from being like man's must be exactly like her creation of children, that it must come out of her own blood, englobed by her womb, nourished with her own milk. It must be a human creation, of flesh, it must be different from man's abstractions. As to this 'I am God,' which makes creation an act of solitude and pride, this image of God alone making sky, earth, sea, it is this image which has confused woman. (Man too, because he thinks God did it all alone, and he thinks he did it all alone. And behind every achievement of man lies a woman, and I am sure God was helped too but never acknowledged it.) [vol.ii, pp.233–4]

When Nin talks so dismissively about the 'nonsense' of Henry Miller and Lawrence Durrell – both close friends – she pretends not to know

what they mean: 'I suppose they mean "I am God, I am not a woman."'
But, in fact, her diaries show that she is all too familiar with the type of
Romantic aesthetic theory that her companions are drawing upon. She
has not been fooled by the fact that Henry Miller thought of great
authors as passive and egoless (even 'feminine') radio-antennae. She
recognises that the model of creativity that underlies her colleague's
work presupposes an individual and arrogant ego, so swollen with pride
as to suppose that its own self encompasses the whole universe. And
Nin is all too poignantly aware of the paradoxes that face the woman
writer who internalises such a model of creativity.

Her *Journals* chart 'the guilt for creating which is strong in woman':

*I tried to efface my creation with a sponge, to drown my creation because my
concept of devotion and the roles I had to play clashed with my creative self.
[January, 1943, vol.iii, p.258]*

A male could be a fully sexual being and remain a creator. But, for a
woman, choosing to be a professional writer, painter or a sculptor was
not just a matter of choosing a career (what one *does* with one's life), it
was also a matter of choosing what to *be*: a woman or a sexual pervert. A
woman accepting that art requires *male* sexual energies would be likely
to see herself as Renoir's George Sand: as an unsexed woman or a 'five-
legged beast'. So Nin carries on:

*I did not want to be a man. Djuna Barnes was masculine. George Sand./I did
not want to steal man's creation, his thunder./Creation and femininity seemed
incompatible. The aggressive act of creation./ . . . I have a horror of the
masculine 'career' woman./To create seemed such an assertion of the strongest
part of me that I would no longer be able to give all those I love the feeling of
their being stronger, and they would love me less./ . . . I have made myself less
powerful, have concealed my powers./ . . . I have crippled myself./Dreams of
Chinese women with bound feet. [ibid., pp.259–60]*

Nin's own solution to this dilemma was to render herself invisible to
herself in the history of high culture. She decides that Henry and Larry
are artists; she is merely a writer. 'I know Henry is the artist because he
does exactly what I do not do. He waits. He gets outside of himself.
Until it becomes fiction . . . I am not interested in fiction. I want
faithfulness' [August 1937, vol.ii, p.233]. The men are 'objective'; she as
a woman could only be 'subjective'. It is the males who are associated
with cultural creation, and the construction of an alternative, fictional
reality. Females are necessarily linked to the body; to the 'real' world; to
feeling, emotion and 'subjectivity'. She wishes to write in a way that
maintains its connections with the womb by a kind of navel-string. And
so she opts for the first-person diary genre: 'a feminine activity, it is a
personal and personified creation, the opposite of the masculine
alchemy' [February 1937, p.172].

In contemporary language what Nin aimed at was *écriture féminine* or
'writing the body' – a solution to the dilemmas of a phallic aesthetics
that has attracted many later feminists [see Chapter 14, below]. There is
something to be said in favour of this type of answer. On one level, after

The Great 'I am'

all, it does negate the false either/or: *either* be a truly feminine woman, *or* be a writer and artist. Nin insists she is a woman; she will write; but she is not an 'artist'. However, by calling Henry 'the artist', and by stepping back from calling her own works 'art', Nin fails to challenge the notion that art itself is a male preserve. For all her creative courage, Nin at these moments adopts the coward's defence, and withdraws into a separate space marked 'women's work'. Nin *is* an artist, and sometimes she sees this – for example, whilst helping Henry Miller to structure his *Black Spring* [ibid., vol.i, p.166]. Her own journals are no more 'subjective' than Miller's novels. In any case, why should 'objectivity' be male and 'subjectivity' female? Why should a woman be more bound by her body than a man? Why should a woman be more emotional, a man more rational and more abstract? These are all dichotomies that Nin used at that time, and they all involve accepting the masculine perspective that views the female as lacking the psychic equipment that enables her to retain her sexuality and also be an artist.[1]

No woman can be blamed for getting trapped by the tradition that denies women the title of 'artist'. Historically the dialectics of exclusion have been so varied, and so inconsistent, that almost every move made by a woman creator will find her presented with another spurious argument that denies or misrepresents either her sexuality or her artistry. The aesthetics of Romanticism treats the woman artist as an isolated and exceptional freak and yet also – and often at the same time – as a sub-human incapable of having a strong and solitary ego. Although Nin talks of the way in which the male artist glorifies the solitary nature of the act of creation, it is in fact the woman artist who is the more isolated figure. The weight of cultural and artistic tradition presses on the shoulders of all writers in our culture who are male, and the male writer is likely to deny his ancestry and insist on his own individual creative power. Tradition, of course, also presses heavily on the shoulders of the woman artist. But it presses in a different way – as a discouragement to all artistic efforts. Dorothy Richardson put it poignantly in *Pilgrimage* (1915–38; vol.ii, ch.xxiv):

If one could only burn all the volumes; stop the publication of them. But it was all books, all the literature in the world, right back to Juvenal . . . whatever happened, if it could all be avenged by somebody in some way, there was all that . . . the classics, the finest literature – 'unsurpassed'. Education would always mean coming in contact with all that. Schoolboys got their first ideas . . . How could Newnham and Girton women endure it? How could they go on living and laughing and talking? [Original ellipses; extract in Goulianos, 1974, p.270]

A lot of the metaphoric language of collectivity and the denial of creation as a solitary act that we find in texts and works by women artists is an expression of their need to find a group to which they feel they can belong. There are alternative traditions of women's art that, picked out, would promote a better understanding and appreciation of female creativity. But Romanticism does not bring these continuities into focus. Indeed, feminist critics are only just managing to peer round the edges of orthodox cultural histories to confront these distinctively female forms. In *The Madwoman in the Attic*, for example, Gilbert and Gubar have revealed a community of isolated female voices in which women creators are not second-class citizens. They show how, condemned to 'Otherness' by a phallic aesthetics that treats the female artist as a 'five-legged beast', nineteenth-century women writers are bonded into an alternative tradition. The characters these women writers create are (like themselves) presented as semi-human: their fictional witches, monsters and madwomen are credited with fully human emotions and capacities that make them worthy of sympathy or empathy . . . whilst still (somehow) remaining thoroughly monstrous. This mode of ambivalence towards craziness, abnormality and terror – of authorial identification and simultaneous distance – constitutes a distinctively *female* genre.

Despite its subtitle 'The Modern Prometheus', Mary Shelley's *Frankenstein* [1818] helps create a tradition of female authorship that speaks with the voice of a modern Pandora. Like the first Pandora, these women are the offspring of a mythology that gifts to males the psychic fire and wisdom of the gods. Just as we could feel despair or anger at the way the first woman was blamed (instead of Prometheus) for introducing disease and suffering into the world, so also we could see the Romantic notion of genius in a purely negative light. It has, after all, obscured the alternative traditions of cultural achievement into which these individual female writers fit. But, as in the original myth, Hope lies concealed at the bottom of the jar of horrors opened up by the modern Pandora. Unfortunately, we have to fumble deep into the darkness of the jar of patriarchal myth before we can bring out Hope. But if we look deep enough we can find a continuum of women creators struggling to position themselves amongst the ancient and modern myths that bind together the concepts of male sexuality and of creativity. We find Another Otherness: as female writers, artists and musicians subvert the notion that artistic production is a *male* task.

Nin knew that she had been trapped into seeing creativity as a male attribute. But although she was aware of her own strength, she could not bring herself to 'want to steal man's creation, his thunder'. Her *Journals* show her trying to re-trace the route out of the maze that imprisons thought about creativity in the grounds of a male God. She rejects as 'confusing' the Old Testament version of the genesis of the universe and its paradigmatic status in accounts of artistic production. Creation cannot be 'an act of solitude and pride': rather, 'behind every achievement of man lies a woman, and I am sure God was helped too but never acknowledged it'. Nin's words here serve as a stunning illustration of the way that women artists, lacking easy access to the female traditions of creativity, have – on an individual basis – to re-establish those insights for themselves. Writing in the late 1930s and early '40s, Anaïs Nin could not have known of the buried texts that would be dug up just a few years later, which also rejected the notion of a male god 'alone making sky, earth, sea'. Nin was unaware of the Gnostic cosmogony, condemned by the Church authorities to centuries of oblivion. So, instead, out of her own imagination, she re-invented

The Great 'I am'

part of the Gnostic alternative.

In December 1945, four months after the thunder of two explosions had brought to an end the Second World War, a jar containing thirteen ancient papyrus books was dug out of the cliffs edging the Egyptian desert by a local farmer collecting fertiliser. Amongst the fifty-two texts contained in the leather-bound books was a poem, called 'Thunder, Perfect Mind', written in the voice of a female divine power. The metaphoric language of omnipotence could not have been used of a male god; but neither did the power of this female creator stem simply from the specifically feminine tasks of motherhood.

For I am the first and the last.
I am the honoured one and the scorned one.
I am the whore and the holy one.
I am the wife and the virgin . . .
I am the barren one,
      and many are her sons . . .
I am the silence that is incomprehensible . . .
I am the utterance of my name.

[Nag Hammadi Library, *1977, VI,2; Pagels, pp.16–17*]

In *The Gnostic Gospels* [1980], Elaine Pagels has exposed some of the detail of these early Christian works, translated into Coptic in AD *c.*350–400 from much earlier Greek texts, including some perhaps as old as – or even older than – those of Matthew, Mark, Luke and John. Pagels points out how much work remains to be done on the manuscripts, which (for reasons of greed and national and professional jealousy) only came fully into the public domain in the late 1970s. But from her account many things are already clear. Buried in Upper Egypt, condemned by the authority of the Fathers of the Church to the fate of unorthodoxy, is a rich tradition of writing and thinking about power and divinity that gives a different role to the female. Several of the texts provide Eve with a more positive part in the drama of the garden of Eden: she is associated with wisdom and the awakening of Adam to life and understanding. Mary Magdalene is also given a more central role, as a knowledgeable and perceptive apostle. A number of the gospels also present us with the prehistory of Genesis. God the Father of the Old Testament is made the self-promoting and boastful offspring of the female procreative force, Sophia (Wisdom). After he was created, the male God

became arrogant, saying, 'It is I who am God, and there is none other apart from me.'

When he said this, he sinned against the Entirety. And a voice came forth from above the realm of absolute power, saying, 'You are mistaken, Samael' – which is, 'god of the blind.'

And he said, 'If any other thing exists before me, let it become visible to me!' And immediately Sophia stretched forth her finger and introduced Light into Matter . . . ['The Hypostasis of the Archons', Nag Hammadi *II, 4, 94–5]*

Gender and Genius

These early Christian gospels thus undermine the orthodox under-standing of the famous first verse of the Gospel of St John: 'In the beginning was the Word, and the Word was with God, and the Word was God.' In the King James version of the New Testament, 'word' is used to render the untranslatable Greek term *logos* – glossed elsewhere as 'speech', 'doctrine', 'measure', 'reason', 'principle' or even 'propor-tion'. This noun, so important in the metaphysics of ancient Greece, was associated with the capacity for rational discourse: that characteristic which, in Aristotelian metaphysics, is what makes human beings super-ior to the rest of the animal kingdom. But *logos* belonged to the males, in the sense that it was claimed that it was through the father that the attributes of the species were passed on from generation to generation. In the Stoic elaborations on this Aristotelian idea, *logos* was the formula contained within the male seed that enabled the father to reproduce his own likeness in his offspring. The *logos* was a kind of mystical (genetic) code, which only males carried.

Logos spermatikos – 'the spermatic word' – was a central concept in ancient Greek and Roman Stoicism. Whether or not the writer of St John's Gospel was himself influenced by Stoicism is a matter of dispute. But it seems clear that the Fathers of the Christian Church read St John through the spectacles of Stoic cosmology, which traced the origin of the universe to the coding contained within the male seed. In Chapter 3 I argued that the Greek philosophers did not themselves have the concept of a self-creating God. Creation in Aristotle was procreation: the male principle was the active shaping force applied to the inert matter provided by the female. But, via Roman Stoicism, Christianity combined Judaic ideas of a self-creating God with Greek ideas of the origins of the universe. For the Church Fathers, God remained male – even though the Christian God was supposed to have created himself *out of nothing*, by processes utterly unlike those of biological reproduc-tion. The 'I AM THAT I AM' was Father, Son and Holy *male* Spirit . . . as '*Genius*' was for the Stoics.

'*Genius*' was one of the key terms in the Stoics' spermatic cosmogony: it was used to conjoin (male) human beings with the universe and Jove (its personification and the father of the gods). The *logos spermatikos* made all three divine. Historians of ideas have, on the whole, pretended that it is the history of the Latin term *ingenium* that is important in the history of our modern concept of genius, and that the Latin word *genius* matters hardly at all. Anaïs Nin, quite instinctively, knew better. She recognised that the model of creation that her male companions drew on in thinking about genius used as its model God the Father. 'I am not a woman' is the whispered implication of the 'I am God' that Nin detects at the heart of Romantic and Modernist aesthetics.

In Chapter 1 we saw Carl Gustav Jung (1875–1961) confining the *logos spermatikos* to the males. Jung, the product of Romanticism, joined a patrilineal tradition that stretches back all the way to Aristotle, the Stoics, and the founding Fathers of the Western Church. Jung would have us believe that this tradition represents ancient wisdom. But the

The Great 'I am'

Gnostics knew better: they suggested that it is wilful male blindness that shapes this ancient prejudice. The Gnostics' primordial creative power is *bi*sexual: it is an androgynous voice which asserts, '[I] am the real Voice. I cry out in everyone, and they know that a seed dwells within' ['Trimorphic Protennoia', *Nag Hammadi* XIII, 1, 36; Pagels, p.77]. The Gnostic female is associated with that which underlies *logos*: with sound (out of which words are shaped), and with matter (out of which the seed itself is moulded). Matter was also female in Aristotle, but was downgraded in a way quite foreign to many of these Gnostic texts. The Gnostic universe was formed by forces which include the psychic and reproductive powers of the female. 'Yahveh' – literally 'I am' – was one of the Old Testament names for the God. 'I am', 'I am', 'I am' thunders the counter-voice of the perfect female mind – adding, 'I am the silence that is incomprehensible . . . I am the utterance of my name.'

The Gnostic codices demonstrate that the Christian account of the creation of the universe could have severed the links between divinity and male procreativity. Christianity offered women the opportunity to be considered the spiritual equals of males. But instead of embracing women as 'brothers in Christ', the Christian Fathers closed ranks . . . and developed a canon that condemned to the desert of forgetfulness the words of those who spoke out for female spiritual power. In much the same way, the Romantics' revaluation of all 'feminine' values should have given female artistic creators equality with males. But the Sons of Romanticism still represented creativity as bonded to male sexual energies, and hence as alien to women. An examination of the pagan worship of male virility – and the subsequent history of its uneasy alliance with Christian orthodoxy – will, I believe, cast light on the later orthodoxies (of post-Romantic aesthetics, and even of some forms of feminism) that *still* represent *logos* as necessarily male. The next chapter does, therefore, move back to explore the original meaning of *genius* for the ancient Romans, and gives the background to the Stoic links between *genius* and the *logos spermatikos*. And then, in Chapter 7, I outline the survival (and transformation) of Roman beliefs about *genius* in medieval Christian texts.

What I will be arguing is that, via Christianity, the (divine metaphysical) *genius* of male procreativity shrivelled into a (mundane, physical) penis . . . the pen was used as a kind of penis-extension (to re-establish male divinity on a new non-physical level) . . . and then, eventually, via Romanticism, 'genius' was, once again, worshipped – although in an entirely different form. As Christian males grew ever more uneasy about the powers embodied in male flesh, 'genius' was excavated out of the classical past, and given an increasingly important role in the misogyny of Western culture. The Romantics re-worked the Roman and Christian myths that derided God the Mother, God the Daughter, and God the Holy *female* Spirit. We need the outlines of this history to grasp the reasons why the mouths of women creators – like the mouths of the Gnostics' earthenware jars – should have been covered with rocks. I do not pretend that the sketch that follows is in any way complete. I am neither a classicist nor a medievalist, nor even a historian

Gender and Genius

of religion. Specialists will have to go back and fill in more of the details of this narrative, with rather more awareness of the gender-implications of classical scholarship than I have found in much of the material that I have consulted. But the silhouettes of this history deserve to be established – however tentatively and however provisionally – to help us understand the processes whereby, in the nineteenth and twentieth centuries, the *logos* was once again decreed male.

The Great 'I am'

6
The Genesis of Genius

The cult of *genius* emerged in prehistorical times in the countryside around Rome. *Genius* was one of a number of household spirits that were all connected in some way with the ownership, protection and cultivation of property and land by a family or a clan. There was, for example, Janus: later the god overseeing beginnings, but to start with the object of ritual worship associated with the entrance or doorway to the family home. Other cults grew up around Vesta, the hearth or fire at the centre of the wigwam-like living space; Penates, the store-cupboard or larder; and the Camenae, the spirits of the springs of water that are so essential to life on the land. These water spirits later evolved into the Muses which cause inspiration to flow. According to most historians of religion this development suggests that the early Romans were animists whose superstitions were designed to placate the protective spirits that were thought to live in objects and lands, as well as in people [Bailey, 1932, pp.35ff.].

These cults emerged at a time of primitive agricultural settlements, when what mattered first and foremost was ownership of land by families and *gentes*. The *gentes* were great clans made up of families, all descended from a common father. Each of these families was a patriar-chal structure, headed by a paterfamilias, who was a living offshoot of the spirit of his *gens*. From the time that a man became a paterfamilias he exercised authority over his *familia* (which included slaves and women in his 'guardianship', as well as his children and his wife). At his death the status of paterfamilias passed to the adult married sons, each of whom then set up a *familia*. The families were patrilocal: for a woman to leave the place of her original family and live, in an uninter-rupted fashion, with another man was a clear sign that she had become a wife [Lefkowitz and Fant, 1982, pp.175, 190]. The *gentes* themselves were patrilineal: the powers associated with them passed from fathers to sons. As Bailey writes, the term *genius* both represented 'the virile powers of man which make for the continuance of the family' and, in a broader sense, 'the spirit that dwells in the man [he means "male"], as a spirit dwelt in the hearth or the store-cupboard' [pp.51,52]. In early Roman art the *genius* is often represented in the form and likeness of the paterfamilias who also acted as the main priest in the family prayers and rites to the *genius* and other ancestral deities of his *gens*.

Roman civilisation was built upon an élite, divided into family groups and working the lands which they owned. Perry Anderson argues that the urbanisation of Rome was only possible through the growth of

Gender and Genius

slavery [1974, pp.59ff.]. The slaves carried on working the land and providing their Roman masters with wealth, whilst the families of slave-owners gradually freed themselves from agricultural labour – and, indeed, from all labour. The *genius* was not only connected with the vital forces of the *gens*, but also with the ground that it owned. The dependence of city life on continued land-ownership might explain why the worship of agricultural deities persisted even after the élite moved into the town. Originally, in the country, at the boundary of each family's land, were boundary stones (*termini*) which were objects of great sacredness, and linked with ritual observances. All land within the boundary stones was watched over and imbued with the *genius* of the *gens* as represented by the paterfamilias. There is thus a connection between the celebrated *genius loci*, 'genius of the place', and the rites associated with the virility and divinity of the paterfamilias. In urban Rome crossroads remained sacred places; and stones – bound round by the old country rituals – continued to mark important boundaries within the city [Bailey, pp.6–7,147ff.]. Indeed, Rome itself became a place with a *Genius* who watched over and guarded the interlinked *gentes* that made up the Roman State. The *genius* was first of all simply the spirit, and later the personification of patrilineal and patriarchal power.

After Augustus had been proclaimed Emperor in 27 BC, worship of the Emperor's *Genius* became part of institutionalised State religion. The Emperor was the paterfamilias of the State, and his *Genius* was worshipped as a kind of god [Taylor, 1931]. By this time, however, another level of complexity had been added to the *genius* cults. We find the first literary allusions to *genius* in the dramas of Plautus in the third century BC. Although *genius* was still associated primarily with the paterfamilias, now each free male (each potential paterfamilias) was seen as having a *genius* from the time of his birth. The *genius* was his potential virility, energy, or life-giving force. Although it could only be truly released with marriage and procreation, it was there in a latent state from the start. A male was expected to 'indulge' his *genius*, which depended on a life-fluid or 'sap' (*sucus*) that circulated throughout the body, but which was particularly associated with the head and the knees. A man who 'defrauded' his *genius* by denying his appetites for health-giving food and sensual pleasures became 'dried up' (*aridus*). The man who nourished his *genius* was, by contrast, 'genial' (*genialis*) [Nitzsche, 1975, pp.10ff.].

By the last century BC this individual *genius* had become a god, who was born with, died with, and was celebrated by each male on his birthday. A woman, by contrast, honoured her *juno*. The nature of the *genius* that ruled over a male's life depended on the stars that were in the sky at the time of his birth. The Romans had come into contact with polytheistic cultures (like that of Greece, for example), and the worship of a family of gods had overlaid the animist cults. But animism and polytheism combined. The *Genius* of individual gods (especially the father = Jove/Jupiter/Zeus) was also worshipped. Modern commentators gloss the oaths and prayers directed to Jove's *Genius* as being directed to his

The Genesis of Genius

'generative spirit, virility, energy' [ibid., p.13]. Eventually under Christian influence the *genius* evolved into a Guardian Angel, which could be good or evil – like the stars themselves [ibid., pp.38ff.].

It is, however, hard to be really sure how important the cult of *genius* was in the earliest traditions of Roman civilisation, and how much or little it took from the cults of family worship that existed in the agricultural communities that preceded the foundation of the city-state of Rome. Paintings, statues and cult objects remain, but we are dealing with a time that predates the written records of the area. It suited later Romans who wrote about that time to idealise it, and to interpret it as one in which male authority had been unquestioned by the women, and in which the deities associated with masculinity were powerful. Modern scholars confront a concerted campaign, mounted in the time of the Emperor Augustus, which used the cult of *genius* to stress the merits of patriarchal authority. Augustus was touted as the new Romulus: the father of a new Rome and of an Empire. He would carry on the traditions of the *gentes*, and restore to the Roman State the order and glory that had been lost during the civil wars and in the last years of the crumbling Republic. The propaganda machine tried to re-animate the old laws, old myths and old religions: including those of *genius*. As a consequence, we can only see the religion of *genius* through a distorting mirror that exaggerates the role of male authority in the classical past.

Legends of male power over women were of the greatest importance in the culture of Rome. This might be, as writers like Bachofen have argued, because an older matriarchal (Etruscan) culture was being replaced by a patriarchal culture. It is hard to know. Roman myth tangles historical fact into male fantasies. In the beginning, we are told, a gang of fighting men under the leadership of the legendary Romulus (traditional dates 753–716 BC) came down from Alba to found the city of Rome. There was a shortage of women in the new city, and the Romans used guile to steal women from the nearby tribe. The settlers arranged a festival and invited their neighbours, the Sabines. At a given signal from Romulus, the Roman men carried off an appropriate number of attractive young Sabine women. According to several old versions of the myth, the Sabine women were not physically molested by the Romans during that first night. The Roman men had in mind a more sophisticated form of sexual oppression. The next morning the women were once again forced – this time to hear a lecture by Romulus on the virtues of the marriage laws that were to govern their lives with the Roman settlers. According to this story, the marriages then took place: the Sabine women having been persuaded to accept their lot by the smooth talking of Romulus and their prospective husbands [Balsdon, 1962, pp.24–25; Grant and Hazel, 1973].

We are used to seeing this myth portrayed in Renaissance and neoclassical paintings as brutal physical rape. But these later pictures miss the subtleties of the Roman story. What is being celebrated is not just male control of women's bodies; it is rather control of their minds. The ancients tell us that the origins of Roman civilisation lie not merely in

Gender and Genius

male power, but in a social contract between males and females. We are asked to believe that women were willing prisoners, and assented to the laws that consigned them to permanent inferiority. Carved in bronze amongst the tablets of law in the Roman Forum is the decree, 'Women, even though they are of full age, because of their levity of mind shall be under guardianship . . . except vestal virgins, who . . . shall be free from guardianship' [Lefkowitz and Fant, p.174]. A young girl was her father's vassal. Complicated legal procedures were devised for the transference of this power from the father of the growing girl to her husband, or to another male guardian. Unless a woman promised thirty years of chastity, she had to remain a minor – under the legal thumb of a man (until she had performed her duty and produced three children by her husband) [ibid., p.249]. The most sacred types of marriage ceremony left a woman in *manus*: literally 'in the hand of ' her husband and under the authority of the family to which he belonged [ibid., p.190 and n., p.249]. Another of Romulus's laws reads: 'If a daughter-in-law strikes her father-in-law she shall be dedicated as a sacrifice to his ancestral deities' [p.174]. The wife had to agree that the *genius* and other household gods of her husband's family should have power over every aspect of her life.

Roman marriage ceremonies contained ritual elements that symbolised the bride being carried away from her family by force. The ancestral laws forbade women from divorcing men, but enabled men to divorce women quite easily. Indeed, divorce was expected 'for the use of drugs or magic on account of children or for counterfeiting the keys or for adultery' [ibid., p.173]. All deformed children were killed; and it was permissible to refuse to rear all except the first born of the female children [pp.173,174]. The laws governing marriage and procreation were designed to reassure the men that their wives' children were quality products of their own *gens*. But precisely because the continuity of the male line was important, and because of the difficulty of guarding women every moment of the day, it was essential that wives should be trusted. Generally speaking the Roman male did not lock his wife away in Southern seclusion; instead the culture mythologised the wives' complicity in the patriarchal institutions. It was a rape of the mind – not the body.

There were, of course, benefits for women within the marriage institution. In particular, a wife was allowed to share in her husband's property. Without this, the myth of consent would not have had the slightest ring of truth, and would thus have failed to reassure the men. And since unforced female assent mattered more than physical compulsion, Roman women were eventually able to negotiate for themselves a surprising degree of freedom – whilst remaining under the overarching patriarchal structures of Roman law and the Roman family. This was why the Emperor Augustus could link a decline in Rome's status to a breakdown in patriarchal law, and to a collapse in morality and traditional religious observances. When the Emperor was promoted to a god, worshipped indirectly through elaborate rites of homage to his *Genius*, a vision of a golden age was conjured up. The

The Genesis of Genius

State cult drew on a rhetoric of rustic families honouring and offering sacrifices to the *genius* of the paterfamilias. Those were the days! . . . Days when the authority of the male was not questioned! . . . A time when there was order, harmony and decency in everyday life! The rites of worship to Augustus's *Genius* were used to cement together the patrilineal *gentes* into one family-State under the greatest paterfamilias of all: the Roman Emperor himself. Feminist classicists and historians of religion need to be suspicious of the Emperor's story, especially since most modern scholarship seems determinedly blind to the masculinist biases embedded in Roman history.

In recent years some aspects of this history of *genius* have been questioned. But the remarks of Dumézil, the most celebrated of these critics, do not take feminist scholarship much further. Dumézil argues (convincingly) that in prehistorical paintings and cult objects the *genius* is not represented by the phallus. But his remarks here only serve to obscure the connection between masculinity and *genius*. Dumézil criticises Altheim for adopting the 'the theory in fashion' and asserting a close link between the phallus and *genius* [Dumézil, 1966, i, p.359]. But this is totally to misinterpret Altheim who made sophisticated modifications to Bachofen's account of prehistorical Rome. To prove that patriarchy involves a higher stage of cultural evolution than matriarchy, Bachofen had alleged, in *Mother Right* (1861), that the matriarchal society of the Etruscans had bordered on – and been eventually absorbed into – patriarchal Rome. Altheim, unconvinced that Etruria was a matriarchy, was nevertheless sure that it was matrilineal. He claimed that it was the Etruscan *woman* who personified the house and family, and who connected the spirits of past ancestors to those of future generations. Altheim suggested that in a matrilineal society the primary value of males is a reproductive one, and hence in a matrilineal society what represents the male is his procreative tool [1938, pp.50ff.]. This is quite different, he contended, in the patrilineal Roman society, and that is why the phallus never symbolised *genius*.

In other words, Altheim agrees with Dumézil that for the Romans *genius* was never symbolised by the male genital organs, but Altheim still argues that *genius* represented masculinity. Dumézil seems to believe that there was no such link, but his structuralist analyses do not establish this conclusion and serve instead to muddy the useful distinctions that Altheim made between symbolic values in matrilineal and patrilineal societies. Clearly there are aspects of Altheim's thesis that need revising. Our society is not matrilineal; but it is still obsessed with the phallus-as-penis. Why this should be will become clearer in the next chapter which deals with the story of what happened to *genius* in a Christian culture in which males were taught shame (instead of pride) in their own bodies. Since there was no longer anything meritorious about procreativity as such, male sexuality was reduced to a set of (physical) genital organs . . . which took on *metaphysical* dimensions and came to signify male *spiritual* power. From our post-Christian perspective it is easy to suppose that in all cultures the penis-as-phallus was always the universal signifier of male power. But this was precisely what Altheim denied.

Gender and Genius

The early Romans seem to have inhabited a pre-dualistic universe, in which the spiritual was an aspect of the (male) body, instead of being merely temporarily housed (Christian-fashion) in human flesh. For the later Romans (including the Stoics) – subject to Greek (especially Platonic) influences – there was already a problematic relationship between soul and body. Nevertheless, even for the Romans of Augustus's time, the worship of *genius* involved homage to male sexuality in its most noble form. It was his forehead, not his genital organs, that a Roman male touched whilst honouring his *genius*. Even if some of the Stoics did claim that it was possible to over-indulge the *genius*, there was nothing intrinsically base or malevolent about this aspect of maleness. *Genius* remained linked to 'geniality': to laughter and happiness. As Altheim put it,

although the name of the Roman genius *does indeed mean the 'begetter', and although the function of a divine force, which works in and beside the human father, is everywhere the same, yet the Roman* genius *is far removed from any relation to the sexual in its narrower sense, not to speak of its ever being conceived or expressed in phallic form. [p.61]*

For the patrilineal Romans, *genius* was 'a simile for the male seed, which from the father begets the son and from the son goes on to continue the race' [p.59]. This seed was not simply mundane (physical) sperm; it was a seed that was ripened in the bodies of heroic male ancestors, and in the soil that had been cleared and planted by generations of males. *Genius* was a sort of genetic coding that entitled a male to property, lands, rights and power over women and slaves.

A woman's *juno* seems to have been by no means an exact female equivalent to the male's *genius*. In Rome a woman's primary power stemmed from her years of fecundity; a man's power was linked with his genetic inheritance, as well as the lands and slaves that he owned. Thus, Onians suggests that the *juno* was only 'the power manifest in a woman more particularly in the period of fertility, the body's prime' [1951, p.264n.]. And Dumézil has argued the worship of the *juno* was much less ancient than that of the *genius* [1966, i, p.293]. For the Romans the head seems to have been the most divine part of the human body, and the house of the *genius* in males. The head of the paterfamilias was covered over only at death – to signify transmission of the *genius* from father to sons? – and during certain religious ceremonies. But, in early Rome, a woman had to cover her head whenever she appeared in public [Onians, pp.145ff.; Lefkowitz and Fant, p.176]. It seems to have been eyebrows – not foreheads – that were dedicated to *Juno* . . . a symbolic reminder of the low status of females [Onians, p.129n.]. Analogously, a slave was compelled to wear a single band round his forehead. Since a male slave had to join in the worship of the *genius* of the paterfamilias – rather than his own *genius* – the banded forehead seems to have indicated a bounded *genius*, as well as simple inferiority.

Even if the Roman *genius* was especially located inside a male's head, it must not be supposed that the Romans made a special connection between it and intelligence. We have seen that in the physiology of the

The Genesis of Genius

Renaissance the head was the place where vapours rising from the heated blood were supposed to condense and turn into animal spirits (analogous to male sperm) which then flowed back down through the body. In *The Origins of European Thought* [1951], Onians finds similar models in ancient Roman and Greek texts. It was out of his forehead, for example, that Jove/Jupiter/Zeus was supposed to have given birth to Minerva/Athena, the warrior maiden and goddess of all activities involving mental skill. Jove was said to have swallowed Minerva's wise and powerful mother, and transferred the foetus he had fathered to his own head. Onians gives other evidence that makes the head a privileged site for masculine procreativity [pp.93–168]. The only other place in the male body that serves as a womb-substitute in Roman and Greek myths seems to be the thigh. Jove, for example, took the foetus of Liber/Bacchus/Dionysus and sewed it into his leg until the godlet was due to be born. Is there some connection between these stories and the fact that the other place in the male body supposed to be especially linked with *genius* was the knee? It's hard to be sure. It is tempting to explain the connection through some form of linguistic confusion, in that the Latin term for 'knee', *genu*, is very close to the word '*gignio*' 'to engender' and also to '*genius*' itself. But Onians has also observed that the links between the masculine power of procreativity and the knee are by no means confined to the Latin language [pp.174–87].

If we think of the fertility of the body as patterned by primitive man on the fertility of the earth, then there is a hypothesis that could explain this bizarre observation. Just as rain is heated by the sun to form a vapour that falls back to earth, so blood was seen to be heated by the heart and liver to form vapours which then rose to the cool, dry regions of the brain where they condensed into liquid life-force. This liquid then ran back through the body, down the marrow, to the genitals, thighs and knees. The head is the source of the river of life; the genitals the place where the actual fertilisation takes place. Perhaps the thighs and knees were seen as analogous to the river delta, where the river joins the sea and ceases to be a separable entity. Interestingly, this model also helps us understand what was supposed to be the matter with the body of a woman. The male body was like the carefully balanced ecology of the ideal river valley; a woman's body (overflowing, it was supposed, with unheated blood) was pictured as a cold land in flood. The heat and moisture levels were out of balance.

If all this seems fantastical, it is not half as wonderful as some of the uses to which the *genius* was put by the Stoic philosophers whose traditions (starting in Greece in the late fourth century BC) endured for more than five centuries. In Stoicism different strands of mysticism and morality (taken from Rome and the East, as well as from Greece) wove together into patterns that greatly influenced Christian theology. But Stoic accounts of the creation of the world embodied a very different attitude to sexual reproduction than did mainstream Christian cosmology. The Stoics explained the origins and workings of the universe in terms of the reproductive processes of a male body. Just as human physiology seems to have been originally understood by adopting models of

Gender and Genius

evaporation and condensation taken from nature, so now the process was reversed. The universe reproduced itself like an enormous, male animal.

In Stoic cosmology we find a universe created by the *logos spermatikos* [Hahm, 1977]. Just as the male body was supposed to distil semen out of heated vapour, so it was argued that nature itself is permeated by a fiery breath that constitutes the *Genius* or spirit of the universe [Nitzsche, pp.24ff.]. It was this *Genius* that caused nature and the universe itself to exist and to reproduce itself, to die off and be born again in a process of eternal recurrence. This fiery breath was supposed both to permeate the whole of nature, and to actually constitute the living being that is nature. It was *spermatic*: an active, forming principle analogous to the male seed. And it was also *logos*: it involved a kind of coded linguistic formula (like a genetic patterning) which ensured continuity of form in the way the universe unfolded. In the beginnings of time, and at the origins of space was *logos* (as the Gospel of John says) . . . and that *logos* was male. The universe was like a great male animal, panting with hot fiery breaths and ejecting sperm out of which a new universe grew when the old one died.

The *logos spermatikos* was *Genius* on a cosmic scale. But there was a real puzzle here. What role did the female play in this eternal drama of creation? The Stoics personified the cosmic *Genius* as Jove/Jupiter/Zeus, the father of the gods. The Roman name for Zeus's wife, Hera, was Juno. Thus, just as each male needs a woman with a *juno* in order to reproduce his stock, so Jove/Jupiter apparently needed his wife Juno. But did he? It is Jupiter's sperm that is said to be the creative principle. What role (if any) did Juno play? About this the different Stoic writers disagreed, as the Greek and Roman medical writers also disagreed about the role that actual women play in the reproductive process. Some made Juno merely the container for Jupiter's sperm. They adapted the Aristotelian 'flower-pot' theory of reproduction: women contribute nothing to the processes of procreation except the soil and the container in which the seed will grow. According to other Stoic writers, Juno *does* contribute more than this: she also has a seed. This is the kind of weak, inferior, but nevertheless active semen like that which Galen found in the bodies of his female patients. On the third Stoic model all Juno provides is the occasion for Jupiter to become sexually excited and to emit his semen into space:

Zeus, remembering Aphrodite and genesis, softened himself and, having quenched much of his light, changed into fiery air of less intense fire. Then having had intercourse with Hera . . . , he ejected the entire seminal fluid of the All . . . Thus he made the whole substance wet, one seed of the All, he himself running through in it, just as the forming and fashioning pneuma *(= soul) in seminal fluid. [Dio Chrysostom, quoted in Hahm, p.61]*

The Stoics seem to have agreed that the creation of the universe comes from a procreative act and requires seed distilled from the body of a male god. They disagreed only about the precise degree of female impotence. But it was this lack of unanimity that St Augustine eagerly

The Genesis of Genius

60   seized on in his attack on pagan metaphysics in *The City of God* [413–26 AD]. He points out, for example, that the Stoics speak of 'Almighty Jupiter/Sovereign of all things, and of all the gods;/Father and mother of the gods; himself/The only god and, in himself, all gods.' He quotes Varro (116–27 BC), who explains that, 'By the male we mean the emitter of the seed, the female being the recipient; so Jupiter is the world, emitting all seeds and receiving them in himself ' [p.267]. How, asks Augustine, is this reconcilable with the other Stoic view that makes Jupiter inhabit the upper atmosphere of the heavens, and Juno, his wife, inhabit the lower atmosphere? Is Jupiter everywhere? Is he the mother of the gods as well as the father? Is he the only god? Or is Juno a separate entity, and also important to the processes of cosmic creation [pp.146ff., 261ff.]?

Augustine puzzled over Varro's words, delighting in the muddle that identifies Jupiter with the cosmic *Genius*, and which also locates a *genius* in the soul of every reasonable (= male) human being:

And what is Genius? 'A god', says Varro, 'who is put in charge of the generation of things, and has the power of generation'. But do they believe that this power belongs to anyone else except the world, which is addressed with the words, 'Jupiter, father and mother'? Now in another passage Varro says that genius is the reasonable soul of the individual, and thus each one has a personal genius, while the corresponding function in respect of the world is fulfilled by the World-Soul, which is God. Here he comes back to the same point; the Soul of the World is believed to be the Universal Genius. This is the god whom they call Jupiter. For if every genius is God, and the soul of every man is a genius, it follows that the soul of every man is God. If they are forced to recoil from such an absurdity, it remains for them to give the name Genius, in this singular and pre-eminent sense, to the god whom they call the Soul of the World, that is, to Jupiter. [pp.270–71]

This is a difficult passage – Augustine would like the reader to simply laugh off such absurdities. But there is a kind of logic to these Stoic arguments, once it is realised that the *Genius* is the *logos spermatikos*. This logic is, of course, entirely obscured by the use of the word 'man', instead of 'male'. For the Stoics it was not that 'the soul of every man is God', but rather that the soul of every *male* is *genius* – and, as such, a chip off the old patriarchal block. As in Romantic aesthetics, Stoic males act as junior God-the-Fathers . . . but it was procreativity, rather than creativity, that made males divine.

7
The Genitals of Genius

'Lord, give me chastity, but not yet!' St Augustine prayed, as he contemplated his Christian future. For the Romans, male procreativity made men god-like. But Augustine equated entering the new religion with celibacy, and with a complete rejection of the notion that the divine might be embodied in the flesh of ordinary males. Although not evil from the start, sexual activity had been transformed to Carnal Sin the moment that Adam and Eve had eaten of the Tree of Knowledge. Indeed, male bodies had themselves become shameful things: it was only by an act of grace that God had deigned to assume the male shape of Jesus. Augustine thought that all bodily urges and desires should be subject to the will; but that at the time of the Fall Adam had lost the power to freely choose his sexual desires. In the beginning, according to Augustine, there was a kind of innocent sexuality which, if it had continued, would have been appropriately celebrated by the Romans as an object of male pride. But it did not continue and, since it was useless to aim at the kind of *control* of (or indifference to) male lusts that the Stoics advocated, Augustine was left to pray for a future in which sexuality would be entirely *repressed*. His analysis thus exaggerates the importance of the genital drives, whilst simultaneously denying any validity to those drives, or reality to the body. Augustine emblematises the way that the implicit dualism of Christian metaphysics (soul *and* body) would be transformed by the Church authorities into ontological conflict (soul *versus* body). The Christian male came to be alienated from his own body and his sexuality.

The Christian 'City of God' emerged from the ruins of Roman Paganism. Since *genius* had been the apotheosis of the most noble aspects of male procreativity, it might be thought that pagan notions of *genius* would have been altogether excluded from the new religion. What – on the surface – could be more at odds with the Christian account of eternal life than the Roman mysteries that ascribed the immortality of the tribe, the human race, and even the universe, to the instincts of male procreation? But many of the rituals of paganism remained: even the Christian communion rites incorporated the ceremonies of sharing wine and cake with the Roman *Genius* [Nitzsche, 1975, p.18]. And although much of the detail of the Roman beliefs about *genius* was lost with the fall of Rome, ancient teachings about *genius* survived into the medieval period in four main forms. First, there were the texts and traditions of popular magic, demonology and angels which drew on beliefs about good and evil *genii*. Second, classical texts that referred to *genius* were preserved in the isolated libraries that survived. Third, there were the words of those early Christians who, like Augustine, had attempted to assess the pagan past. Fourth, and most important, there were works by later authors who attempted to comprehend the ancient manuscripts, to moralise *Genius* and treat it allegorically.

To be influential in anything more than a marginal way, classical writings about the Roman and Greek gods had to be interpreted by Christian scholars, and fitted into an overall Christian history and metaphysic. This was obviously difficult in the case of *genius*, precisely because it was in writing about *genius* that the Romans glorified the male sexual drive. But although *genius* fitted very awkwardly on to the medieval clerics' distaste for the sin of 'concupiscence' (lust), these Churchmen were used to reading the fragmentary records of the classical past in the manner of exceptionally obscure crossword puzzles. The monks tried to fill in the blanks from clues provided by Christian doctrine. The result was an extraordinary hodge-podge of attitudes and tones. And, since it was the Church that first took on the task of recalling and comprehending the classical past, even the secular scholars and the allegorists of courtly love who wrote about *Genius* during the Middle Ages could not escape a fundamentally monkish view of the body.

Genius is a character in a number of medieval allegories, and in these allegories we can detect the following pattern:

1 *Genius* is always personified as a male – whatever the gender ascribed to the other Greco-Roman gods.

2 This male always seems to be connected with male reproduction of the most divine or perfect type.

3 *Genius* is described in a mystical fashion and, also (often simultaneously) in a kind of jocular, or even pornographic way. In describing the sexual act, the allegorists adopt an uneasy tone. Behind the metaphysical or moralising language there is a belly laugh which sometimes bubbles to the surface of the texts.

4 The Stoics claimed that *Genius* is both cosmic and within each individual man. The medieval writers agree. *Genius* is up in the heavens, but also in man on earth.

5 In one of his aspects, *Genius* becomes creative, rather than procreative. He is a being who wrote, drew or painted reality into existence. Less important than God Himself, but more important than Goddess Nature, *Genius* is transformed into a kind of Platonic demiurge whose job is to create a spatio-temporal reality.

6 This creative *Genius* has special responsibilities both for forming human beings, and for maintaining quality controls over the processes of their production. *Genius* makes men (especially males) god-like. Even on a cosmic level, therefore, *Genius* retains his connections with male procreative power.

Gender and Genius

within the male self: to reproduce, and to produce artistically. The pen,
paintbrush and sculptor's chisel are made substitutes for the penis.

The twelfth-century work by Alain de Lille (Alanus de Insulis), *The
Complaint of Nature*, provides the most straightforward demonstration
of the connection between medieval *Genius* and the generative power of
the male. Alain tells us that after God created the universe and 'clothed
all things with the forms of their natures', He delegated the power to
carry on the work to various other subordinate deities, especially the
goddess Nature [Alain, p.43]. Nature superintends a process of mould-
ing: she has to make sure that 'the face of the copy should not be
changed by any additions of any other elements from the face of the
original' [p.44]. She is also a scribe: 'on [clay] tiles, with the aid of a reed
pen, [she] called up and pictured various images of things' [p.19]. Alain
is envisaging Nature as involved in a manufacturing process not unlike
that of minting coins. Unfortunately, however, 'the pictures would not
keep closely to the material beneath them, but quickly vanished and
died away, leaving no traces'. Nature has 'the weakness of the womanly
nature' and can't carry out her copying task alone [p.19]. To create
proper, lasting pictures she has to be helped by Venus (goddess of love),
Hymen (her husband) and Cupid (their son). She is also overseen by
her shadowy double, 'her other self ', *Genius* [p.85].

Genius represents the continuity between grandfathers, fathers and
sons. 'His head was clothed with locks of hoary whiteness and bore the
marks of wintery age; yet his face was delicate with the smoothness of
youth' [pp.90–91]. In his right hand he holds a pen or 'reed' of 'frail
papyrus, which never rested from its occupation of writing'. In his left
hand he carried 'an animal's skin from which a knife had cut and bared
the shock of hair'. On this he writes with his 'compliant pen', thus giving
life to images which turn 'from the shadow of a sketch to the truth of
very being, the life of their kind' [p.91]. *Genius* writes on animal skins
with his pen (phallus), while nature only writes on clay tiles (earth/
matter). While Nature's task was to form all living things, *Genius* specia-
lises in the creation of animals (including human animals). *Genius* assists
Nature by bullying (excommunicating) those who refuse to fulfil their
sexual duties of marrying, remaining faithful, and producing offspring. Nature complains that her job is being made harder by those
who will not stick to their allotted gender roles: male, active; female,
passive. Those whose sexual identities are uncertain should be expelled
from 'the temple of *Genius*, for they deny the tithes of *Genius* and their
own duties' [p.5]. *Genius*'s special role is to oversee sexual activity,
especially that of the males.

It is scarcely possible to overlook the fact that *Genius*'s pen is a substitute
penis. Alain uses a series of coy metaphors taken from grammar,
writing, logic and rhetoric to describe sexual activity. The euphemisms
are insistent. Men should be adjectives (active) and come before nouns
(passive). Men are the subjects of a sentence, and need a predicate as
their proper addition. The rules of grammar should be observed and

The Genitals of Genius

'only the natural union of the masculine with the feminine gender' permitted [pp.51 ff.]. The active voice should not become passive, nor the passive active. A syllogistic conclusion should result from the kiss of a major premise and a bound, subordinate premise. The long syllable in rhyme (masculine) must be completed by a short (feminine). Although the similes are used to condemn all forms of copulation not designed for the production of children, male homosexuals are the primary targets for *Genius*'s sermonising:

The sex of active nature trembles shamefully at the way in which it declines into passive nature. Man is made woman, he blackens the honour of his sex, the craft of magic Venus makes him of double gender. He is both predicate and subject, he becomes likewise of two declensions, he pushes the laws of grammar too far. [p.3]

Male homosexuality is a vice, 'an inexcusable and monstrous solecism' which cannot be excused 'by any beauty of figure' [p.51]. This, apparently, is Venus's fault – and hence, presumably, the fault of women. Venus became bored with always performing the same old act. She committed adultery with Antigamus ('enemy of marriage') or, in some manuscripts, Antigenius [see Nitzsche, pp.100ff.]. The bastard child of this union, Jocus ('mirth', 'joke', or 'play'), provides a foothold for the sins of non-serious, non-heterosexual sexual activity [Alain, p.56]. Alain condemns playfulness and advocates a sexual work ethic by making *Genius* legitimate only those sexual acts which are designed to repro- duce the species. Further metaphors adapted from Plato's *Phaedrus* suggest that even within marriage sexual motivation has to be carefully controlled.[1] Where lust or ungovernable passion are forces that direct the penis, the children produced will be monsters. Under these circum- stances the figures that *Genius* sketches into existence will be those of imperfect, botched human beings . . . including failed writers [pp.91ff.]. Heroes, heroines and great artistic achievers are produced only when *Genius* functions properly, and reason and male sexuality are harnessed together. The drawing and writing metaphors that started out as simple euphemisms for copulation lose their one-dimensionality as Alain tries to bless the tool that nestles between the legs of a male. Paradigm, semi-divine human beings are produced when the pen/penis is controlled by a reasoning (male) brain.

What is Alain up to in this tedious text? Is it clever paradox? Or is it simple minded? Jocus (and hence verbal artifice) is condemned as a type of perversion. But Alain seems to take a self-satisfied pleasure in rhetorical play within the text. Is this a redeeming feature? Or should the modern reader react in the same way as C. S. Lewis? In discussing his feelings about the over-elaborate language of another of Alain's works, Lewis comments: 'how speedily amused contempt turns into contempt without amusement, and how even contempt at last settles into something not far removed from a rankling personal hatred of the author' [1936, p.100]. Jane Chance Nitzsche, however, who must be the most qualified person to judge Alain's literary allusions – and to whom in general I am deeply indebted – feels that there is a way out for Alain. She claims that *Genius*'s 'stark eloquence at the end of the poem'

Gender and Genius

exorcises the previous stylistic excess [Nitzsche, p.111]. On this occasion, however, Nitzsche fails to convince me. Alain's text lies there for me, somewhere between self-parody and pomposity. It is hard to bless the marriage bed with any degree of honesty when all sexual desire is seen as something shameful.

A second twelfth-century text, slightly earlier than Alain's, shows its uneasiness with male sexuality in a very different way. In Bernardus Silvestris's *Cosmographia* [*c*.1147–8] God the Father delegates the tasks of creation to a collection of inferior deities right from the start. There is *Genius*, the architect (but not the creator) of the universe, and a predominantly female cast of subordinates. Silva or Hyle is Aristotelian formless matter. She is a 'vast womb', born before the beginning of time, who 'yearns to born again', and to be shaped and formed [Wetherbee, 1973, p.68]. Bernardus departs from the Aristotelian tradition, however, by making matter active, and also by rendering reason and the other formative forces female powers. Nature is helped in her work by her mother Noys (divine reason) and her sisters: Endelechia (soul of the world), Urania (principle of celestial existence) and Physis (principle of earthly existence). Like the ancient Gnostics, centuries before, and William Blake, centuries after, Bernardus does not lack images of female power.

Genius, however, is male. Bernardus calls him Pantomorphos or Omniformis (the All-Former), and Oyarses, the supreme ruler or governor of the highest sphere of the heavens. He is 'given to the skills and business of a painter and draughtsman', and whatever he pictures and draws comes into existence somewhere in the heavens or on the earth. *Genius* 'confers all the forms that are attributed to things' in such a way that their shapes mirror a truer, eternal, 'invariable' higher reality to which he has access [Wetherbee, p.96 *corr.*].[2] This *Genius* is an artist-god whose drawings create an alternative reality; but for Bernardus this second-order reality is the world of space and time within which we live. *Genius* acts like Kant's or Coleridge's primary imagination. The extent of this resemblance is, however, somewhat obscured by the other *genii* that Bernardus strews round the universe. Still up in the heavens he places a *Genius* in charge of each planet: Saturn, Jupiter, Venus and the rest are all aspects of, and subordinate to, the chief Oyarses or *Genius*. Then there are *genii* who act as planetary messengers and intervene between the gods and men. Since the planets and stars are thought in the astrological scheme of things to influence everything that happens on earth, there are also *Genii* assigned to the twelve signs of the zodiac who have charge of human life. And it is in writing about these *Genii* that Bernardus's real unease with male sexuality emerges.

Cosmographia ends in a kind of mystical pornography. There are apparently two aspects of the human body that produce a tendency to evil. The context makes it clear that these shameful bits are the excretory and sexual organs. Man is redeemed from evil by *Genii* who erase the foul marks that unformed matter (Silva) left on human beings [Wetherbee, pp.118 ff.]. In a final ecstatic poem to the 'joyful and satisfactory'

The Genitals of Genius

use of the genital organs which 'lie hidden' in the 'lustful' groin, Bernardus invokes 'two *Genii*' who perform the tasks of reproduction which were once assigned 'to twin brothers'. In astrological lore the star-sign of Gemini was symbolised by fraternal twins, and Gemini was also supposed to exercise special control over the arms or hands of an individual human being. Gemini was a propitious star for an inventor to be born under. Bernardus writes of 'genial arms' (pun = arms/armaments of *Genii*) and the very last words of the book make 'all-purpose hands' compensate for bodily organs which should never have been in existence. The *Genii* of Gemini redeem the 'male member', and enable man to wage war on human mortality. Blood with 'the appearance of whitish sperm' flows 'from the region of the brain' down to the area of the kidneys or loins. Here Bernardus is once again referring in elaborate astrological code to the Roman legend of the origin of the twin stars [p.126 *corr.*].[3]

The twins were born Castor and Pollux. They were 'the Dioscuri', fathered by Zeus/Jupiter/Jove/*Genius* when he turned into a swan and raped Leda. When they emerged from the cosmic egg, one of the twins was divine and the other mortal. The divine brother loved the mortal one so much that he made a gift of half his own immortality to his twin when the latter died. The two became twin stars who spent half their time in the heavens, and half visiting earth or the underworld. Roman legend and religious cults celebrated the journey of the Dioscuri ('sons of Jove') to earth bearing arms (cf. Bernardus's pun: 'genial arma-ments') and riding on white steeds. Their intervention in battle saved the Republic of Rome [*Oxford Classical Dictionary*; Grant, 1971, pp. 189–94]. In the medieval period the Dioscuri were, unsurprisingly, interpreted allegorically as Jesus and John the Baptist. The overlay of Christian and pagan mythology allows Bernardus to prophesy the time when man will die, and 'at last the tottering structure of his bodily dwelling' will fall, so that he can 'ascend the heavens' and 'assume the place assigned him among the stars' [Wetherbee, p.114].

Bernardus's language combines in a most extraordinary way a Christian distaste for the body, and a Roman pride in male sexuality. The *Cosmographia* is divided into two books: *Megacosmos* and *Microcosmos*. Like the Stoics, Bernardus quite explicitly made the microcosmic world of the male human body mirror that of the heavens. The greatest *Genius* of all is up in the highest point of the heavens. In the male body the equivalent house of *Genius* is the head [ibid., pp.123ff.]. From here the heavenly white sperm flows down to redeem male sexuality. Man does not just 'sweat' or 'wipe out' his life as 'the whole man flows away' (at the moment of death, in excretion, or in male sexual emissions). 'Crafty Nature moulds and fashions [this] liquid/So that reproduction brings back [something] like [one's] ancestors in appearance.' Decay is outwitted 'by the hand of the Fates' [ibid., pp.126–7 *corr.*]. Further-more, the *Genii* of the astrological star sign of Gemini provide human beings with the power to invent and the power to use hands (presuma-bly to paint and draw like the all-powerful *Genius* who painted them into existence as a poor copy of his own divine image). The 'pollution' of human flesh is erased by the male brain sending messages to male hands to mimic the greatest *Genius* of all and draw or paint things into existence.

Bernardus's *Cosmographia* and Alain's *Complaint* were both sources for the most famous characterisation of *Genius* during the Middle Ages: Jean de Meun(g)'s continuation of Guillaume de Lorris's allegory *Le Roman de la Rose* [*c.* 1225/77]. De Meun offers us one of the most sustained and prolonged dirty jokes in the history of literature. But *The Romance of the Rose* was never just a scurrilous story, it was also the narrative of a mystical (male) quest. De Meun found exactly the right semi-serious tone and vernacular in which to convey contemporary ambivalence about male sexuality. The popularity of this work was enormous. It was read and re-read throughout the Middle Ages. Around two hundred and fifty manuscripts still survive; many more must have been lost. By 1538 at least twenty-one editions had rolled off the printing presses that had been introduced into Europe around 1450. The *Romance* was adapted into the different dialects of France, and much translated (most famously by Chaucer). Its influence on later European literature was also enormous. John Gower, Chaucer's friend, used the figure of Genius in his own key (English) text, *Confessio Amantis*. It was via this route that the notion that *Genius* as a male procreative force made sublime/sublimated into artistic creativity escaped from the monasteries into mainstream European Literature.

De Meun makes Genius a priest of Nature. Like Alain's Latin *Genius*, de Meun's French priest also excommunicates all males who fail to use their procreative tools (pens, hammers, ploughs, etc.). But de Meun offers no straight-faced sermon in the manner of Alain. Venus is 'O'erwhelmed with laughter' as she listens. She assists Genius by handing him 'a taper bright,/Which certainly was not of virgin wax'. Meanwhile, the rest of Genius's audience, the barons, sprawl on the ground, and 'with wink and nod' listen attentively to the words which Genius delivers [p.412]. Mankind has been given 'a tablet and a style' (pen); men should 'set themselves to work/To write their names upon the tablets fair/Or stamp their likenesses which might endure!' Man must not 'Neglect the instruments' that God has lent Nature, 'That she with them may reproductions form/To give a mortal race eternal life' [p.414]. All men must reproduce. There are to be no exceptions – not even priests. Men should be hanged 'who with their stylets scorn to write/Upon the precious tablets delicate/By means of which all mortals come to life'. '[W]e all should scriveners/Become' [p.415]. Those who so despise Nature 'that they read her rules/All upside down' should 'be deprived/Of that convenient stylus they refused/To write withal upon the tablets fair!' [p.416]. Genius's speech is greeted with boisterous approval by his non-homosexual, non-monkish audience of males.

Modern critics disagree amongst themselves as to whether or not de Meun intends Genius's lesson to be taken seriously. Can the author be in earnest when he preaches to men about the virtues of lechery? Perhaps Genius is just a character who does not really express the views

The Genitals of Genius

of the author? Perhaps this is just a way of debunking the medieval conventions of courtly love? It is around the figure of Genius, who plays a major role in the eight books of verse, that the disagreements centre. Christine de Pizan (1365–*c*. 1430) had no such hesitation. As the first recorded professional woman writer outside the monasteries, she was also the first to mount an attack on Genius from a feminist perspective. How apt! From 1399–1403 she played a major part in the 'The Quarrel of *The Romance of the Rose*'. Backed by Jean Gerson, the influential chancellor of the University of Paris, she lined up against the *Romance* – and against the most celebrated humanists of her day. In academic circles the resulting 'quarrel' still makes passions run high. Modern feminists are also often alienated by de Pizan's highly moral tone. But it is probably because of this that we can still read her. Christine found influential allies within the Christian establishment that, for quite different reasons, wished to attack the blending of pagan and Christian morality that the *Romance* represented. Fragments from earlier women writers show that de Pizan was not the first to realise the problems that women face in a culture in which the most learned and wise men adopt ideals and a mythology taken from patriarchal Rome; but Christine was the first woman to argue out her anger systematically in a body of manuscripts that survive.

De Pizan defends women vigorously against the misogyny of de Meun and other well-established authors. In *The Book of the City of Ladies* [1405–], de Pizan confronts Europe's pagan past – as St Augustine did in *The City of God*. She re-interprets myth and history (Christian, as well as Latin and Greek), exposing the strong, clever and saintly women hidden behind the patriarchal façade. She writes of her feelings as a woman when she sees her sex put down by wise and learned men. But elsewhere she also describes herself as having become male as she became an author:

. . . from female I became male
By Fortune, who wanted it thus;
So (she) changed me, both body and will,
Into a natural, perfect man;
Formerly, I was a woman; now
I am a man, I do not lie,
My stride demonstrates it well enough.

[Le Livre de la Mutacion de Fortune *(1400–03)*, Altman, 1980, *p.11*]

Although this might seem at odds with de Pizan's self-conscious feminism, it is only to be expected. Every time Jean de Meun and the others use writing as a metaphor for the sexual act, the substitution works in the same way. The pen/stylus/style is a substitute penis; the scrivener/writer is always male; the blank tablet/material waiting around to be written upon is always female. To write at all de Pizan has to make herself metaphorically a man.

Being a born-again male does not blind Christine to the misogyny of Genius [1405– , p.134]. She quarrels with de Meun's attack on women for their inability to keep secrets. Nature was about to confess to Genius her part in the origins of sexual evil. Instead of just listening, Genius launches into a diatribe against women. At first sight, this seems a digression. Looked at closely, however, Genius's argument is that men should not place themselves in the power of women. Women are all Delilahs; men Samsons. Access to secrets gives women power [*Romance*, pp.348ff.]. Genius fantasises about a Golden Age, the Age of Saturn, before Jupiter 'Bereft his regal father of his testicles' [pp.425 ff.]. It was with this act of castration that Jupiter became the paterfamilias of the pantheon of Greco-Roman gods. Whilst Saturn reigned there was perpetual Spring (season of maximum fertility). Afterwards the world divided into seasons, numbers, names, and the arts and mathematics became possible. All of these (even the development of the arts and sciences) represent a decline from the Age of Gold.

Unity was destroyed, along with Saturn's testicles. Jupiter inaugurated the Silver Age. But after Jupiter the decline continued, with the Age of Brass. Contemporary man is living in thoroughly corrupt times: in the Age of Iron, de Meun says. Sexual relations have become degenerate. True love flourished at a time when men and women were hunters and gatherers. Now that matches are based on mercenary considerations, love has degenerated: '"There's no companionship/'Twixt Love and Seignory"' [p.171]. This view of the equality of lovers should not mislead us as to de Meun's view of women. It is women who are 'covetous of gain,/And gluttonous to swallow and consume/Until there naught remains to those who claim/Themselves their lovers' [p.167]. De Meun suggests that ideal love can only exist in an ideal world without money or land-ownership. But in the ideal world the Laws of Nature will be at work, and men will assert their natural supremacy: the supremacy of the uncastrated male.

In *Symposium* Plato told the story of another perfect state which preceded the present state of things. In the beginning men had two faces both looking in different directions, with four legs, four arms and two sets of genitalia. The gods were jealous of these self-sufficient beings, and cut them in two. Each man or woman has to spend his or her life searching for the other half that would re-establish that original unity of being. Finding that Other is love. In Plato the original roundness of being was not necessarily bisexual; and the noblest search was that of a male homosexual for his lost male other self. But in a Christian context, of course, the original wholes became androgynous, and the wrench of flesh from flesh was caused by sin and the consequent expulsion from paradise. This story was of the greatest importance in the Middle Ages, and provides the basis for the vocabulary and metaphors of the alchemists. As the menstrual and spermatic language of the *Dictionaire Hermetique* (1695) shows, the hermaphrodite and the androgyne were important stages in the task of trying to turn base metals into gold. De Meun turned the alchemists' metaphors back on themselves. Gold (the Age of Gold) would not be created by the arts and sciences (which are connected with Jupiter, not Saturn). A perfect neoplatonic unity of Being should be reached through the act of love.

The Genitals of Genius

In his portrait of the Shepherd's Park, de Meun's Genius conjures up a vision of a state of primal bliss that males can re-create by procreating in the way that Nature demands. Despite all the humour at the idea of a metaphysics and ethics premised on the satisfaction of male (heterosexual) lusts, de Meun remains a mystic . . . closer to Bernardus Silvestris than to Alain de Lille. Wholeness of being can be reached before death, on this earth, through the use of the male sexual organ. It sounds absurd (and de Meun laughs at himself); but it was also meant seriously. Art is only a poor substitute for the real male quest for the Rose: the shared ecstasy of the lovers which takes them beyond time and space, and in which self and Other become one. Jean does not distance himself from the character of the Lover, who says,

Truly I tell you that I better love
My scrip and hammers than my lute and harp.
When such equipment Nature furnished me,
Much was I honoured; and I learned its use
Till I became a craftsman wise and good. [p.455]

The 'scrip' (leather purse) and 'hammers' are here euphemisms for the testicles that accompany his 'pilgrim staff so stiff and stout' [p.454]. The 'lute and harp' seem, however, to be meant as emblems of the minstrel. Earlier Orpheus (archetypal player of the lyre) was blamed for having neglected his procreative duties [p.416].

If we focus on the issue of gender, we can see that the history of the term *genius* is by no means irrelevant to our modern concept. In fact, the ties turn out to be so close that already in the Middle Ages we find the first professional woman author feeling the need to oppose the mythology of *genius*. Although de Pizan describes herself as male, she did not, of course, appropriate genius for herself – that would have been absurd, given that *Genius* was still a god of male procreative activity. Indeed, the medieval male's discomfort with his own sexual instincts placed much more insistence on the purely physical aspects of *Genius* than did the classical Latin texts. Genius flashes his penis before picking up his pen, paintbrush or chisel. Although there was not yet the theoretical back-up for an aesthetics that stressed creativity over imitation, in de Pizan's world the archetypal artist is already Pygmalion, whose story de Meun re-tells [pp.441–51]. God brings to life the perfect statue carved out by the sculptor's tools. The artist is male; the beautiful art-object is female. The artist is trying to make love to/through his art. If skilful enough, a male can be a Pygmalion and produce an art-work that is in harmony with his procreative drive. For a male, art is already *displaced* sexuality; for a female it is already *misplaced* sexuality. It is only males who can sublime (alchemists' language) or sublimate (Freudian language) their sexual drive into art. The School of Spermatic Art has a lineage which is impressively (and depressingly) ancient.

8
The Passionate Revolution

Genius and *ingenium* – and the related words in Western European languages – were central to rationalisations of male supremacy throughout the medieval and Renaissance periods. The terminology of *genius* linked human divinity to male procreativity. *Ingenium*, by contrast, was used to explain why a female's 'wits' – her judgement and talents – should be inferior to those of a male. The first necessary step in the founding of our modern concept of genius was the blending of the two sets of terms: a process that took place in English during the seventeenth century. By the start of the eighteenth century, 'genius' had become a vogue catch-all term, and there were many complaints about its over-frequent and ill-defined use. 'Genius' could still mean a spirit or guardian angel, who was supposed to watch over, and protect, the lives and fortunes of individual human beings. There were also evil genii, or demons. Early eighteenth-century 'genius' thus encompassed the senses – including the connotations of masculinity – of the Latin term *genius*. But 'genius' was also being used to mean a person's abilities and judgement: old *ingenium*.

The term 'genius' had moved one stage nearer to the Romantic concept of genius, but was by no means identical with it. Although the Romantics talked of somebody as *being* a genius, during the opening years of the eighteenth century 'genius' was only something that human beings *possessed*. In so far as a person had a character, he also had a genius. Whether or not this was thought to include women is a moot point, given the contemporary use made of Pope's couplet in *Epistle to a Lady* (1735): 'Nothing so true as what you once let fall,/Most women have no *characters at all*' [Duff, 1807; and see Nussbaum, 1987, p.147]. Moreover, even if a woman was granted a genius, it might be one of an inferior type: in the *Spectator* no. 10 of 1711 Addison moves effortlessly from addressing 'the female World' to mocking 'men of a little smart Genius'. Since genius was a kind of innate talent, there was no *necessary* connection between genius and greatness. Nor was originality one of its essential components: indeed, 'imitation' – following artistic rules, or copying previous masters – was generally thought to improve genius, rather than to be a blemish.

Our modern notion of genius finally crystallised out during the closing decades of the eighteenth century. At this time fundamental changes occurred in conceptions of what made some humans superior to others, and why man had dominion over the animal kingdom. The neo-classical view that made human supremacy a matter of mental and physical skill was gradually replaced by various forms of pre-Romanticism in which 'originality' was more important than talent. In his widely-read essay 'Conjectures on Original Composition', Edward Young offered a eulogy to genius: 'the stranger within' [1759, p.289]. This stranger was a kind of inner god, and Young exhorted his readers: '1st. *Know thyself*; 2ndly, *Reverence thyself* '; 'let thy genius rise (if a genius thou hast) as the sun from chaos' [pp.288–9]. In the breasts of an élite of civilised Europeans this eighteenth-century clergyman (and poet) placed a primitive god or force, and then paused to wonder if it was too bold to 'say, like an Indian, *Worship it*' [p.289]. Young's 'genius' worked below the level of consciousness, and was allied to instinct, feeling and imagination – rather than to reason, judgement or ingenuity:

An original may be said to be of a vegetable nature; it rises spontaneously from the vital root of genius; it grows, it is not made. Imitations are often a sort of manufacture wrought up by those mechanics, art and labour, out of pre-existent materials not their own . . .

. . . A genius differs from a good understanding, as a magician from a good architect: that raises his structure by means invisible; this by the skilful use of common tools. Hence genius has ever been supposed to partake of something divine. [pp.274, 279]

Although Young drew on imagery that derived from the Latin mythology of *genius* – that pagan god of male procreative power – and although he clearly thought of genius as a male characteristic, it is notable that human excellence was now given characteristics that would previously have been associated with females. 'In the fairyland of fancy, genius may wander wild: there it has a creative power, and may reign arbitrarily over its own empire of chimeras' [p.283]. Edward Young describes what (for him) are the most exalted beings on earth in terms appropriate to Renaissance fairy-queens. And this is not atypical of the late eighteenth century. For a time the stock descriptions of women and of genius were so close as to suggest that if only women could be released from domestic duties, they would prove an important reservoir of future genius . . . and might even turn out to be superior to males.

Young's metaphors in this essay provide a clue to the reasons that underlay the change of attitude towards the primitive and the instinctual. The eighteenth century saw a mass exodus from the countryside into the rapidly growing cities. Factories began to replace the small family-based enterprises of agricultural life; and even the landscape outside the towns was carved up into larger, more economic, units. Out of this transformation of the processes of production, our present class-society emerged. And, as power began to pass out of the hands of the traditional landowners and towards the newly formed bourgeoisie, urban man began to feel intense nostalgia for the old way of life. 'Organic' and 'natural' means of production were contrasted favourably with the alienating and 'mechanical' labour of the towns. For centuries, male philosophers had described women in ways that made them inferior: as emotional, instinctive, moved by nature rather than by

Gender and Genius

reason, governed by their procreative functions rather than by judgement. Now, gradually, with the fundamental change in values that industrialisation brought about, males began to covet the stock descriptions of femininity . . . and began to appropriate that vocabulary to refer to themselves. Since most of the men who made a career out of the arts in the late eighteenth century belonged to the new middle classes, their aspirations to 'genius' were at the centre of the whirlpool that re-shaped European values.

It is thus no accident that the Romantic concept of genius came into existence at the moment at which the old pre-industrial world disintegrated. The concept of woman was in crisis, and so were aesthetic and moral values. Indeed, because the eighteenth-century revolutions fundamentally undermined the old stereotypes of female nature and human excellence, it could never again simply be taken for granted that women were cultural inferiors. Male supremacy would require new rationalisations – and would receive them from the new ideas of genius and the new stereotypes of female nature that were developed in the nineteenth century. But, because these new stereotypes were both amorphous and unstable – mixing the old and new without ever thoroughly fusing them – some women have managed to benefit from the Romantic notion of genius, despite the fact that the male supremacists have wielded this concept like a metal bar to try and beat back the female hordes invading the male space of European Culture.

In Chapter 3 I argued that from the Renaissance until the eighteenth century 'ease' and 'facility' were qualities that great artists were said to possess. The Renaissance craftsmen had sought to emulate the effortless elegance of the idle land-owning classes who acted as their artistic patrons. By the nineteenth century, however, the rhetoric of genius was different: the 'passivity' of the creator was stressed, but so also was the 'labour' involved in the work of genius. For fully-fledged Romantics like Carlyle, a great man struggled to produce, driven ever harder by unconscious forces within him. Creation involved suffering, pain and tears. Work (even sweat) was involved; but the outcome was not a soulless 'mechanical' product. It was 'natural' and 'organic', and was likened to the (previously despised) processes of being impregnated and giving birth.

At the start of this transformation, the valued 'natural' kind of labour was endlessly described by metaphors taken from the plant and insect kingdoms. The early Romantics appealed to spiders spinning webs, bees building hives, seeds sprouting, and plants burgeoning and blossoming. Organic work was only occasionally described using similes based on animal or human gestation. As the nineteenth century drew on, however, the metaphors of male motherhood became commonplace – as did those of male midwifery. The artist conceived, was pregnant, laboured (in sweat and pain), was delivered, and (in an uncontrolled ecstasy of agonised – male – control) brought forth. These were the images of 'natural' childbirth that the male creators elaborated. Anaesthetics were rare (except for alcohol and opium). As we will see in Chapter 12, this tendency to promote the artist as a male mother reached its apogee in the writings of Friedrich Nietzsche. But, as Nietzsche also proves, male appropriation of the images of motherhood did not make men any kinder, or more understanding, towards real-life female creators. His verbal brutality towards women artists (and even towards all *educated* women) coexists with his own identification of himself as psychically female.

The revaluation of 'nature' and the 'organic' did not, of course, come about in a sudden single moment, and the pre-Romantics of the late eighteenth century seem in many respects different from their nineteenth-century offspring. But the Romantics inherited from the pre-Romantics a taste for 'nature' in its most savage and unimproved mode: for primeval and desolate landscapes, untouched by agriculture and untamed by gardening. Gaunt mountains, thunder and lightning, the immensity of the ocean, all were dubbed 'sublime' – and contrasted with the delicacy and 'beauty' of the tranquil and cultivated valleys. We now take an appreciation of wild mountain scenery so much for granted that we don't realise how uncommon it was before the eighteenth century: before improved roads and transport made it possible for the traveller to enjoy the frisson of danger that these lonely and bleak places produced. It was only when nature was tamed – and there was a good chance of escape from the wolves, the snows or the barren and wind-swept heights – that the luxury of aesthetic appreciation of the sublime could flourish. The eighteenth century saw the beginnings of the tourist industry to 'sublime' and 'picturesque' parts of Europe. In James Boswell's *The Journal of a Tour to the Hebrides with Samuel Johnson* (1785), we can see Johnson's neo-classical distaste for rude nature in conflict with Boswell's more modern enthusiasm for its raw power.

The revolutions in taste that occurred during the eighteenth century affected every aspect of life, including fashion (especially male fashion) and taste for faces and figures. The most admired males of the early eighteenth century were well fed (fat), wore bright, highly ornamented costumes, floured wigs, perfume and rouge – a costume that required leisure and servants to maintain. The moves to drab colours, simple (functional) trousers and a lack of ornament were perhaps the most obvious aesthetic offshoots of the agricultural and industrial revolutions; but there was also a new appreciation for gaunt masculine features, as well as for the wild and sublime aspects of nature. Raw nature gained a *male* face, as it became more admired: hence contemporary references to the 'Father of nature'. [See Mary Wollstonecraft, 1787, p.107, discussed Chapter 10, below.] Indeed, the 'sublime' was often explicitly, and nearly always implicitly, gendered as male. Thus, in his influential *Philosophical Enquiry into the Origin of our Ideas of the Sublime and Beautiful* [1757], Edmund Burke seems to have deliberately adopted the language of sexual power to explain the psychological thrill that comes from the sublime. The latter is exemplified by kings and commanders discharging their terrible strength and destroying all obstacles in their paths, as well as by the grandeur of the Alps [pp.64ff.]. By contrast, the 'beautiful' – small, smooth, delicate and graceful – is

Gender and Genius

claimed to be what men (= males) love in the opposite sex [p.42].

In much of the aesthetic literature of the period, the sublime is described as overpowering and overwhelming the spectator by a kind of mental rape. In the pre-Romantic excesses of the late eighteenth century, whatever incited a kind of awed mental trembling was 'sublime'. The muscular dynamism of Michelangelo's art was 'sublime'; Raphael's gentle and rounded forms were merely 'beautiful'. But if the contrast between the two kinds of aesthetic appeal was useful in confining the beautiful – and hence female faces and forms – to the category of the second-rate, it was in other respects a blunt kind of critical tool. Shakespeare and Homer might have been 'sublime' . . . but so too was 'Ossian'. James Macpherson picked up on the contemporary taste for the rude and primitive, and wrote reams of poetry which were presented as being by this supposedly authentic, ancient Highland bard. Many of the pre-Romantics found 'Ossian's' descriptions of wailing ghosts, crashing storms, bleak landscapes, barbaric battles and ravished maidens truly sublime. They titillated the passions and imagination that the eighteenth-century 'man of sensibility' was so proud of. Since pre-Romantic aesthetics judged sublimity in terms of its effects on the audience, it encouraged a kind of swooning approach to art. In Germany the resulting rapture over genius became so extreme that the decades between 1770 and 1790 have been labelled *die Geniezeit* ('The Genius Age'). The *Sturm und Drang* ('Storm and Stress') writers of this era were fans of genius, but lacked the critical apparatus that permitted the later Romantic analyses of artistic achievement.

Most eighteenth-century artists, authors and even musical composers still saw the artist as a copyist of nature. Shakespeare, for example, was presented as the archetypal 'natural' genius, who produced his works as painlessly, as effortlessly, and as automatically as a bird on a bough in a forest produces its song. He was sublime because his subject-matter was sublime: blasted heaths, ghosts, storms, shipwrecks and terrible passions. Shakespeare was a lawless, wild 'child of nature', who broke all the rules of neo-classical drama, and who was none the less still (mysteriously) awe-inspiring. Shakespeare was a 'primitive': untutored; artless; producing his works in a blank ecstasy of imaginative and passionate inspiration; merely imitating the strong emotions that nature induced in him. For the Romantics, by contrast, the art-work was no longer simply a mirror held up to nature. Thus, although in Chapter 4 we saw Percy Bysshe Shelley drawing on the traditions that gendered sublimity, Shelley escapes the pre-Romantic view of art. It remains true that Percy and Byron inhabit the sublime (male) heights of the Alps and produce great works of poetic genius, while Mary remains in the beautiful, domesticated (female) space of the valleys and invents a simple ghost-story. But it is no longer the case that Shelley and Byron are considered sublime just because they overwhelm the mind of the audience with the refracted thrills of nature. The emphasis has switched from the reactions of a passive spectator to the actions of the artistic producer. The Romantic genius is the ruler of the world of art; but his imagination is no longer the 'arbitrary' and 'capricious' empire

The Passionate Revolution

of 'fancy' that Edward Young had written about. He is, instead, a kind of junior God-the-Father who shapes matter into form according to rules. He imposes order on chaos; but does this not by applying artistic maxims that had been laid down in advance (as the neo-classicists had supposed). The order derives from the depths of the personality of the 'I AM'. The new (artistic) reality is as highly structured as the cobweb spun out of the bowels of the spider, or the child that emerges from the womb. The imagination, too, is provided with laws.

In Chapter 5 I wrote about the way that Romantic aesthetics built on the metaphysics and epistemology of the late eighteenth-century German philosopher Immanuel Kant. Kant's own treatise on aesthetics – *The Critique of Judgement* [1790] – contains one of the most influential and celebrated definitions of genius ('*Genie*'):

Genius *is the talent (or natural gift) which gives the rule to art. Since talent, as the innate productive faculty of the artist, belongs itself to nature, we may express the matter thus: Genius is the innate mental disposition* (ingenium) *through which* nature gives the rule to art. *[§46, p.150]*

For Kant, genius is an inborn talent (*ingenium*); but it also involves autonomy and the power to shape the material according to one's own will. The genius does not 'rule' art by imitating the natural world he sees around him. Nor are there artistic rules that must be slavishly copied and obeyed if a great work of art is to be produced. Kant takes a step beyond both pre-Romanticism and neo-classicism. Like the Romantics, Kant emphasised that genius is a law-giver, and like them he gives the personality of the artist as the source of the new law. But Kant does not value the dark, instinctual forces from the unconscious that became so important in the next century. It is still reason, understanding and memory – as well as the imagination – that makes Kant's genius sublime. It is through the exercise of these faculties that humans can begin to envisage what God's own infinite and divine powers must be like.

Like other writers in the late eighteenth century, Kant contrasts that which involves mere prettiness, harmony, good proportions and formal perfection – beauty or '*Schönheit*' – with the energies and grandeur of the sublime ('*das Erhabene*'). The former appeals primarily to the senses, and is consequently downgraded in comparison with the appeal that the sublime exerts on rational and imaginative man. Kant knew Burke's influential essays on the sublime, and keeps the same gender connotations. But he is much less explicit than Burke. Only in two minor texts, *Observations on the Feeling of the Beautiful and Sublime* [1764] and *Anthropology* [1798], does it become clear that the sublime – and hence true genius – is properly a male preserve. It is not *women* who mimic – even in a pale kind of way – the awesome and terrifying powers of a God who can think the universe, and even Himself, into existence.

Although, in *The Critique of Pure Reason* (1781), Kant had made God a Being who combines active intellect and passive intuition, Kant seems clear that there could be nothing in any way female or effeminate about genius itself. In Section 3 of his *Observations* Kant tells us that women

Gender and Genius

are motivated to act by a taste for the beautiful, and that this explains the prevalence of emotion and sympathy in their moral make-up. But, according to Kant, the best human beings (= males) act out of duty, rather than love; and rules and principles are what make men god-like and sublime. Women, consequently, are amoral beings. They also have inferior understandings. It is not just women's appearance that makes them beautiful: it is also their minds. Indeed, since women's overriding duty is always to be beautiful, the whole of their'education and upbringing should be entirely directed to this end. Intellectual pretensions (or even too much knowledge) defeminise them. Males can study the stars, mathematics, the sciences, metaphysics and Greek, history and geography: 'The content of woman's great science, rather, is humankind, and amongst humanity, men ["*der Mann*" = the male or husband]. Her philosophy is not to reason, but to sense' [1764, p.79]. Women who know Greek or know mechanics 'might as well even have a beard': their knowledge makes them ugly [p.78].

Kant does not deny that some individual women might be capable of masculine intellectual pursuits. But what is a perfection in a man is an imperfection in a woman; only the males should attempt the sublime:

The fair sex has just as much understanding as the male, but it is a beautiful understanding, *whereas ours should be a* deep understanding, *an expression that signifies identity with the sublime.*

. . . strivings and surmounted difficulties arouse admiration and belong to the sublime. Deep meditation and a long-sustained reflection are noble but difficult, and do not well befit a person in whom unconstrained charms should show nothing else than a beautiful nature. Laborious learning or painful pondering, even if a woman should greatly succeed in it, destroy the merits that are proper to her sex . . . [p.78]

For Kant a woman genius is not impossible; but for a woman to aim at the sublime makes her merely ridiculous . . . and, even worse, '*ekelhaft*' (loathsome). She is an unbeautiful, unnatural freak who is disobeying nature and aping the genius of the male – who is her (and nature's) lord and master [p.83].

Kant allows that women have a passion to dominate. However, this passion 'naturally' expresses itself via charm. Nature gives women a taste for the beautiful, so that they can beautify themselves more efficiently and hence help nature fulfil its goal of reproducing the species [1764, pp.90ff.; 1798, pp.140, 166ff.]. A man has his own goals and purposes; but a woman has only nature's purposes. Kant's female sex is an aesthetically pleasing sex, but not a fully human sex – nor a sex capable of wielding the kind of quasi-divine power that makes a male a junior God-the-Father. Only males are capable of true justice and sublime genius. Males are the natural rulers; females their natural subjects.

What is so disturbing about Kant's notion of genius is that he dissents from the pre-Romantic emphasis on passion as an integral part of genius, whilst maintaining their emphasis on the *maleness* of genius.

The Passionate Revolution

Rousseau was one of Kant's great heroes, and in Chapter 4 we have already seen Rousseau declaring that women lack genius because they are deficient in passion. How ironic! For Kant women are passionate creatures; genius is a matter of reason; and women lack reason. For Rousseau passion is valued, and it is therefore passion that women are seen to lack. This is typical of these late eighteenth-century theories of genius . . . whatever faculty is most highly prized is the one that women are seen to lack. In the case of William Duff, for example, genius is primarily a matter of imagination . . . but a female imagination is, of course, inferior to that of a male.

In 1767 William Duff's influential *Essay on Original Genius* was published, followed three years later by his *Critical Observations* on genius. This Scottish aesthetician, clergyman and novelist was one of the most extreme of the pre-Romantic writers. He stressed the *primitive* nature of genius, and suggested that education was likely to mar the strong passions and warm imagination required for the most 'sublime' genius. In 1807, however, Duff felt obliged to publish his *Letters on the Intellectual and Moral Character of Women*. The introduction to a recent reprinted edition suggests that the spur to the original publication was the impact of Mary Wollstonecraft's writings. This might have been the spur; but it was not the reason underlying the writing of the *Letters*. Duff was engaged in a dialogue with himself. Given his earlier writings on genius, how could he exclude women from the ranks of original geniuses? Didn't his account of the psychology of genius make it overwhelmingly likely that, as female literacy increased, males would come to occupy a subordinate place in European culture? Duff wished neither to *discourage* the education of women, nor to *encourage* their entry into the artistic professions: 'a general passion for literary fame' would produce 'the most obvious disadvantages, by inducing women to desert their natural and proper sphere, by interfering with their most important duties, and by disturbing the order and harmony of domestic society' [p.99]. In his *Letters* Duff determinedly rationalised the confinement of women to domestic roles.

Duff's *Letters* went through eight editions during the course of the nineteenth century. His woman is more virtuous than man. She has more taste than man. He refuses to say whether women have more judgement than men, because, he says, it would be mortifying 'should the result prove unfavourable to my own sex'; but he does indicate that with more education women might outclass men here [pp.32 ff.]. In other words, Duff is willing to allow women the superiority over men in more or less every area – except the one that matters most to him, the imagination. Although it is still theoretically possible on Duff's model for women to produce imaginative works, the 'delicate organisation of their frame' makes this improbable. For success, 'a creative energy and masculine vigor of mind, are indispensably requisite', and woman's physique is 'obstructive of, if not incompatible with' such energy. According to Duff, 'Imagination in women is for the most part more gay and sprightly than in men, but it is usually at the same time, as I am inclined to think, less vigorous and extensive.' Women lack 'that crea-

Gender and Genius

tive power and energy of imagination, which is exerted in calling into existence things that are not, and, in bestowing on shadowy forms all the colours of life and reality' [p.29–30]. Duff 's language suggests that the artist is himself a god – and not just one who copies God's handi-work – but women are carefully excluded from any direct participation in that which makes humans divine.

Duff recognises in Mary Wollstonecraft an apparent exception to his generalisations; but her 'energy' and 'contumacious spirit' only make him angry. Apparently she has overstepped the 'natural and proper bounds' of female nature by entering the lists to do battle with men in the fields of literature and learning. Only in males is vigour prized. Duff claims that those women with 'true feminine sensibility' and 'a delicacy of sentiment' will recognise this [pp.100–101n.]. It is 'by his singular activity of mind and body' that the male is 'qualified for all the dangerous and toilsome, for all the busy and bustling scenes of life, which are his peculiar province' [p.98]. Inconsistently ignoring his earlier criticism of savages for taking their women with them on hunt-ing expeditions, Duff writes as if only the male savage is active. Then he claims that

In the civilized state of society, man is still the same active being; only his activity and enterprize are employed in a different manner, and on different objects. [p.98]

Obviously, there are examples of women writing and painting with mental energy. But these are examples of unnatural women. A woman can have a powerful imagination only by being unsexed: by being a freak of nature; a kind of mental hermaphrodite. Duff makes genius a (sexually chaste) male. Having reported that the ardour and warmth of a genius makes him 'peculiarly susceptible of the charms of the fair sex', he quickly points to the harm that a passion for women can do to a youthful genius. The genius might waste his powers either in indolence, or 'in fomenting this pleasing, but in the present case highly dangerous passion' [1770, pp.342, 343]. For Duff – as for Jean de Meun, Sigmund Freud and present-day members of the Virility School of Creativity – being an author involves (sublimated) male procreativity. The shameful (physical) sexuality of males has been elevated to the god-like (mental) sublime.

Despite these continuities in the aesthetics of virility, we can see, how-ever, that at the point in history at which substantial numbers of women invaded the male domain of the arts, the rhetoric of exclusion took on new forms. As William Duff shows, this rhetoric is complex. On the one hand, he seems naïvely open about his motives. Women must be excluded from the literary professions for purely practical consider-ations: society would collapse unless they acted as domestic servants. On the other hand, there is an appeal to female physiology to buttress this exclusion. But, with the revaluation of passion, instinct and imagina-tion, the rationalisations of male superiority flounder in disagreement. A sublime understanding? Sublime passions? Sublime imagination? Kant, Rousseau and Duff seem eager to justify the cultural subordina-

The Passionate Revolution

tion of women as a matter of historical necessity, even though there was no longer a consensus about which features of the psyche doomed females to perpetual inferiority. In the eighteenth century 'natural law' replaced 'divine law' as the rationale for social custom. But 'natural justice' was wheeled in on the side of the males. 'Universal harmony' required that a woman should be a homemaker, and that the wage-earner and the head of the household should be the husband. It was for offending against 'Nature's plan' that female creators were condemned as monsters or freaks. 'Sublime Nature' was not just a father, but the personification of patriarchal power.

9
The Gender Revolution

The breakdown in established stereotypes of female nature that occurred during the closing decades of the eighteenth century was a product of the agricultural and (subsequent) industrial revolutions. The emergence of the urban middle classes caused, as we have seen, a change in attitude towards the natural and the primitive. But this profound re-structuring of society also affected women in a variety of other ways. In particular, patterns of marriage altered as more wealth was accumulated through commerce, and less through the inheritance of land. During the course of the eighteenth century, a new ideal of love-marriages was set against the arranged marriages that had previously been the norm for the landed gentry. The middle classes wanted partners who would share in life's enterprise – not just property transfers and family alliances – and this new ideology of marriage produced shock-waves that affected contemporary portrayals of female nature [Davidoff and Hall, 1987, pp.149ff.].

The newly emergent novel celebrated these 'love' matches, as did much eighteenth-century drama. But, for stable life-partnerships, it was important that such marriages should be based on something other than lustful infatuation. Undesirable pairings had to be prevented by a process of rearing that played down the importance of sexual desire, and which promoted acceptance of parental distinctions between sensible love and mere passion. But this meant encouraging women to think of themselves as rational, and as being in control of their bodily needs. Female literacy – and suitably edifying reading – was seen as a key factor in developing the 'judgement' and 'good taste' needed to counterbalance emotion and sexual instinct. 'The Ladies' became the target audience for a large proportion of works on morality and aesthetics. Even works on science and metaphysics were written in the form of essays, letters or dialogues, so as to broaden their appeal to both sexes. Thus, in a sense, 'The Fair Sex' came to symbolise the refinement that made European man superior to the animals. Very few eighteenth-century men (or women) would have adopted the view that 'a woman is but an animal, and an animal not of the highest order'. Indeed, Edmund Burke presented this demystification of woman as a symptom of the French Revolution and the end of civilised values [1790, p.103].

Middle-class education was directed towards the production of discerning, lovable, loyal and chaste wives who had moral worth, and not just economic or strategic worth. Furthermore, the men were also being educated . . . into believing that a woman should only be picked as a mate if she had mental beauty, as well as physical beauty. But this meant ranking women's minds, and crediting them with special, feminine gifts. Males were anxious to discover what gave the female mind or soul inner beauty, and also the extent to which women could be 'improved' by education and social conditioning. Thus, eighteenth-century writers both emphasised the power of untamed women, and sought ways of controlling and 'civilising' them in order to make them more suitable as wives and mothers . . . and less destructive to the fragile edifice of bourgeois society. Women were portrayed as a natural resource, with minds to be cultivated, enriched and made more beautiful (like gardens). Thus, by a kind of irony, we see that just when the primitive and the wild came to be valued, women themselves were being prized precisely in so far as they were domesticated. There might have been a new admiration for the sublime aspects of Nature; but only by disciplining her anarchic desires could a woman become a mate worthy of the European male . . . that being who had dominion over the whole of the animal kingdom, and also over the 'savages'.

In the eighteenth century 'nice girls didn't' sleep around; but even 'Ladies' were credited with voracious sexual needs. In the past, arranged marriages had made this a convenient belief. An upper-class woman had rarely been able to choose her mate. How convenient, therefore, that she should be pictured as an always-willing sexual partner! Amongst the aristocrats who relied on property marriages, the new middle-class ideology of love-matches even coexisted for a time with the institution of arranged marriages and led to a degree of toleration for female infidelities – especially in pre-revolutionary France.[1] Of course, most contemporary moralists condemned this toleration, and asserted the importance of female restraint. The anti-Christian Scottish philosopher David Hume, for example, both saw women as sexually hungry, and imposed on them the 'artificial' virtue of chastity [Battersby, 1981]. Although males were only advised to practise sexual moderation, Hume argued that female chastity was essential to social order. Without it, a man could not know that his wife's children were his own, and the handing on of property through the male line would be jeopardised. Hume did not believe in the Divine Right of Kings; but he was insistent that only patrilineal inheritance could ensure a stable and moral society.

During the eighteenth-century 'Enlightenment' period, female virtue was seen to be based on female self-control. But gradually, in the nineteenth century, middle-class ideology made believe that nice girls didn't sleep around *because* they didn't have sexual appetites. Of course, the older stereotype of woman's sexuality never died out entirely, and the image of woman as the sexually devouring partner can be found right through the anti-bourgeois literature and art imagery of the nineteenth century. But in the pre-Victorian period – in which even middle-class women were still generally credited with strong (if misguided) appetites and passions – Aristotelianism was undermined. Women were not just simply failed males, nearer to the animals than to humanity. The middle-class concern to stress the good – improvable –

Gender and Genius

qualities of the female mind opened a kind of psychic window which allowed quite ordinary women to become authors and artists – and even to conceive of themselves as equal (or superior) to males. Indeed, the stress on the passion and imagination of genius should have encouraged women to see themselves in these terms. In point of fact, however, very few eighteenth-century writers (of either sex) were willing to grant women genius.

There were (predictably) a few exceptions. In 1766 the authors of the *Biographium Faemineum* asserted polemically that 'Souls are of no sex, any more than wit, genius, or any other of the intellectual faculties' [p.vii]. Before this, in 1757 John Duncombe subtitled a poem in praise of women 'Female Genius', and this was a theme taken up and extended by Mary Scott in her 1774 reply, 'The Female Advocate'. Scott used the word 'genius' in the new sense, whereby a person does not just *have* a genius, but rather *is* a genius – and Scott also allowed 'female geniuses'. It was no longer a contradiction in terms to talk about women with genius. But, in general, writers denied this. As Francis Hutcheson put it in *A System of Moral Philosophy* (1755):

If the males more generally excel in fortitude, or strength of genius; there are other as amiable dispositions in which they are as generally surpassed by the females. [Extract in Rendall, 1978, p.88]

Women were credited with some intellectual merits – which compensated (to a larger or smaller extent) for their deficiencies – but genius was seen as a distinctively male form of mental strength.

It is tempting to explain this gendering of genius simply by reference to the history of the term – which clearly still affected eighteenth-century usage. Thus, for example, the famous essay on genius in issue no. 160 of the *Spectator* [3 September 1711] – with its influential distinction between 'natural' genius and a genius 'formed by rules' – is preceded by another essay [no. 159] in which Addison uses motifs and images drawn from the previous classical tradition of *genius*. He writes about a male spirit-Genius who haunts the rocks above Baghdad, and about several 'little winged Boys' who are minor spirits who hover over the first stage of human existence. These are clearly adaptations of the major and minor genii that were so common in Renaissance art. Another of the classical motifs is taken up again a week later in no. 166 where Addison writes of the 'Legacies' that 'a great Genius leaves to Mankind, which are delivered down from Generation to Generation, as presents to the Posterity of those who are yet unborn'. Words are said to be the most efficient means of 'propagating' the ideas of 'great Masters'; and books carry on the traditions of an Aristotelian God-the-Father who transcribed the universe into existence. Thus, Addison's discussion of genius as varieties of talent is sandwiched between two other essays which link genius with male spirit-powers, male procreation, the Aristotelian (male) *logos*, and patrilineal inheritance. Such connotations must have increased the reluctance of eighteenth-century authors to credit women with genius.

The Gender Revolution

84   However, the gendering of genius in this eighteenth-century period cannot be put down simply to verbal association. It needs also to be related to the limits of the Enlightenment project for educating and improving women. Ladies commanded respect as *companions* to the sublime European males; but they were not granted the psychological potential that would have ensured intellectual or social equality between the sexes. As we have seen in the last chapter, there was no general agreement about the factor that made European males superior to the rest of humanity: reason, understanding, imagination and even passion, all had their advocates. But, in each case, women seem to have been allowed *some measure* of the relevant faculty – a 'beautiful' understanding; a 'gay and sprightly' imagination; 'delicate' passions – just enough to qualify them as suitable helpmates to their marriage partners. Women were, consequently, encouraged to educate and improve themselves up to a certain point. If there was no general agreement on what that cut-off point 'was, there was a consensus that *some* physiological limits debarred women from Addison's two types of genius: from both inborn 'natural' genius, and from the genius acquired as a consequence of education.

We can see this from the pages of the *Spectator*: a periodical specifically aimed at an audience that included 'the Ladies'. The *Spectator* was a magazine in the forefront of the new approach to female nature: its women were definitely worthy both of education and of male respect. But if we scratch behind the 'Enlightened' surface of these pages, we find some ancient prejudices about the physiological inferiority of the female. Thus, for example, Joseph Addison claimed that

Women in their nature are much more gay and joyous than Men; whether it be that their Blood is more refined, their Fibres more delicate, and their Animal Spirits more light and volatile; or whether, as some have imagined, there may not be a kind of Sex in the very Soul, I shall not pretend to determine. As Vivacity is the Gift of Women, Gravity is that of Men. [no. 128]

Although it does not advertise itself as such, this comment in effect recycles ancient beliefs that consigned females to cultural inferiority. The description of women as 'gay and joyous' has to be read in the context of the tradition – explored in Chapter 3 – that linked the *ingenium* of a great artist with a tendency to melancholy and to gravity . . . and which then (implicitly) gendered melancholy as male.

Addison suggests that both the ideal and the average woman will find fulfilment of nature's purpose adding cheerfulness and charm within the family circle. He seeks to domesticate women: to position them within the inner space of the new middle-class home. He wishes to educate women – and in such a way as to play down innate sex differences [*Spectator*, no. 128] – but he takes for granted that females will always be cultural subordinates. Although the *Spectator* does not harp on this point (and it has to be inferred from what is *not* said, as much as from what *is* said), women lack genius. Thus, given the monotonous regularity with which the *Spectator* mentions 'genius', and given the fact that this journal wished to encourage and foster female talents – and given that 'genius' was being used to mean a kind of talent – we might have expected to find in its pages frequent reference to the genius of women. But, in all its moralising, I have only been able to spot one such reference – and that is a half-humorous, half-serious (and altogether unpleasant) dig at female authors. The essayist recommends needlework as 'the most proper way wherein a Lady can shew a fine Genius', and adds his wishes 'that several Writers of that Sex had chosen to apply themselves rather to Tapestry than Rhime'. 'Pastoral Poetesses' and 'Heroick Writers' could 'vent their Fancy' in silk and mohair [no. 606]. This last phrase suggests that all women writers have the 'vapours' – a disease of the imagination which (once again) draws on the Renaissance tradition of female imaginations merely simulating the divine madness of the great (male) author.

It might be thought surprising that we can find hints of such a traditional view of female physiology in the most 'enlightened' writers of the eighteenth century. 'The vapours' was a curious disease that should have ceased to exist the moment it was proved that the blood is circulated round the body by the heart, and not boiled by the entrails. But instead of dying the death it deserved, the disease lingered on well into the nineteenth century. Nor was it simply men of letters who appealed to the 'vapours' to rationalise female incapacity for genius. Eighteenth-century medical men adopted a similar strategy. While medical theories had remained based on the theory of the humours, doctors had access to a (relatively) consistent explanation for the Aristotelian view of the female as a failed male. By the Enlightenment period, however, the humours were outmoded, and there were consequently several competing theories of the functioning of the body, all of which were deployed to place the supposed inferiority of women on a new pseudo-scientific footing. Medical texts on 'the vapours' are thus particularly revealing about the ways in which the 'female' continued to be derided, even though the 'feminine' was being revalued as integral to creativity. Only males, apparently, had a physiology that could withstand the debilitating effects of genius – whether it was innate, or derived from extensive study.

When it originated round about the year 1600, the term 'vapours' seems to have been used as a euphemism for hysteria [Veith, 1965, p.122n.]. Fumes were sent up by the womb which clouded the female mind, and which mimicked the effects of the melancholy madness produced in hot (male) bodies by the malfunctioning of the spleen. In the nineteenth century 'the vapours' no longer meant hysteria, but the label was attached to a large number of unspecified, but definitely *female* complaints. In the eighteenth century, however, things were quite different. The gendering of types of madness had broken down. Sometimes the term 'vapours' was reserved for female madness; sometimes the label was used in an apparently gender-neutral way. Although the vapours were still said to be more common amongst women than men, many of the detailed case histories offered by doctors were accounts of male patients. 'Melancholy', 'Spleen', 'The Disease of the Learned' and 'The English Malady' were often used as synonyms for the vapours.

The Gender Revolution

In these texts, we see a most curious thing. Before the eighteenth century there had been a direct link between the word 'genius' and male fertility; now 'genius' was presented as both an expression of, and a threat to, maleness. Genius was seen to feminise the male body and mind. But genius was also a male preserve, in that only the highest and best males could withstand it. The unisex surface of the medical explanations thus masks a deep prejudice against women. Medical men agreed that the female physique made genius either dangerous or impossible for women, even though they could not agree why or how. As I will show, doctors of the period examined male and female bodies via a microscope which seemed shiny and new, but which was used to try and maintain the perspective of lack through which Aristotelian tradition peered at women's minds and bodies.

Some eighteenth-century authors still believed in 'animal spirits' which were supposed to resemble (and sometimes even seem identified with) the seed-bearing part of the male sperm. These authors explained the threat that learning and genius posed to masculinity in terms of an interference in the processes of the production of these spirits. In 1772 an English translation of Tissot's 'On the Diseases of Literary and Sedentary Persons' was published in the same volume as his notorious essay on onanism. From comparing the two essays we can see that, in terms of their effects on the body, learning and genius simulated masturbation. Even reading what Tissot called 'the masculine style' – he means the 'sublime' – could have terrible consequences. '[T]he innermost part of the brain has been affected by a troublesome heat' which results from 'the force of the thinking soul' [pp.14,13]. Books 'composed without any strength of genius . . . only tire the eyes; but those that are composed with an exquisite force of ideas . . . fatigue it with the very pleasure, which, the more compleat, lasting, and frequent it is, breaks the man the more' [p.15].

Tissot's 'evidence' included four males driven to epilepsy by excessive study; one whose beard, eyelashes, head hair then body hair fell off; several more made mad, and driven to frenzy and idiocy. The blood was driven to the head by intense study – witness the nose bleeds that result [pp.19ff.]! 'The seminal fluid, which has been thought by some great men not to be very different from the nervous liquor, is likewise deprived of its force'. The reason why so few eminent men have eminent offspring is because 'whilst the mind of the father was entirely given up to meditation' his 'vivifying liquor was perhaps defrauded of that part of elaboration which it should have had for the brain of the embryo' [p.34]. Although Tissot is in favour of what he calls 'a polite learning', prolonged study is considered dangerous, especially to 'boys of a penetrating genius' [pp.72,42]. Except for one female French mystic (treated as deluded) women are absent from Tissot's discussion of genius. This makes sense since the animating nervous fluid that produces genius is made analogous to the male semen. Just as female masturbators are treated by Tissot as both physically and psychologically pseudo-males, so on this model the female genius would be some kind of monster ['On Onanism', pp.41ff.]. Tissot's rhetoric suggests the

Gender and Genius

model of the androgynous mind in a male body that Coleridge and other Romantic theorists were to put forward as the model for genius at the start of the nineteenth century.

Women's physiology was not treated any more favourably, however, by those doctors who denied that the vapours are linked to animal spirits. In *The English Malady* [1733], George Cheyne put the disease down to a loss of elasticity in the nerves. Human bodies were, he thought, made up of three types of solid woven fibres, each with a different texture and lubricated by different bodily liquids. The elasticity of the nerves could be gauged from the quality of the other two types of fibre – bone and muscle. Signs of nerves which had lost their elasticity included small bones; little muscles; a pale complexion; fleshiness; a soft, low voice; 'Evacuations of any Kind' including loss of blood (and hence menstruation); and those (remember Aristotle's woman) 'who are naturally of a cold Constitution' [pp.100–105]. Other symptoms include wind, tumours and other swellings of the body. Cheyne even observed 'monthly Periods' in the symptoms of the disease 'especially towards the *Conjunctions* of the *Sun* and *Moon*' [p.198]. Incredible though it may seem, these observations are also supposed to apply to males – even to Cheyne himself who recounts all the symptoms of his own previous attacks of the vapours in sickening detail. In other words, for Cheyne the male with vapours has a feminine physique: even (sometimes) simulating menstruation and pregnancy.

Cheyne's labelling of the vapours as 'The English Malady' is also explicable by the same lunatic logic. The British fogs and the richness and heaviness of British food send up cold fumes and mimic the effects of femininity. On the Aristotelian model the mind of a female is inferior to that of a male because her body is naturally cold and wet. But living in England, learning, genius and a sedentary life have the same effect and make men resemble women. Since 'the Arts of *Ingenuity, Invention, Study, Learning,* and all the contemplative and sedentary Professions' are listed as amongst the causes of the disease, a rationale is given (once again) for the exclusion of women from these occupations that 'affect and deaden the whole *System,* and lay a Foundation for the Diseases of Lowness and Weakness' [p.54]. On this model, even a healthy and psychologically well-balanced female is like a male made mad with nervous disorders.

Cheyne asks rhetorically,

The original Stamina, *the whole* System *of the Solids, the Firmness, Force, and Strength of the Muscles, of the Viscera, and great Organs, are they not owing to the male?* [p.96]

On the original theory of the humours these parts of the body had been nourished by the black bile of melancholy. This was one of its main functions in terms of the economy of the human body. What was once put down to bile, is later put down simply to maleness. These eighteenth-century writers have lost the theory of the humours; but they retain the framework of assumptions on which the theory was

The Gender Revolution

based. Women remain inferior; they remain metaphorically cold and moist; but Cheyne searches (in vain) for a more mechanistic account of the inferiority. Women, this popular and influential writer informs us, are made of different, less elastic fibres.

Other eighteenth-century medical models attempt the same impossible dream of combining ancient prejudice with new-fangled scientific explanations. John Purcell, for example, uses chemical explanations and makes the origin of the vapours the absorption of mineral salts into the blood. He still insists, however, that women are more likely to suffer vapours than men. Their menses; the foods they eat; their 'violent Passions' and the 'still and unactive Life' of middle- and upper-class women are given as causes [1702, p.32]. Purcell explains chemically why strong passions boil the blood, sending the wrong mixture to the brain [pp.85ff.]. He also explains why women are more efficient boilers of blood than males. Later in the century genius was described as having similar effects. William Rowley linked madness with too much blood to the brain, and *'stronger* and *sublimer* ideas in the mind'. 'Poetical sublimity, superior reasoning faculties, clear conception, penetration, judgment, a refined imagination' all require blood to the brain; and a strong inclination to 'any particular art, science, or pleasure, an ambition and constant desire to excell the gross of mankind' can all produce 'symptoms little short of madness' [1788, pp.245, 246].

The medical texts imply (without ever making the implication explicit) that the human being who possesses genius will have the sexual organs of a male but will also have feminine characteristics. It was not, of course, until the nineteenth century that the modern concept of genius became firmly associated with madness. But it is interesting to explore the prehistory of this link, and to see how in the eighteenth century the ground was being prepared for the re-gendering of the vapours as female and as especially dangerous for women with pretensions to genius. Women were denied that 'excellent constitution of the fibres' which even Tissot supposed might be what 'produces great geniuses' ['On the diseases', p.27]. On the old system of the humours the symptoms of female hysteria and melancholy faked the powers of the male seer's great *ingenium*. In the eighteenth century it was genius that came to mimic the effect of vapours, and vice versa. If women are by nature vaporous, they would need great strength (maleness!) to withstand its effects without succumbing to disease.

Elizabeth Barrett, lying on her sick-bed, awaiting Robert Browning's invigorating presence and overflowing life-force, was a logical extension of this form of medical reasoning. From her confinement in a quiet room away from all excitement, to the glass of porter she was forced to drink with meals, Elizabeth Barrett's cure seems a classic late eighteenth-century remedy for the vapours. Cheyne even made tuberculosis (the disease ascribed to Barrett by her modern biographers) a possible final symptom of the most severe form of vapours. Barrett herself reacted with 'vexation' – and an ironical 'smile' – to the doctors who diagnosed her illness in this fashion. Writing to Robert Browning

Gender and Genius

(her husband-to-be) on 11 August 1845 she recorded her treatment by "'the faculty,'" who 'set themselves against the exercise of other people's faculties'. One of her doctors

thought poetry a sort of disease . . . a sort of fungus of the brain – & held as a serious opinion, that nobody could be properly well who exercised it as an art – which was true (he maintained) even of men – he had studied the physiology of poets, 'quotha' – but that for women, it was a mortal malady & incompatible with any common show of health under any circumstances. And then came the damnatory clause in his experience . . . that he had never known 'a system' approaching mine in 'excitability' . . . except Miss Garrow's [. . .] the only other female rhymer he had had the misfortune of attending. And she was to die in two years, though she was dancing quadrilles then (& has lived to do the same by the Polka), & I, of course, much sooner . . . [Browning, 1969, i, pp.151–2]

Since Elizabeth Barrett Browning was, in her own words, taken over by 'the religion of genius' we can understand her claim that such medical diagnoses – and the weight placed on them by her family – caused her long-term harm [1954, p.50; 1969, loc. cit.]. The young poet had internalised the models of her age: that condemned her to freakishness, to (fatal) sickness, and to maleness for her pretensions to genius. Thus she wrote to Miss Mitford in 1842:

. . . through the whole course of my childhood, I had a steady indignation against Nature who made me a woman, and a determinate resolution to dress up in men's clothes as soon as ever I was free of the nursery, and go into the world 'to seek my fortune'. 'How', was not decided: but I rather leant towards being poor Lord Byron's page. [1954, p.126]

To serve genius, Elizabeth had to will herself to be a man. She was, therefore, ecstatic in 1838 (at the age of thirty-two) when she finally discovered that to meet a female genius was *not* to 'see a *woman of the masculine gender*, with her genius very prominent in eccentricity of manner and sentiment'. There was no '*terribleness*' in Lady Dacre (a celebrated dramatist and poet); but only 'gentleness and womanlyness . . . And that is what I like in a woman – yes, and in a man too' [pp.29–30].

Elizabeth was embarrassed by her extremity of relief at finding a woman genius who was no hermaphrodite. But she couldn't help it. It was, after all, less than two months since her first volume of poetry had been published under her own name. Still awaiting the reviews, she must have pondered her father's brutal reactions – recorded (word for word) in her notebooks – to the earlier (unpublished) poem, 'The Development of Genius' (1727). Modern critics have read this poem as 'the moment when Mrs. Browning's own authentic voice as a poet was first heard aloud'. But Elizabeth's father thought that the subject of genius was 'beyond her grasp', and that she had parodied Byron's "'melancholy mind'", transforming heroic genius into egotistic madness [Hayter, 1962, pp.23, 24]. Her father's literary outrage echoes the tones of medical 'science'.

The doctors made Elizabeth Barrett Browning into a morphine addict: who had to employ the euphoric side-effects of her medicine to counter

The Gender Revolution

the discouragement that was also doled out to female authors. But when in 1845 she commented laconically, 'Those physicians are such metaphysicians! It's curious to listen to them. And it's wise to leave off listening . . .', her words convey much more than a mere personal tragedy [1969, i, p.152]. There had, after all, already been a century and a half during which cultured women had tried to align their own artistic ambitions against the shifting category of 'genius'. All found themselves confronted by fathers and doctors – and even by mothers and sisters – anxious for their welfare: eager to tell them that Nature had provided women with a physique that would punish them with madness and disease if they attempted to rival the males. Throughout the nineteenth century, the figure of the mad woman would haunt the texts of women poets and novelists. This spectre is foreshadowed in the eighteenth-century medical and literary texts on the vapours.

10
The Daughters' Dilemma

When Johann Georg Hamann wrote to Johann Gottfried Herder in 1760, 'My coarse imagination has never been able to imagine a creative genius without genitals', we can be sure that it was *male* genitals that he was imagining, despite the fact that this 'Magus of the North' was one of the least conservative thinkers of his age [Wellek, 1955, i, p.180]. Indeed, since the most revolutionary artists of the late eighteenth century were also the most likely to attempt honesty about the relationship between sexual energy and creativity, they were also the most likely to use metaphors and symbols of maleness in a bold fashion, thus increasing the difficulties for the women who aimed to emulate their achievements. To a certain extent the 'first English Romantic' – William Blake (1757–1827) – might seem to be an exception to this model. He did, after all, remark that 'A Poet, a Painter, a Musician, an Architect: the Man Or Woman who is not one of these is not a Christian' [1820, p.776]. He also attacked Aristotelianism and other static modes of thought that produce 'reptiles of the mind' – and a distorted view of reality [1790–93, pp.156–7].

According to Blake we are not passive perceivers or knowers of the external world. Instead, we construct barriers (of beliefs and dead 'Aristotelian' categories) to protect us from reality. To break through these and access truth requires an inner conflict of contrary forces. Creativity thus grows out of tension and opposing energies. There are, however, some inner struggles that are unproductive. These Blake associates with the 'hermaphrodite': a being who has ambiguous genital organs, or the primary sexual characteristics of both sexes. Creativity, by contrast, requires an 'androgyne': a body with a clearly-defined sexuality, but a bisexual soul [Damon, 1965]. Since Blake allows women artists, he can be read as implying that there can be androgynes of either sex, and that within women too there are the powerful semi-divine (and largely sexual) energies that he calls 'genius' [1790–93, p.153]. Blake seems to be crediting females with the inner deities that produce poetry, art and all true vision.

But Blake's symbolism undercuts his revolutionary potential. In his prophetic books the 'female' is always associated with receptivity, passivity, softness and emotional support – not with the destructive and sublime power of the true artist. In his poetry, paintings and engravings, Blake tries to tear apart the 'Aristotelian' fiction that constitutes reality for most human beings. He seeks to wipe away those aspects of language, custom, tradition and inherited memory that obscure the five

The Daughters' Dilemma

senses. He opens up the 'sixth' sense (of imaginative vision) to reveal that an androgynous creative being is actually still a *male* with a counter-active feminine soul (or 'emanation'). The artist accesses 'eternity' – beyond the false time-order of the fake reality – but 'In Eternity Woman is the Emanation of Man; she has No Will of her own. There is no such thing in Eternity as a Female Will' [1810, p.613]. As David Aers puts it, in Blake's eternal 'Eden'

there is no equal and true reciprocity but an ancient sexist hierarchy of being. The great creative acts are allotted to males, 'man to man', for the females, Blake assures us, simply could not live in Eden 'because the life of Man was too exceeding unbounded'; so the females seek a shadowy place, gratefully promising their 'Fathers and Brothers' that they will dutifully 'obey your words'. [1981, p.37]

How disappointing! Blake's universe is the creation of *androgynous* forces, and his prophetic books continue the mythological traditions of Gnosticism. Indeed, many of Blake's female spirits appear to have stepped out of the pages of the buried *Nag Hammadi Gospels* or out of the obscurity of Bernardus Silvestris' *Cosmographia*. But Blake is closer to twelfth-century Bernardus than to the original Gnostic texts. Like the medieval monk, Blake makes the hands and mind of the artist a product of *male* sexual energies, and of *genius* in the ancient Roman sense. The perfect female mind that thundered 'I am' in the *Nag Hammadi* texts has been silenced. There is *no* female will, and no female creator with the power of the Christian God the Father, nor of Blake's heroic (Saturnine) Satan. Thus, the Aristotelian tradition that makes *logos* the province of males remains fundamentally undisturbed by Blake's artistic revolutions.

Blake was engaged in a kind of intellectual warfare with the literary and artistic establishment of his day. But he never doubted his own genius: he drew spiritual sustenance from the ancient traditions of male power that shaped his creative theory and practice. Blake's female contemporaries had no such inner support. Indeed, if we examine the writings of Mary Wollstonecraft – a member of Blake's circle of friends and one of the authors whose books he illustrated – the contrast is marked. For all her feminism, Mary Wollstonecraft's writings betray no confidence in her own female strengths. Wollstonecraft wants to increase the power that women can exercise over their own lives; but she tends to equate all power with maleness. Her essays and novels are, consequently, fractured by a series of dichotomies: strong/weak; masculine/feminine; sane/mad; sick/well; reason/sensibility; sublime/beautiful; genius/non-genius. Only in the travel-journal, *A Short Residence in Sweden, Norway and Denmark* [1796], does Wollstonecraft find a literary subject which can successfully contain these tensions. Here she can thrill to the power of her absent demon-lover and the omnipresent demon-Nature, while simultaneously appropriating the masculine sublime for *females* (by exploring it herself, and by describing the women who live there). In the rest of her writing, Wollstonecraft works out on paper her puzzled indignation at the changing ideals of femininity and of genius

Gender and Genius

and the way that her favourite authors seem both to describe her and exclude her when they portray the man of genius. Could a woman be a genius? How? What is it about male genius that merits female admiration? How does a female genius love? Her answers change; but the questions are constants.

Most of Mary Wollstonecraft's literary output reads like a dialogue with Rousseau, that other 'revolutionary' thinker of the late eighteenth century. Women were often portrayed as childlike, and Rousseau was the first to take really seriously the understanding of a child. Wollstonecraft was overjoyed when she first started reading *Émile*, Rousseau's utopian novel about the transformation of a supposedly average (fictional) boy into an ideal human type. Emile was to be educated in such a way that, with the limited mental capacities at his disposal, he could discover for himself facts and values. He was to learn not through rote lessons or rules, but by his tutor's manipulation of his desires, his needs and his imagination. On 24 March 1787 Mary wrote to her sister, Everina, full of enthusiasm for Rousseau's 'paradoxes. He chuses a *common* capacity to educate – and gives as a reason, that a genius will educate itself ' [Wollstonecraft, 1979, p.145]. Rousseau – counted by himself and by many of his contemporaries as the one modern genius – was preoccupied with the problems of replicating 'genius'. We can understand Mary's delight at discovering a system in which human perfectibility was dissociated from the powers of reason assigned by nature to an élite group of males.

In the letter to Everina Mary compares herself with Rousseau: 'he rambles into that *chimerical* world in which I have too often [wand]ered'. He is a 'strange inconsistent unhappy clever creature' who combines 'sensibility and penetration'. She also identified psychologically with Émile . . . until, that is, she discovered Book V of Rousseau's utopia and the description of Sophie, the 'ideal' woman who is Émile's vacuous and pretty companion. It was her outraged reaction to this discovery that turned Wollstonecraft into a professional author. She wrote and wrote, as a way of trying to work out how to modify and extend Rousseau's conclusions so as to include women. According to Rousseau, only those who work out for themselves what is right and wrong can be called virtuous: 'This was Rousseau's opinion respecting men; I extend it to women' [Wollstonecraft, 1792, p.25].

It must have seemed easy to extend Rousseau's conclusions about the education of boys to the education of girls. Rousseau's refusal to do this must have seemed inexplicable and inconsistent with his desire to produce better human beings. It must have come as a shock to Mary Wollstonecraft when she suddenly discovered that women were being denied the imagination, the passion and sensibility that made them worthy of the education of a genius. But, although Rousseau's treatment of women seemed an inconsistency and a mere afterthought to his system, it was more than this. Despite all the rhetoric about dispensing with money and learning a simple, useful craft, Rousseau's 'natural' genius could only exist in the world behind somebody who could act as

The Daughters' Dilemma

a buffer between him and others. A class of selfless servants was needed to prop up a society of strong, unique, authentic male egos. For Rousseau, women were the obvious candidates: they were needed as professional mothers, housekeepers, managers, wives and sex-objects.

One of Mary Wollstonecraft's first attempts at countering Rousseau was never completed. In 'The Cave of Fancy' [1787], a tiny female child is saved from a shipwreck by Sagestus, a wise old man who serves the 'Father of nature' [p.107]. A kind of magician, Sagestus seems to be modelled on Prospero from Shakespeare's *Tempest*. Rousseau's Émile was isolated from the rest of society, and brought up by a tutor to become the ideal boy. In order to find a counter to Rousseau's woman, Wollstonecraft seems to have tried to re-think Shakespeare's island universe. The sage adopts the girl as heir to his name and his powers. ('*Sagesse*' is French for 'wisdom'. The girl's name, 'Sagesta', thus substitutes for Émile's partner, Sophie, whose name was an adaptation of the Greek word for wisdom.) Having pondered 'the best method of educating this child', Sagestus initiates her into the secrets of a magical underworld of spirits that provide her lessons in 'the cave of fancy' [pp.125ff.].

The characters in this story draw a contrast between those who are, and those who are not, born geniuses. From looking at the face of a drowned sailor, Sagestus could tell immediately that the man was born to be a sailor. From looking at the face of a drowned woman, he knew that 'this female was intended to fold up linen and nurse the sick' [p.122]. Genius, on the other hand, overcomes all social obstacles in its path: 'The genius that sprouts from a dunghil soon shakes off the heterogeneous mass; those only grovel, who have not power to fly' [p.118]. In this alternative utopia, the lower classes are being used to substitute for Rousseau's class of selfless women. Even so, nothing in the fragments of educational tales that survive teaches the perfect girl that she could become a genius. The only lesson preserved is one that teaches women to attain the 'melancholy' and the 'sublime' not through creativity, but through love for another [p.151]. The female spirit who is teaching Sagesta compares herself to Galileo, 'who when he left the inquisition, looked upwards, and cried out, "Yet it moves."' In an analogous way the teacher exclaimed, '"Yet I love"' [p.147]. We can only be pleased that the tale stopped short, and Wollstonecraft escaped from the cave of fancy – which offers a utopia as deluding as the analogous cave in Plato's *Republic*.

Wollstonecraft finished the other novel that she started while reading *Émile*. *Mary* [1788] was a rather more radical affair. A quotation from Rousseau in French stands as its epigraph: 'The exercise of the most sublime virtues rears and nourishes genius'. And the words 'genius' and 'sublime' are frequently used in the description of its heroine. However, although 'Sublime ideas filled her young mind' and 'genius animated her expressive countenance', a woman of such 'melancholy' sensibility is still fated to a life of love . . . a kind of doom, since the fictional Mary is already bound to another via an (arranged) marriage [pp.5,27,6]. The

Gender and Genius

man Mary falls in love with has 'rather ugly, strong lines of genius' written on his face [p.22]. He is not, however, healthy. His habitual melancholy is transformed into terminal tuberculosis; a disease then associated with the vapours, and hence with genius. His death sends Mary into a 'phrensy' from which 'her nerves were not to be restored' [pp.66,67]. Thus, in this first completed novel, female genius dies of empathy with an unhealthy male genius, and love remains woman's destiny. All Mary can do on her deathbed is dream about a different world – 'where there is neither marrying, nor giving in marriage' [p.68] – in which a woman could combine genius with love.

A year later Wollstonecraft can be found tackling the question of genius in a different way, through a translation of an abridgment of Lavater's *Essays on Physiognomy* [4 vols, 1775–8]. The appearance of another English translation meant that her own was never published, but 1789 saw the publication of *The Female Reader*. This book of readings for young ladies (published under a male pseudonym) was stuffed full of quotations from Lavater. But this Swiss-German author was a most depressing choice for Wollstonecraft as she tried to think through the puzzles of female genius. What Lavater provided was a 'science' of the external features of humanity as a guide to the inner human nature. This was the art of reading faces that Sagestus practised in 'The Cave of Fancy'; and these were the 'lines of genius' that the heroine in *Mary* read on the face of her beloved the first time she saw him [p.22]. But for Lavater the typical human being is a male, and the most perfect human is also a male.

Elaborately illustrated with sketched caricatures of actual and imagined human 'types' (many of which appear to be inmates of lunatic asylums), Lavater's *Essays* seek to define the animal, intellectual and moral nature of man,

the essence of creation. The son of earth, he is the earth's lord; the summary and central point of all existence, of all powers, and of all life, on that earth which he inhabits. [p.6]

The work was revised many times. But only about eleven of 497 pages of the abridged edition are on the subject of women. Lavater is already three-quarters of the way through the book before he remembers to tell us that he is

but little acquainted with the female part of the human race. Any man of the world must know more of them than I can pretend to know; my opportunities for seeing them at the theatre, at balls, or at the card table, where they best may be studied, have been exceedingly few. In my youth I almost avoided women, and was never in love . . .

I frequently shudder while I think how excessively, how contrary to my intention, the study of physiognomy may be abused, when applied to women. [pp.396–7]

In other words Lavater has written a 'science of human nature' in which human nature does not include female nature.

It is significant that Lavater believed that a game of cards revealed most about the female mind. For his woman lacks gravity – and the kind of

The Daughters' Dilemma

moral and physical uprightness – that marks man off from the animals. A woman's gentleness, charm, beauty – even her playfulness – make her second-rate:

Man is most firm – woman the most flexible.
Man is the straightest – woman the most bending.
Man stands steadfast – woman gently trips.
Man surveys and observes – woman glances and feels.
Man is serious – woman is gay.
Man is the tallest and broadest – woman less and taper.
Man is rough and hard – woman smooth and soft.
Man is brown – woman is fair.
Man is wrinkly – woman less so.
The hair of a man is more strong and short – of woman more long and pliant.
The eyebrows of a man are compressed – of woman less frowning.
Man has most convex lines – woman most concave.
Man has most straight lines – woman most curved.
The countenance of man, taken in profile, is more seldom perpendicular than that of the woman.
Man is most angular – woman most round. [pp.402–3]

The environmental, racial (and sometimes straightforwardly false) features on this list are obvious. Lavater chooses not to see the brown, weathered, wrinkled women working on the land. His woman is young, upper-class and European. Flexible, soft, bending, curved (concavely), she trips along gaily on dainty (tapering) ankles, feelingly glancing from side to side. She lacks the confidence to stare boldly, and instead peeps at the world in a shy (or coquettish) manner that limits the amount of external information that can be taken in. It is the straight, serious, magisterial male that Lavater has defined as 'the earth's lord' who frowningly surveys and observes his kingdom. It is the male who 'stands erect' as the storm bursts around him. The *typical* and *ideal* 'Woman trembles at the lightning, and the voice of distant thunder; and shrinks into herself, or sinks into the arms of man' [p.401]. Woman, as an afterthought, might be a worthy helpmate for man – but she is part of nature's kingdom, not nature's king [p.402].

Because Lavater's image of women is so thoroughly second-hand, contradictions mark the places where the old and new stereotypes of female nature collide. Thus, on the one hand, his male seems to personify the pre-Romantic sublime, his female the beautiful who swoons at the exercise of force. On the other hand, Lavater accepts the (conflicting) medical orthodoxies which made female bodies and nerves more 'flexible, irritable, and elastic' than those of males [p.400]. And, since 'melancholy' and mystical frenzy were also associated with nervous diseases, Lavater's thoroughly domesticated and coy woman is permanently threatened by mental derangement [pp.400ff.]. It is only the Christian religion that keeps this tendency in check: 'a woman without religion is raging and monstrous' [p.402]. Because of their propensity to become 'the most irreclaimable, the most rapturous enthusiasts', Lavater goes so far as to ally his idealised women with the 'sublime'

Gender and Genius

[p.401]. But this should not mislead us: 'incurable melancholy' – and even the 'enraptured heights' of mystical vision – do not make female minds (or faces) those of god-like geniuses [p.402]. 'The female thinks not profoundly; profound thought is the power of the man.' Even if 'Women feel more', they are not designed to use this capacity to rule except 'with tender looks, tears, and sighs'. Anything more, any 'passion and threats', makes them 'no longer women, but abortions' [p.401].

Mary Wollstonecraft read all this and, for a time, was infatuated with the new science of physiognomy – as was a great part of 'civilised' Europe for much of the next century. She was also infatuated with Fuseli (a Swiss painter living in England), who wrote steamy, erotic letters to Lavater about the times they had spent together wandering round Germany [Tomalin, 1974, p.115]. As William Godwin (later Wollstonecraft's husband) remarks, Fuseli argued for

*the divinity of genius. This is a power that comes complete at once from the hands of the Creator of all things, and the first essays of a man of real genius are such, in all their grand and most important features, as no subsequent assiduity can amend . . . I believe Mary came something more a cynic out of the school of Mr Fuseli, than she went into it. [*Memoirs*, 1798, p.234]*

Wollstonecraft grew out of this infatuation for primitive, inspired genius. She also lost faith in Lavater as an accurate observer of genius [1796, p.179]. But 'genius' remained an ideal – as *A Vindication of the Rights of Woman* [1792] and *The Wrongs of Woman* (an unfinished, late novel) reveal. Mary Wollstonecraft developed towards literary maturity still wrestling with the difficulties involved in extending the category of 'genius' to women.

In her most famous work, *A Vindication*, Wollstonecraft expressed her anger at the contemporary ideals of female excellence which encouraged women to decrease, rather than increase, their mental and physical strengths. She therefore mounted an attack on any notion that weakness can be a hidden strength – and this meant taking issue with the doctors who portrayed the genius as an emasculated male. Wollstonecraft did not dispute the medical orthodoxy that decreed 'People of genius have very frequently impaired their constitutions by study'. But she refused to infer from this that 'men of genius have commonly weak, or, to use a more fashionable phrase, delicate constitutions' [p.43]. Bodily strength and mental strength go together – in both men and women. Shakespeare's hand was not 'nerveless', 'nor did Milton tremble'. Their writings 'were not the ravings of imbecility, the sickly effusions of distempered brains'. Geniuses have 'iron frames' that can withstand poetic visions and strong passions [pp.44, 43].

Of course, Wollstonecraft recognises that here she is caught in a trap: 'I am aware that this argument would carry me further than it may be supposed I wish to go'. She has said that bodily strength and mental strength go together; but she also allows (as she must) that 'bodily strength seems to give man a natural superiority over woman' [p.44]. Wollstonecraft refuses to back down having seen the consequence of

The Daughters' Dilemma

her position: that males are 'naturally' women's mental superiors as they are their physical superiors. She makes genius a machismo male. She even goes so far as to 'imagine' that, just as Newton 'was probably a being of superior order accidentally caged in a human body', so 'the few extraordinary women' thrown up by history 'were *male* spirits, confined by mistake in female frames' [p.39]. The masculine 'sublime' is king, and women can only serve and become more like the 'demi-gods' of which she dreams [p.51]. Women, she suggests, should aim to become as strong, and male-like as possible.

Wollstonecraft tried to think through the paradoxes implicit in the contemporary portrayals of genius and of femininity. She was certain that there *could* be women of genius – even if that meant imagining *male* souls trapped in female bodies – but her own voice was always hesitant about her own status as a 'genius'. Indeed, it was left to William Godwin to outrage the establishment by his confident presentation of his dead wife in terms of the contemporary expectations of the 'genius'-personality [see, for example, *Memoirs*, pp.216–17]. There was, however, one woman of Mary Wollstonecraft's generation who managed a degree of confidence in herself as a genius. But Germaine de Staël, née Anne Louise Germaine Necker, (1766–1817) had the advantage of having, from the start, been educated into this role. Her mother – influenced by Rousseau, but rebelling against his idealisation of maternity and the 'artifice' of Sophie – had taken the 'amiable and honest' Émile as a pattern for her daughter's upbringing [Gutwirth, 1978, p.31].

Like Mary Wollstonecraft, Mme Necker obviously thought it a simple matter to extend Rousseau's philosophy of man to encompass woman. Wasn't Rousseau himself a creature of strong sensibilities, imagination and passion? Wasn't Rousseau simply being eccentric in denying women the same innate capacities as men? Reared by educational devices directed at making her *want* to learn, Germaine developed into a precocious teenager used to holding her own in her mother's celebrated salon. As daughter to one of the most important figures in pre-revolutionary France (her father was Finance Minister to Louis XVI), Germaine was in the public gaze and, from an early age, heard herself described as a 'genius'. Later – after the arranged marriage that was still expected of women of her class – Germaine de Staël retained her high public profile, despite being banned from post-revolutionary Paris. She became a celebrated novelist, literary critic and political exile, who toured the sublime sights (and literary figures) of Europe. Like Rousseau, she drew curious crowds who inspected her and gossiped about her wherever she went. She lived (almost) like a man, with considerable social and sexual freedoms. She attracted admiration; but also outspoken animosity – most notably from Napoleon whose obsessive hatred of her contributed to her notoriety.

The concepts of the 'female' and the 'genius' had come close enough for Germaine to be flattered into the belief that in her they combined. But de Staël knew that the only man she really doted on (her father)

Gender and Genius

disapproved of women authors. Even if her many admirers could help her blank out the image of the woman genius as a kind of 'monster', there was no escape from being a 'phenomenon'. In her most celebrated novel, *Corinne, or Italy* [1807], de Staël tried to align the image of the 'feminine' woman with that of the 'genius' – by creating a fictional counterpart, Corinne, who is the perfect representative of both. '*Long live Corinne! Long live genius! Long live beauty!*' is the chorus that echoes throughout the pages of this novel [p.21]. Carried by enthusiasm and inspiration beyond the trembling timidity expected of women, Corinne hurls poetry at the crowd: 'No longer a fearful woman, she was an inspired priestess, joyously devoting herself to the cult of genius' [p.32]. Then she kneels down and lowers her bare head, modestly awaiting the crown of myrtle and laurel that the Senators and the populace of Rome would bestow on her. Everyone cheers; there is not a single dissenting voice . . . even a 'melancholy' (and tubercular) Scottish Lord melts into love, overwhelmed by this combination of the beautiful and the sublime.

The author is determinedly deaf to all mocking voices – including her own inner voice. She would like to deafen the reader also by turning up the volume on the tumultuous applause for Corinne. In her own time, de Staël seems to have been successful in this ploy. *Corinne* was one of the most influential novels of French Romanticism – and the reference point for generations of women trying to wrestle with the shifting categories of 'female' and 'genius' [Moers, 1976]. To us – less obsessed with the physiological and aesthetic impossibility of female genius – this seems extraordinary. The novel reveals in hypnotic detail a woman fascinated by her own image. But it does not reveal 'genius', since de Staël could never simply allow her heroine to enact genius. She lectures us insistently on the subject of Corinne's excellence; but this leaves an overwhelming impression of dishonesty, and fails to engage the sympathies of even the most sensitive of modern feminist critics [see Gutwirth, 1978].

Without a trace of irony or embarrassment, de Staël uses her novel as a kind of looking-glass in which to grimace at herself. She rehearses the grand gestures of genius, but then remembers that she needs to adjust the posture of the truly womanly woman. The contortions produce tensions in the prose that now seem like simple pretentiousness. The Cumaean Sibyl whose powers de Staël appropriated for Corinne had prophesied the introduction of the worship of the Great Goddess into Rome. Romantic aesthetics looked within the artist's own self for the gods. De Staël exclaims loudly that she has found a goddess (not a god). But she finds the goddess in her mirror, not her heart. It seems there was no easy escape for even the most doggedly optimistic woman from the false dichotomy: become *either* a genius *or* a woman. Nor could Germaine de Staël, for all her apparent confidence, foresee a future for woman that combined her mission as a genius with great love for another – that more conventional view of a woman's destiny. At the start of the novel Mme de Staël's heroine is the great 'I am' of the Romantic artist; at the end she is a woman, her life and her genius

The Daughters' Dilemma

destroyed by passion. The forces in our society that encourage a woman to drown her own self in egoless love cannot easily be reconciled with the driving ego necessary for The Great Artist.

Clara Schumann's father discovered this not many years later. Like de Staël's mother, he had educated his daughter using principles taken from Rousseau's *Émile* [Reich, 1985, p.27]. He went much further than Émile's manipulative tutor, however, and tried to make his daughter an extension of his own boundless ego – to the extent that he even dictated the wording of Clara's diary for her to write down! He refused to understand why Clara should prejudice her own career as a pianist and composer by the compromises necessitated by her love for her composer-husband. Rousseau's attempts to exclude women from genius actually helped them attain artistic success. But success was flawed by the fact that no models existed that could help women maintain their precarious balance on the parallel bars of being both an artist and a woman. As the nineteenth century drew on, female achievements put heart into women artists. But keeping the confidence up was a struggle, as the changing stereotypes of woman combined with the new Romantic aesthetics to produce a deterioration in the situation of the exceptional woman artist.

One symptom of that decline was the way that 'fancy' was systematically downgraded in Romantic theory. When William Duff decided that women had the wrong kind of 'creative imagination' for genius, he did not altogether deny women imagination. Instead, he allowed them a 'vivacity of fancy' [1807, p.30]. Duff gendered the vocabulary of imaginative vision – but in an unsystematic way. However, this distinction between 'imagination' (a good thing, and characteristic of the genius-mind) and 'fancy' (an inferior thing, and characteristic of those who merely fake genius) lies at the heart of Coleridge's literary theory. Coleridge used theoretical distinctions developed by the German Romantics to systematise the qualitative distinction between 'fancy' and 'imagination' that had become a commonplace in late eighteenth-century Britain [Engell, 1981, e.g. pp.172ff., 234].

The distinction between creative ('productive') and pseudo-creative ('reproductive') imagination is integral to all the Romantic theorists of art. The lower grade of imagination – in English 'fancy' – was described in contradictory and puzzling ways by different authors. Sometimes it was 'gay'. Sometimes it was associated with the 'beautiful'. Sometimes it was deluding. It is always puzzling . . . until we notice that it re-works characteristics of mind previously attributed to females who ape the great male *ingenium*. A weapon to downgrade the productions of women who pretended to genius had been picked up and sharpened by the Romantic theorists of genius. And this was characteristic of Romanticism and its privileging of *male* madness, the androgynous *male* ego, and *male* power and activity.

In Chapter 4 we saw Percy Bysshe Shelley also gendering the capacity for imaginative vision. We should not therefore be surprised that his wife – despite being the daughter of Mary Wollstonecraft – was unable

Gender and Genius

to reconcile her image of herself as a woman with an ambition to be a great writer. As a young adolescent Mary Shelley used to take the volume of *Posthumous Works* that contained the unfinished 'The Cave of Fancy' to her mother's grave to read. This story must have seemed particularly poignant to the young Mary. Her mother had died not long after her birth, and had left behind the story of an infant who lisps a plea to a powerful magician to save her dead and shipwrecked mother. Her request is not granted, but the child is instead transformed into the perfect woman and the personification of wisdom. Mary Shelley read this story; but the message that her own fiction sends back to her dead mother transforms Enlightenment dreams into Romantic nightmares.

Mary Shelley's novel *The Last Man* [1826] starts – as did 'The Cave of Fancy' – in a cavern near the sea. Like her mother, Mary Shelley writes of the future, and of death by drowning. But in the daughter's novel the last woman is already dead. Drowned at sea. The storms have put the final touches to the plague that depopulated the earth. There was no sage to rescue her. No girl child to be rescued and transformed by a magical education. Only the male narrator remains alive. Unlike Mary Wollstonecraft, Mary Shelley finished her novel. But her message is one of despair. She could foresee no grand future for womankind. The epigraph to her book (taken from Milton) reads like a response to her dead mother: *'Let no man seek/Henceforth to be foretold what shall befall/Him or his children.'*

Mary Shelley opens her story in an actual cave that she visited with her husband near Naples. It is 'the Sibyl's cave', and Mary is deciphering the leaves on which the Cumaean Sibyl wrote her vision of the future. The Sibyl was an ancient crone with prophetic gifts, rewarded with long life because she was loved by Apollo, but denied eternal youth because she refused to grant his favours. The Sibyl was a kind of witch. Mary Shelley's choice of this name for the cave suggests that she is more distrustful of the powers of her own poetic imagination than was her mother. During the Renaissance it required divine intervention before a woman's madness could be as prophetic as a man's. A woman could become a Sibyl more easily than she could become a great artist. It is only in the shadow of a female Sibyl that Mary Shelley dares predict the future – and then she will only enter the cave cautiously led by the ambition of her companion. It is also only with his help that she can decipher the message left by the inspired woman who has preceded her.

Mary Shelley's last woman died because she insisted on crossing the sea to Greece to visit the tomb of her parents rather than visit Rome. '"Why go to Rome? what should we do at Rome?"' she asks [p.319]. But Rome was the depository of the nine books written by the Cumaean Sibyl prophesying the introduction of the worship of the Great Goddess. Rome was also the scene of the success of that more recent woman-genius, Corinne, who appropriated sibylline powers. Shelley's last man returns to Rome alone bewailing the fact that he is the sole remaining representative of 'Corinna', and the grandeur and romance of Rome

The Daughters' Dilemma

[p.336]. He is the last of a great race 'wondrous in their achievements, with imaginations infinite, and powers godlike' [p.339].

Mary Shelley chooses to look backwards at the tombs of those she has loved, rather than project a future for women as geniuses, sibyls or poets. She has her mother as a model. But the great future that her mother had foreseen for women was in the past. It is no accident that Mary Shelley gives the name of her real-life dead daughter, Clara, to the last fictional woman to remain alive. And here, as in her *Frankenstein* [1818], Mary Shelley has her finger on the pulse of Romantic myth. Her mother had dreamed about female geniuses: divine male spirits trapped in female bodies. As the new category of 'genius' collided with older notions of 'femininity', de Staël could even change the gender of the inner god. But the privileged historical moment was passing. Mary Shelley responds with instinctive pessimism to the way that the stereotypes of the female were changing. Women were being increasingly denied any share in the strong passions, imaginations and sexual drive that the Romantics made essential components of genius. The female soul was being determinedly shoved back into the prison of female flesh.

11
The Third Sex

By the end of the eighteenth century, 'genius' had acquired Romantic grandeur: it had been transformed from a kind of talent into a superior type of *being* who walked a 'sublime' path between 'sanity' and 'madness', between the 'monstrous' and the 'superhuman'. The creative success that could be ascribed to 'mere' talent was opposed to that bound up with the *personality* of the Romantic 'genius'. From its inception and up to our own time, this notion of a genius-*personality* would trap women artists and thinkers. On the one hand – even before Freud – the driving force of genius was described in terms of *male* sexual energies. On the other hand, the genius was supposed to be *like a woman*: in tune with his emotions, sensitive, inspired – guided by instinctual forces that welled up from beyond the limits of rational consciousness. Real-life women who confronted this model of genius during the post-Romantic era found themselves in difficulties, since the stereotypes of woman had changed. The Victorian 'Angel in the House', and her twentieth-century 'housewife' daughter, lacked spiritual ecstasy, as well as sexual desire. The simultaneous survival of the older conceptions of female nature only created a further level of paradox, especially since non-rationality is perceived differently (and evaluated differently) in men and women.

Reviewing a recent book of photographs of poets, Russell Davies wonders why all the women look as if they could be mistresses of some Oxbridge college, whilst the men all look like priests or like rogues at a country fair [1986, p.23]. I think the reason is not hard to find. Who gets counted as a poet depends in part on obtaining the audience's trust that what you are doing is art. The stance of the stereotypical poet is, however, awkward for women. Emotion and sensitivity are expected of women, and therefore not generally valued in them except in controlled circumstances. Sylvia Plath's suicide might be popularly viewed as confirming her 'genius' by proving that she lived in the psychic no-man's-land between sanity and madness. But, in poetry workshops, I always know that when my poetry is likened to that of Plath the comparison is not meant as a compliment. It means that my poems are perceived as too subjective; too raw; too emotional. And, since there are very few similarities between Plath's voice and my own, I also know that my audience is hearing my words (and Plath's) through an ear-trumpet that amplifies all female anger as 'hysteria' and all female sorrow as 'confessional'. In creative writing a woman has always the problem of aligning Romantic notions of art as an instinctive, non-rational activity

The Third Sex

against her need to assess (rationally and consciously) the likely reactions to a *female* voice.

Even the most successful women authors have experienced these tensions. Virginia Woolf, for example, measured her own aesthetic achievement against Romantic ideals of creativity . . . and her own inability (as a woman) to immerse herself completely in the unconscious. Thus, in 'Professions for Women' [1931], Woolf used 'the image of a fisherman lying sunk in dreams on the verge of a deep lake with a rod held out over the water' as a metaphor for the first stage of the writing process. Authors have to wait passively, in 'a state of perpetual lethargy', for the impulses that will move the hand to shape words. But, where the writer is a woman, there will be difficulties in dipping into the unconscious:

The line raced through the girl's fingers. Her imagination had rushed away. It had sought the pools, the depths, the dark places where the largest fish slumber. And then there was a smash. There was an explosion. There was foam and confusion. The imagination had dashed itself against something hard. The girl was roused from her dream. [p.61]

Woolf elaborates. What the young woman author had found was 'something about the body, about the passions which it was unfitting for her as a woman to say. Men, her reason told her, would be shocked.' The trance ends, the creative processes are blocked. The woman can write no more. The ultimate battle for creative women is – says Woolf, as she goes on to identify herself with the defeated writer – to conquer the consciousness of the way men will react [p.62]. Thus, despite her extraordinary accomplishments, Woolf's acceptance of romantic norms led to a feeling of literary failure. The models of the 'feminine' unconscious offered by male aesthetics disguise a vicious woman-trap. Like Plath, Woolf eventually committed suicide.

In ways that would continue to tug at the imagination of women artists and writers, Romanticism linked genius to a *type* of personality, and to concomitant (non-conscious) *modes* of creative process. But early eighteenth-century ways of talking about genius have also survived, mainly in recent psychological and sociological research (discussed in Chapter 13, below). In this alternative tradition, genius is neither a psychological type, nor a variety of psychic act, but rather a diversity of human talents that, developed, lead to success. Paradoxically, it is the talent/success model of greatness that is the more useful to women now, despite the Romantics' admiration for the 'androgynous' genius, and despite the ways in which the notions of 'talent' and 'success' have been employed. The lack of *success* of women artists has been used as 'evidence' for their lack of *talent* and consequent *incapacity* for genius. For the pre-Enlightenment period – when there were few women in the arts and sciences – such arguments can seem plausible . . . at least, if the educational and environmental obstacles placed in women's way are determinedly discounted. But as more women became literate and had sufficient finance, education, leisure and social back-up to begin to enter the artistic professions, the number of *great* female creators also

In the writings of Simone de Beauvoir, we can see how Romantic
presuppositions about art made even the 'mother' of second-wave
feminism unfair to women. Taking Van Gogh as the example of the
paradigm genius, de Beauvoir asks rhetorically:

*How could Van Gogh have been born a woman? A woman would not have been
sent on a mission to the Belgian coal mines in Borinage, she would not have felt
the misery of the miners as her own crime, she would not have sought a redemp-
tion; she would therefore have never painted Van Gogh's sunflowers. Not to
mention that the mode of life of the painter—his solitude at Arles, his frequenta-
tion of cafés and brothels, all that nourished Van Gogh's art in nourishing his
sensitivity—would have been forbidden her. [1949, p. 722]*

By itself the above passage could just be read as a comment about the
narrowness of the lives of past generations of women. We could close
our eyes to the way it glamorises the male personality that matures in
brothels (of dubious value in enriching 'sensitivity'). But de Beauvoir's
comments are more disturbing than this. In the rest of this section from
The Second Sex, she considers various women as candidates for genius,
and rejects them all. She dismisses George Eliot, Jane Austen, the
Brontë sisters, Virginia Woolf, Katherine Mansfield – even Colette,
whose words and works are used so extensively throughout de Beauvoir's own analysis of female consciousness.

De Beauvoir makes similar moves in a lecture that she gave on 'Women
and Creativity' in Japan in 1966. She quotes Stendhal, that 'great
feminist', and asserts that it is *still* true to say that '"Every genius born a
woman is lost to humanity"' [1966, p.18]. She goes on to claim – in a
sentence that should lead us to be very suspicious of the notions of
'genius' and of 'creativity' that she is employing – 'With literature we
come to the sphere where the anti-feminists appear to have the most
trump cards' [ibid., p.24]. What an extraordinary comment! It is 'literature' that is used to demonstrate that there has never yet been a woman
genius . . . and not music (in which, at least, women creators are better
concealed by history). De Beauvoir maintains that the great male
geniuses have produced works which 'contest the world in its entirety',
whereas women writers and thinkers 'do not contest the world in any
radical way' [ibid., pp. 28–9]. But that is equally bizarre! Has she
forgotten her own brilliant analyses of the way that men's vision of
society is limited by their preconceptions about their own sexual superiority? Why does she accept a male view of man's achievement, and of
the female's contribution to civilisation? Why can't our feminist fore-
mother recognise the literary achievements of her own matrilineal
ancestors?

We have to turn back to *The Second Sex* for clear answers to these
questions. There we discover that – for all her radicalism – de Beauvoir
still measures all cultural achievements against the paradigm personality of Romantic genius who walks that narrow path between sanity and

The Third Sex

madness. She writes, 'There are women who are mad and there are women of talent: none has that madness in her talent that we call genius' [1949, p.717, *corr.*].[1] This sentence shows how deeply de Beauvoir is entrapped ·by the ideology of Romanticism. To be a genius, a person has to be *like* a madman – but not a madman. De Beauvoir does not recognise that Romantic genius must also be *like* a woman – but not a woman. Instead, she internalises the Romantic version of man's past: that defines 'genius' in terms of the *male* psyche, and then 'concludes' that in the whole of Western culture there has never been one (real) female genius. She is scathing about the 'eccentric' women whose behaviour is so 'singular that they should be locked up' [p.717]. Women have contributed to 'a literature of protest' with their 'sincere and powerful works'; but they lack 'irony', 'ease', 'calm sincerity', and 'abstract elegance' [pp.718,719]. Their texts (is this consistent?) 'lack metaphysical resonances and also anger' [p.720].

De Beauvoir makes these comments in that part of *The Second Sex* which sets out to envisage a future of true equality for men and women. She insists that women's psychic inferiority is determined not by biology, but by upbringing and social circumstance; and that there is thus no reason why the future should resemble the past. But, if history is always to be inspected through spectacles that blur the great women in the past into fuzzy marginality, we have every reason to doubt the grounds for de Beauvoir's optimism. If we remain within the horizons of Romantic myth – that takes *male* reason, *male* fantasies and *male* sexual energies as the norms for creativity – women will only be able to progress *so far*. Of course, in one sense de Beauvoir is right: Western culture *is* a male preserve. Like her, I have argued that 'Art', 'Culture' and the whole of European 'Civilisation' have been constructed via a process of excluding or denigrating female achievements. Woman is pushed to the outside – an 'Other'. De Beauvoir describes the process well; but it is, nevertheless, a mistake to suppose that such 'Otherness' exhausts woman's (socialised) nature, or that women in the past did not exploit this 'Otherness' to produce valuable and subversive words and works of their own. In the history of culture women have been neither absences nor insignificant zeros. Indeed, there have been *great* women artists, whose achievements have been such as to merit being praised as 'geniuses'.

As an existentialist, de Beauvoir could afford to mis-hear the passion and irony in women's voices. She can re-work the traditions of the splenetic *male* madness that is semi-divine and the *female* hysteria that merely apes genius . . . and *still* represent women as free. For the existentialist, a human being is as free *inside* prison as s/he is outside. De Beauvoir spells out what Jean-Paul Sartre had merely implied: that (in our culture) the female body is more of a prison than that of the male. Since most people seek to conceal their freedom from themselves, and since femaleness (like imprisonment) offers an extreme predicament which challenges such bad faith, de Beauvoir can (paradoxically) combine this *negative* assessment of the female predicament with a *positive* feminist message. Later feminists have, however, refused de Beauvoir's overly metaphysical account of the nature of freedom, while (simultaneously) clinging to de Beauvoir's theory that woman is always Other, even to herself. Many of the debates in current feminist theory originate in this double reaction to existentialist feminism. And we can avoid many of the dilemmas by recognising how de Beauvoir's androcentric 'Otherness' re-works the misogny that patterns Romantic thought.

The very title of de Beauvoir's *The Second Sex* reveals her place in the traditions of Romanticism. This phrase − used ironically, but also, in a sense, endorsed − has been picked out of 'On Women' [1851], the notorious essay in which Arthur Schopenhauer (1788–1860) expressed undisguised contempt for that half of humanity that he dubbed 'the second sex' [p.108]. Since Schopenhauer's views on women are often dismissed as a kind of aberration in his work, it is important to point out that they are positioned at its core. His massive philosophical treatise, *The World as Will and Idea* [1818 and 1844], climaxes in sexual hate. Of course, not all Romantics were misogynists. Nor need misogyny take the extreme shapes that Schopenhauer's does. I know of no other Romantic philosopher recorded as having thrown a seamstress downstairs because her chatter disturbed his work! But what is so revealing about Schopenhauer's position is that he shows how the 'feminine' Romantic genius and a horror of women can, and do, coexist.

On the face of things it seems very odd to describe the Schopenhauerian genius as in any way 'feminine'. Schopenhauer idolised 'genius'; took the individual male human being as the norm for humanity; and despised women utterly. There seems to be nothing about the latter that he admired. For Kant the female sex was, at least, the 'aesthetic' sex − with a 'beautiful' mind and body compensating for the deficiency in genius. Schopenhauer built on Kantian metaphysics in a self-conscious fashion; but saw women as 'the unaesthetic sex':

It is only the man whose intellect is clouded by his sexual impulses that could give the name of the fair sex *to that undersized, narrow-shouldered, broad-hipped, and short-legged race . . . [p.107]*

Kant had allowed women a role as consumers of art. But not Schopenhauer. He quotes, gloatingly, Rousseau's remark in the *Letter to Mr d'Alembert* (1758) that women lack artistic taste, as well as genius. Given this, it is all the more remarkable that there is a considerable overlap between Schopenhauer's portrait of genius and his caricature of woman. As he matures, a 'genius' transcends the motivational drives and urges that are integral to masculinity and acquires feminine passivity. He belongs to a kind of third sex − the female male.

The triad of genius/ordinary male/woman provides the shaping outlines of Schopenhauer's philosophical system. At the high point of evolution is the creative genius who has very little in common with ordinary males − however talented (or even extraordinarily talented) those males might be. The genius is guided not by his own will or desires, but by something over and above him and acting through him. He has 'a double intellect, one for himself and the service of his will; the

The Third Sex

other for the world, of which he becomes the mirror'. This second, special intellect Schopenhauer calls 'objective'. 'The normal man, on the other hand, has only a single intellect'. By 'man' here Schopenhauer means 'male', and this single intellect is labelled 'subjective' in contrast to that of the genius. However perfect and 'acute' this intellect might be in a man of talent, it can never even remotely resemble that of the genius. The ordinary male and the genius live on different planes ['On Genius', 1851, p.71]. The genius is, in fact, closer to madness than to talent because, like the madman, the genius does not act out of self-interest and is not guided by his own individual will or character. He suspends his own self in the act of creation, and lets the 'universal', in other words objective truth, control his mind and his body. He is like some kind of shaman.

The nearest the ordinary male comes to this, according to Schopenhauer, is in his choice of sexual partners. Whereas an ordinary male might think that individual choice and individual taste lead him to select his sexual partner, in fact part of his choice is that of nature dictating to him what sort of mate is to be preferred in order for the human race to continue and to improve. (Schopenhauer can think of no other reason why males should feel sexual desire for ugly, stupid, unaesthetic women instead of for noble, well-formed intelligent males!) He calls that facet of nature that pre-programmes sexual selection 'the genius of the species', and claims that it is in conflict with 'the guardian geniuses of individuals' (= the egos of individual *males*) [*World as Will*, iii, p.369]. Apparently, in the sexual behaviour of ordinary males the two impulses of the species-drive and ego-drive are at war with each other. This is highly reminiscent of Freud, who used Schopenhauer's account of these two conflicting types of drive as a model for the libido and ego of the normal male.

Schopenhauer knew of the connection in the Latin language between the word *genius* and male sexuality, and he is playing with the two meanings of the term. He explains that 'the ancients personified the genius of the species in Cupid, a malevolent, cruel, and therefore ill-reputed god, in spite of his childish appearance'. Sexual love (Cupid) is 'a capricious, despotic demon', a tyrant that is none the less 'lord of gods and men' [ibid., iii, p.370]. Sexual desire (like Cupid) is blind to the interests and even tastes of individuals, and is solely directed to the propagation of the race of human beings. As a young man Schopenhauer was sexually quite promiscuous – with women! Schopenhauer's position is really quite comical. It is not just modern analytical philosophers who practise the kind of mental gymnastics described by Tom Stoppard in *Jumpers*. If we look at great philosophers writing on sexuality, we can see a number of intriguing manoeuvres that philosophers have had to perform in order to fit their prejudices about women into their metaphysical systems.

For Schopenhauer each male has his own separate genius; but a woman lacks a comparable personal genius to guide her on her path through life. She lacks the ego and related drives that operate in ordinary males.

Gender and Genius

For the ordinary woman (and all women are more or less ordinary), the interests of the species and the interests of the individual are not in conflict – given her lack of ego they can't be. Apparently, a woman *instinctively* chooses the partner who is her physical and psychological opposite, and who will produce the best and most harmonious balance in nature. Her choice of sex-partner is dictated entirely by the 'genius of the species', i.e. by nature and the necessity to procreate [ibid., iii, pp.351 ff.]. Women's physique, psychology and talents (such as they are) are all directed towards *nature's* purpose – to reproduce the species. Women's virtues and duties, the legal and social restrictions placed on them, and the rights allotted to them are all traceable to the fact that women (like the lower animals) act in the service of the species, instead of being guided by their own individual wills.

The creative genius resembles woman in that he is guided by something over and above himself: the 'universal' and the needs of the species. This genius is, however, still male: he has an ego which he *surrenders* to an external control. And this outside force is not just 'nature' – as it is for woman – but includes, also, civilisation, culture and the perfection of the race. Woman is a passive pawn of nature. The ordinary male is torn between self and nature. The creative genius actively permits himself to be a pawn; but a pawn of cultural and racial evolution. He *freely chooses* to become a passive thing, to become the mouthpiece of all that is divine in man. The male fulfils his potential in cultural production; woman's only potential is reproduction. These are tasks allotted by nature, and nature's plan for the species. Despite his praise for 'original' genius, Schopenhauer's views on women are not very original!

Schopenhauer's woman is still fundamentally Aristotelian: he even (absurdly) uses as one of his authorities Huarte's sixteenth-century text on how to breed superior (= male) humans ['On Women', p.108; and see Chapter 3 above]. A woman is still a kind of monstrous deviation from humanity, designed by nature solely to preserve the species. Culture is still perfected through the activity of its best (= male) specimens. The female body is still associated with matter; that of the male is still equated with soul (form) and all that is essentially human. Schopenhauer's account of procreation even re-works Aristotle's 'flower-pot' theory of reproduction, according to which women provide the soil and the receptacle within which the male seed will grow. In matters of breeding – including the breeding of geniuses – the *logos* retains its connections with the heat of the male body.

We are told that the matter in the body of a child is inherited from the mother, whereas the energy or form is the father's gift to his offspring. For a genius two things are necessary: a well-formed brain and nervous system (these come from the mother), and a good supply of vital heat and blood to the brain (which come from a father with sufficient vital heat). To some extent the heat of a genius's brain is seen to depend on the mother, because heat is partly dependent on physique. Being short, and having 'especially a short neck' helps: 'because by the shorter path the blood reaches the brain with more energy'. Nevertheless, the heat

The Third Sex

and energy of a creative genius are male energies. The mother supplies the material and the stature: not an unimportant task, since a good supply of blood to an inadequate brain produces 'vivacity without mind, heat without light, hot-headed persons, men of unsupportable restlessness and petulance' [*World as Will*, iii, pp.160, 161]. Women are important to the breeding of geniuses, although nature disqualifies them from ever being geniuses themselves. In Chapter 2 we saw Andrew Gemant still repeating this Schopenhauerian conclusion in *The Nature of the Genius* [1961]. Indeed, Schopenhauer's views on women and creativity were profoundly influential: on Nietzsche, Jung, Freud, and through them on the twentieth century.

Intriguingly, Arthur Schopenhauer's own mother, Johanna, was a writer of quite popular novels and travel journals. After the death of her husband, she ran a literary salon in Weimar that counted Goethe amongst its patrons. Her son had to wait until he was in his sixties before his own writings began to be popular, and he was consequently jealous of his mother's literary reputation and power. Unlike Kant, Schopenhauer couldn't afford simply to assume that women were creative inferiors. He had to spend many pages rationalising his conviction that women should never even attempt to be geniuses. This was one of the many issues over which mother and son quarrelled violently. Some of the bitter exchanges that eventually led to their irreconcilable estrangement have survived. 'Arthur: My book will be available when all your books are completely forgotten. Johanna: Yes, the whole edition will be available' [Hollingdale, 1970, p.27].

In terms of what gets preserved in the European Hall of Fame, the odds were very much stacked in Arthur's favour. Until Women's Studies resurrected an interest in Johanna Schopenhauer, it was impossible to locate any critical literature that bothered to examine the literary merits (or demerits) of her writings. Yet, despite this, generations of male critics have seemed certain of her mediocrity, and of her failure as a mother. William Hirsch described her as 'mentally gifted indeed, but cold', and went on to blame her for the faults in Arthur's character. If he had been given a childhood 'beautified by a mother's love', Schopenhauer might even have avoided misogyny [1897, pp.161, 162]! Seventy-five years later Storr repeated the accusation, but with even more vehemence. Johanna was 'an intellectually pretentious woman with no heart' [1972, p.73]. Hollingdale [1970] felt confident enough to report that Johanna Schopenhauer was '"artistic" in the silly sense and a bit of a culture snob' [p.27]. The adjective 'silly' is used when inferiors (housewives, shopgirls, secretaries, children and the like) aspire to the social and cultural attainments of their superiors. Simple bad taste is not 'silly', neither are attempts at self-improvement that are viewed as socially legitimate. Arthur Schopenhauer's cultural heirs have taken over the son's envious view of his mother's literary fame. The description 'silly' would be much more appropriately used of Arthur Schopenhauer's views on women – if only he had not simply re-formulated the ancient traditions of patriarchal power that Christianity appropriated from ancient Greece and Rome.

Gender and Genius

Like the Gnostic God the Father, Arthur sought to appropriate the role of his mother in the act of creation. But there is a distinctively modern feel to Arthur Schopenhauer's brand of masculinism. On the surface, Arthur and Johanna seem merely to re-enact the Gnostic drama. The Gnostic God the Father had boasted that he was the only God: he had refused to recognise that there is any other kind of creative power different from, prior to, or superior to his own. 'I am the only God,' Arthur choruses with Ialdabaoth. 'You're wrong!' Johanna's angry voice joins the measured tones of God the Mother, as together they respond to the insolence of their sons. Who can blame Johanna for sounding more shrill than Sophia? After all, Arthur (unlike the Gnostic Father) does not pretend to have simply overlooked the existence of a type of being other than himself. No. Arthur sees the Other, envies it, mocks it . . . and seeks to incorporate it into his own universal, greedy (and paradoxically 'egoless') ego.

Arthur ascribes to the genius (and, of course, to himself as typical genius) the aspects of femininity that had been re-valued during the agricultural and industrial revolutions. Schopenhauer covets the passivity, the receptivity and the selflessness that the Aristotelians so despised in the female sex. He even boasts that to ordinary humans his élite males can seem like monsters: nearer to madness than to normality. Having been excluded from the category of the fully-human, women find men even seeking to appropriate their status as Other! Nineteenth-century males aspired to the demonic roles – spirit-medium, priestess, oracle, witch, lunatic, monster – that had left women with a residue of strength in classical (and neo-classical) times. Schopenhauer's females are left as little more than domestic and reproductive slaves: deprived of basic human rights because of membership of an inferior, semi-human race. Although superficially identical to ancient modes of patriarchal ideology, this blend of Romanticism and Aristotelianism is peculiarly vicious, since Schopenhauer does not really despise femininity . . . he only hates women! He puts up with them only because they are essential for breeding purposes. Had it not been for this, we might suspect that Arthur's proposed solution to 'The Woman Question' would have been similar to Hitler's answer to 'The Jewish Question'. Hitler was, after all, a child of the world that Schopenhauer helped to create.

As a teenager, Hitler had wanted to be an artist [see Gimpel, 1968, pp.1ff.]. The young Adolf stubbornly resisted his father's objections to his proposed career as a painter, preferring a bohemian life to the career in the civil service that his father advocated. To Europe's loss, Hitler failed the entrance examination into the Viennese Academy of Fine Arts. He never, however, gave up the Romantic artist's dream of playing God. By the end of the nineteenth century the Romantic notion of genius had been extended to the arena of politics. The political genius was not necessarily a man of high intelligence, but was a special kind of being – shamanistic (and Schopenhauerian) – who was in touch with the mood and will of the people and could express the spirit of the *Volk* through political action. This is how Hitler presented himself to

The Third Sex

the German people. Jung clearly recognised this when, in 1936, he described Hitler in terms of the Romantic stereotype of the genius: Hitler was not just a politician, or even a dictator, but a 'medium', a 'medicine man' and 'the mouthpiece of the gods'. Jung made this even clearer in 1938 when he remarked:

> . . . *Hitler is the mirror of every German's unconscious . . . He is the loudspeaker which magnifies the inaudible whispers of the German soul until they can be heard by the German's unconscious ear.*[2]

Given Jung's own Romantic notions of genius, his use of this vocabulary is disturbing. We have to turn to Thomas Mann's novel, *Doctor Faustus* [1947], for a less ambivalent reaction to the connections between Romantic aesthetics and the phenomenon of Hitler. '[H]ow near aestheticism and barbarism are to each other', muses the narrator, Zeitblom, as he contemplates the way the 'civilised' artist takes on the roles of 'the priest-medicine-man, the priest-wizard' [p.359]. The novel opens with the narrator's 'embarrassment' over 'the word "genius"': at the way its 'noble, harmonious, and humane ring' is infiltrated by 'the daemonic and irrational [which] have a disquieting share in this radiant sphere' [p.10]. Zeitblom stands for humanism in Mann's text: for the belief that there is a distinction to be made 'between pure and impure genius' [p.11]. What Zeitblom does not recognise – but what *Doctor Faustus* itself implies – is that there is more than a simple affinity between the Romantic cult of the genius-personality and the fascists' response to Hitler's frenzies.

Thomas Mann gently satirises the narrator's attempts to separate out the (evil) cult of genius from the (good) culture of modern Germany. Schönberg's modernist music and Friedrich Nietzsche's anti-metaphysical metaphysics are portrayed as remaining within the (decadent) axis of Romanticism. And, through the figure of Schleppfuss (whose name emblematises the dragging foot of the devil himself), we confront views of the relationship between sexuality, genius and art as misogynistic as those of Schopenhauer. Indeed, the term 'genius' runs like a *leitmotiv* through Zeitblom's story of the tragic career of his friend, Adrian Leverkühn, whose creative gifts as a musical composer were intertwined with disease, evil, madness and a warped (male) sexuality. It is, therefore, doubly ironic that – by promoting the novel as 'one of the most convincing accounts of genius ever written' – the jacket of my English-language translation leaves the Romantic notion of a genius-personality fundamentally undisturbed. There are some lessons of history that we are slow to learn. We would rather not register the author's message, that links the rise of European fascism to the cult of genius that is integral to the traditions of European culture.

12
A Degenerate Breed

In October 1903 a young Austrian man of twenty-three, whose Hebrew
name was Schlomoh, made his way to the room in Vienna in which
Beethoven had died . . . and shot himself. More commonly known as
Otto Weininger, in May of that same year, a book of his had rolled off
the presses into instant notoriety. Later translated into English under
the title *Sex and Character*, it offered copious 'proof' that genius is
confined to males. Weininger argued that although real-life men and
women never measure up to the quintessence of maleness and femaleness and always contain within themselves elements of bisexuality, the
perfect male and the perfect female are not symmetrical opposites. In a
late notebook, Tennyson had jotted: 'Men should be androgynous and
women gynandrous, but men should not be gynandrous nor women
androgynous' [*Poems*, p.1424]. Weininger also refused women androgyny. The perfect male includes within himself the female. The perfect
female is, however, always utterly female. It is this 'fact' that means
women can't be geniuses:

*The man of genius possesses, like everything else, the complete female in himself;
but woman herself is only a part of the Universe, and the part never can be the
whole; femaleness can never include genius. [1903, p.189]*

Weininger spelt out the details of this by now familiar, crazy logic. The
genius is the great 'I am' who constructs the universe out of his own
individual, very inflated ego. The great man is 'the centre of infinite
space; the great man contains the whole universe within himself; genius
is the living microcosm' [p.169]. Woman, without a self, is stuck outside
in the metaphorical cold of outer space. Almost as an afterthought to
his two-volume work, Weininger included a chapter on the way men in
different cultural groups approach this Romantic ideal of perfect maleness. Jews failed to measure up and were described in ways that made
them psychological eunuchs. In a gesture of symbolic homage to Aryan
genius, the young Jewish author committed suicide.

The echoes of this deadly shot resounded throughout the 'civilised'
world, transforming *Sex and Character* into the most up-to-date answer
to 'the woman problem'. Even before Weininger had killed himself,
Strindberg had written to the author offering 'reverence' and 'thanks'.
As he remarks elsewhere, Weininger's achievement was 'awe-inspiring':
he had solved 'the most difficult of all problems' [Abrahamsen, 1946,
p.122]. As Ford Maddox Ford noted, the book came to represent 'the
attitude of really advanced men toward woman-kind'. In 1906, after the

work had been translated,

in the men's clubs of England and in the cafés of France and Germany – one began to hear singular mutterings amongst men. Even in the United States where men never talk about women, certain whispers might be heard. The idea was that a new gospel had appeared. [Dijkstra, 1986, p.218]

Evidently the news penetrated as far as Scandinavia where, as early as 1904, Hulda Garborg published an anonymous account of her own life and set it within the framework of Weininger's theories [Abrahamsen, p.197].

The book certainly did have its critics, as Ford Maddox Ford's sarcastic tone makes clear. But often the criticisms that were made of it were over relatively minor matters. The most hostile review was by Paul Möbius who objected that there was nothing really original about Weininger's ideas on the feeblemindedness of women, and that they had been stolen from his own popular essays on this subject! It was only in so far as Weininger had departed from Möbius's own argument that errors had crept in [Abrahamsen, p.138]. We see a similar thing if we look at Freud's recorded remarks on Weininger. As a young student Weininger had taken the first part of the book (then in the form of a doctoral thesis) to the great man to get his opinion. Freud also seems to have been worried about intellectual plagiarism. Freud's later criticisms of Weininger were offered as a defence of himself against Fliess's accusation that by teaching Fliess's ideas on hysteria, Freud had enabled the undergraduate to steal them. Freud was certainly impressed enough by the young man to recall him later as 'a personality with a touch of the genius' [ibid., p.55].

As these debates about intellectual ownership suggest, what Weininger's book did was package in a popular form various ideas about women that had currency at the turn of the century. It was as a second-year Philosophy student that Weininger had begun the work. Asked to do an essay on 'The Problem of Talent', the teenager embarked on a process of reading that would change his life – and bring about his death. Believing that he had 'discovered' the 'solution' to the dual nineteenth-century 'problems' – that of the nature of genius and the nature of woman – he supplemented his studies in Philosophy and Psychology with courses in Biology and Medicine, so as to accommodate his theories to the latest scientific 'facts'. In a sudden shift of perspective, the young student spotted the assumption that underlies Thomas Carlyle's *On Heroes and Hero-Worship* [1840] – and all Romantic discussion of the genius-personality:

[T]he idea is definitely insisted on that genius is linked with manhood, that it represents an ideal masculinity in the highest form . . . Woman, in short, has an unconscious life, man a conscious life, and the genius the most conscious life. [1903, p.113]

Weininger aimed at consistency in his account of the links between genius and maleness. He felt he could put together Kant, Schopenhauer, Carlyle and the rest into one coherent thesis. But although the

Gender and Genius

theories of these authors were consistent in outcome, they were utterly inconsistent in detail. As we have seen, Rousseau's woman lacked passion; Duff's lacked imagination; Kant's lacked a 'sublime understanding'; Schopenhauer's woman lacked free will (or any will of her own). It is hardly surprising, therefore, that Weininger's own arguments should be dogged by contradictions. On the one hand, for example, Weininger made the conventional move that described eminent women authors and artists as 'masculine'. Here, as usual, we find George Sand, George Eliot, Rosa Bonheur and the rest as illustrations of partly bisexual, and partly homosexual women [pp.64ff.]. On the other hand, Weininger parroted the contemporary wisdom that made all women gynogynous. Even imperfect (= talented) females were denied psychic bisexuality:

. . . whilst there are people who are anatomically men and psychically women, there is no such thing as a person who is physically female and psychically male, notwithstanding the extreme maleness of their outward appearance and the unwomanliness of their expression. [pp.188–9].

Women in the artistic professions remained utterly female – and that is why no woman of genius could ever exist! Weininger tied himself in knots trying to rationalise the conclusion that he wanted: 'A female genius is a contradiction in terms, for genius is simply intensified, perfectly developed, universally conscious maleness' [p.189].

To establish this 'truth' Weininger tried yet another variation on the language of lack: women lack memory [p.282]. And, since without a memory there is no real self-consciousness, or soul, a woman is (once again) more like an animal or a savage than a civilised European male. A woman is even said to lack the capacity for 'love' – as well as 'individuality', 'will', a 'sense of worth or value' and the 'faculty of "taking notice"' [loc.cit.]. She is driven, instead, by her 'natural' instinct for motherhood – which is so strong that she will turn to prostitution if she does not meet the man who is her appropriate sexual complement. In terms of the stereotypes of woman then current amongst the middle classes, Weininger's might seem to focus unduly on female sexual depravity. But, as Bram Dijkstra has shown in Idols of Perversity [1986], even here there was nothing very original about Weininger – except in the way that he attempted to systematise the platitudes of 'enlightened opinion'. This stereotype of woman as lacking in love, but sexually greedy, was common amongst the anti-bourgeois élite of the time, amongst the 'overbearing intellectuals' recorded by Ford Maddox Ford.

Weininger's eventual suicide does, of course, make it easy to dismiss him as simply psychically deranged. But I am not convinced that the madness originated in him, rather than in the culture around him. To talk about an ego so extensive that it includes within itself the whole of reality sounds like a classic symptom of psychosis. But Weininger did not make up this theory; he merely abstracted it from the contemporary obsession with genius. It might be thought a clear sign of lunacy that the young Jew should claim that the males of his own race 'adhere together' like women and lack the strong individuality, dignity, self-knowledge and 'greatness' of perfect males [pp.308–11]. But although

A Degenerate Breed

Weininger seems to have added touches of his own – as, for example, when he claims that Jewish men are as sex-obsessed as women – most of this is just *fin-de-siècle* cliché. In any case, Weininger was right to focus on the racial and cultural links between 'genius' and 'maleness'. 'Become a man, my son,' says the father, implying that maleness, like masculinity, is more than simply passing through the biological stage of puberty. We never say, 'Become a woman, my daughter'; but if we did it would have quite different connotations – of *accepting* menstruation, body-hair, breasts and the like. Our conceptual scheme binds 'being female' to a set of biological givens. By contrast, 'male' is ambiguous: it is sometimes purely descriptive; but it can also be prescriptive . . . an honorific title conferred on those who successfully negotiate a cultural rite of passage into maturity. However, since only Aryans (or honorary Aryans) were allowed to test their manhood against the norms of 'genius', the young Jew found himself ensnared by the non-descriptive senses of 'maleness' that he wished to endorse.

According to Weininger's argument, a Jew, like a woman, faces an either/or: he is *either* a Jew *or* a genius, since male Jews 'are found to approach so slightly and so rarely to the ideal of manhood' [p.302]. Redefining Jewishness as a state of mind – instead of some kind of racial or religious fact – Weininger claimed that 'To defeat Judaism, the Jew must first understand himself, and war against himself ' [p.312]. Weininger thus accepted the contemporary caricature of the Jew as 'feminine', even though he drew back from dismissing the cultural pretensions of his race as being as self-deluding as those of women. Arguing (with Fliess and Freud) that female hysteria results when a woman represses her own sexuality, Weininger suggested that a woman who thinks she can choose to give up her femininity and choose genius misunderstands herself. She is hysterical. She has taken on a *male* view of human development and can't see herself except as a pseudo-male. The only *real* 'either/or' facing Weininger's woman was to become either a wife and mother or a whore . . . anything else – any attempt to evade biological destiny – was a form of delusion. By contrast, Weininger insisted that there was a real possibility for Jewish males to renounce their Judiasm and choose genius.

Since the links between 'hysteria' and 'womb-sickness' had been severed by the most advanced writers on psychology (including Freud), it was difficult for Weininger to set up his argument so as to ally Jewish males with Aryan males at this point. Did Weininger suddenly recognise the possible consequences of the fact that 'bisexual' and 'feminine' males were also being classified as 'hysterical'? Did he suddenly recognise that others might hear *him* as a 'hysterical Jew', voicing and acting out his self-deceit as he sought to evade his racial destiny? After the work was published, Weininger anxiously watched the reviews – and wrote aggressive replies to his critics. That has again been seen as proof of his craziness. But was it? According to the logic based on his own false premises, Weininger could be either a genius or a Jew. If he was not a genius, then he might be a Jew after all . . . and, even worse, a self-deluding hysteric whose conclusions could not be trusted.

Gender and Genius

Weininger tried to block the parallels between Jews and women by arguing that the ideal male contains female elements, and that only a small proportion of feminine males have the perverse form of bisexuality that manifests itself as hysteria [p.266]. Also, significantly, after the chapter on Judaism, Weininger suddenly, desperately, looked round for a way out for women, suggesting (inconsistently, and as a kind of postscript) that they could transcend their biology by giving up sexual intercourse. The day Weininger received his doctorate for this questionable piece of research he entered the Christian Church. But, given his transformation of 'Judaism' into a purely psychological state, even this could not put his mind at rest. Did the racial taunts become too much to bear? Did he come to locate within his own psyche the stigma of 'Otherness' that he had tried to transfer on to the body of Woman? Was Weininger's suicide the ultimate act of madness? Or did he suddenly see the trap that had been laid for Jews (and other inferior 'feminine' types) by the shared madness of Austria – that most 'civilised' of countries – in which the teenage Hitler would grow up wanting to be a Romantic genius . . . and a perfect (Aryan) male?

I am not intending to deny that there are elements within Weininger's work which seem quite bizarre, even when situated in the context of contemporary theories of psychology and physiology. What are we to think when, to prove the bisexuality of males, Weininger cites 'several' men that he has observed 'who have the upper part of the thigh of a female with a normally male under part, and some with the right hip of a male and the left of a female' [p.17]? It's hard not to laugh at the distortions in perspective that come from observing male bodies through a prism of paranoia! Had we been able to meet Weininger and accuse him to his face of some form of madness that was not hysterical in origin, he might (paradoxically) have been reassured. Although by this time males as well as females were being described as faking genius by a hysterical form of delusion, it had also become commonplace to represent madness and genius as twin brothers. In *The Mad Genius Controversy* [1978] George Becker has traced the debate on the relationship between genius and madness that so occupied medical and literary writers through the years 1836 to 1949. Between the years 1836 and 1886 Becker finds the view that genius is a kind of madness to be very nearly unanimous amongst writers in English and German. Important critics of this view emerge after 1886; but Becker's sampling of texts suggests that until 1949 majority opinion still made genius a kind of biological disorder.

The exact nature of that disorder was described differently by different medical and psychological writers. It was in France in the 1850s that the account of genius as a form of 'degeneracy' was first put forward by B. A. Morel. Cesare Lombroso popularised this notion with a series of writings that started with *The Man of Genius* in 1863. Lombroso was a celebrated Italian criminologist whose views attracted many disciples, as well as some critics. He argued that geniuses, criminals and lunatics are all degenerate types of humanity. 'Degeneracy' was described as a state of biological inferiority that can occur in a family when children are

A Degenerate Breed

born who are characteristic of earlier primitive stages of human development. Even before Darwin's theories of evolution inked in the detail, it was a common belief that human beings had developed from relatively simple organisms to 'higher', more 'complex' ones. The link that Romantic aesthetic theory posited between 'genius' and non-deliberative modes of consciousness encouraged scientific and medical theorists to regard the genius as a 'throwback' to less sophisticated times, before the 'rationality' of the civilised European male had fully evolved. In 1895 W. L. Babcock provided a convenient summary of the four possible patterns of life open to a throwback:

First, and most prominent in the order of frequency is an early death. Second, he may swell the criminal ranks. Third, he may become mentally deranged and ultimately find his way into a hospital for the insane. Fourth, and least frequently, he startles the world by an invention or discovery in science or by an original composition of great merit in art, music or literature. He is then styled a genius. [Becker, pp.38–9]

Did some (degenerate) women follow the same path as their degenerate brothers and become geniuses? Were all women naturally degenerate? What, in any case, was the relationship between the form of male degeneracy that manifested itself as genius and degeneracy in females? All of these topics were hotly disputed in the latter half of the nineteenth century and the opening years of the twentieth. When Darwin's *The Descent of Man* appeared in 1871, a scientific seal of approval was set on the view that women are always, naturally, degenerate – and that genius is not one of the symptoms of female degeneracy. Darwin pointed to the 'higher eminence' achieved by males in all activities 'requiring deep thought, reason, or imagination, or merely the use of the senses and hands'. Darwin was sure that these differences are the result of inborn male superiority, and he confronted head-on the problem posed by the high evaluation given to some supposedly 'feminine' characteristics:

It is generally admitted that with woman the powers of intuition, of rapid perception, and perhaps of imitation, are more strongly marked than in man; but some, at least, of these faculties are characteristic of the lower races, and therefore of a past and lower state of civilisation. [1871, p.858]

In *The Female Malady* [1987] Elaine Showalter has shown how Henry Maudsley, that pioneer of British psychiatry, used Darwin's views on degeneracy in his theory of mental illness and in his treatment of female patients. Like many other medical men writing during the second half of the nineteenth century, Maudsley was also a writer of essays on literary genius. Showalter also records Maudsley's eventual unease with the way that the rhetoric of 'degeneracy' was being employed in contemporary debate. Whether *all* women are degenerate, or only women who are prostitutes, lunatics, criminal – or talented – was the issue that divided Otto Weininger from his reviewer Paul Möbius. What a choice!

Even those who denied that women manifest the same kind of

Gender and Genius

'degeneracy' as men were likely to phrase this in ways that disadvantaged women. In *The Female Offender* [1893], for example, Cesare Lombroso argued that a specifically female type of degeneracy is rare amongst lunatics and criminals . . . because *all* women have characteristics in common with degenerate and primitive males. According to Lombroso, it is only convention and motherhood which checks the 'evil tendencies' – and sexual appetite – inherent in female nature. Whether or not a woman becomes a prostitute – or turns to other (related) crimes – is no more than a social accident . . . not a matter of reason or moral conscience (which do not operate in the case of women, who are no more than 'big children') [pp.151ff.]. Like Möbius and Weininger, Lombroso allowed women to be inmates of brothels, jails and lunatic asylums and still remain *typically* female. By contrast, a woman who entered the cages of European culture was so *atypical* as to have altogether surrendered her sexuality: hence his approval of Goncourt's maxim 'there are no women of genius; the women of genius are men' [Lombroso, 1863, p.138].

Aristotle had suggested that a woman is a failed biological experiment. Many of these genius theorists echo his voice in their presentation of woman as a failed evolutionary experiment. Women's creative inferiority became a scientific 'fact', unquestioned by most of those who spoke up for women [Alaya, 1977]. Cesare Lombroso was not alone in noting (with glee) that even John Stuart Mill accepted a 'deficiency of originality' and a lack of 'great and luminous new ideas' in modern women [Mill, 1869, p.285]. Although Cesare's daughter, Gina Lombroso-Ferrero, contradicted her father's account of sexual difference in her own *The Soul of Woman* [1924], she also accepted the 'fact' that a woman is incapable of genius:

It is true that there is no Dante, no Shakespeare, no Newton among women, but it is also true that it is not woman's business to write poems or to determine the laws that rule the universe. [p.180]

Gina's 'defence' of women thus had to rest on the claim that males might be culturally superior, but they are biologically inferior; passive machines, driven by their own selfish and gross egos to compensate for the strong other-centred drives that motivate the females. Since Gina had acted as a research assistant to her famous father and to William Ferrero (her husband and co-author of *The Female Offender*), her own book – addressed to her daughter – reads as a rationalisation of collaboration with the enemy. In its own way, *The Soul of Woman* is as disturbing as Weininger's *Sex and Character*. Like Weininger, Gina Lombroso-Ferrero becomes entangled in fantasy 'facts' about sexual difference.

At least Friedrich Nietzsche (1844–1900) seems to have recognised that so-called scientific facts about women are projections of male desire, hopes and ideals: 'Man has created woman – out of what? Out of a rib of his god – of his "ideal"' [1889, Aphorism 13, p.468]. According to Nietzsche, all so-called 'truths' are constructed via a similar mechanism: each self is a force-field of desires and appetites which functions by

A Degenerate Breed

seeking to incorporate all that is not-self within the boundaries of its own ego. The physical struggle to survive is matched by a psychic struggle: the mind projects order and stability on to the world as a way of containing the threat from the alien Otherness of all that is not-self. Nietzsche suggested that the whole of reality is a fiction, created by language which expresses a kind of collective (male) will-to-power. 'Truth' is a fiction, and so is 'woman' – and so also is the very notion of a stable, unitary and coherent ego. Writers like Schopenhauer had contrasted the (noble) individuality of the Indo-European male with egoless (and ignoble) females. But, for Nietzsche, even the supposedly strong and stable self of the normal male is a shifting focus of energies which is given an appearance of permanence by the way (male) language is structured.

According to the currently fashionable way of reading Nietzsche, this makes him a 'feminist'. Such an interpretation of Nietzsche takes its cue from Jacques Derrida's *Spurs* [*Éperons*, 1976]: a text in which the guru of deconstruction playfully confronts Nietzsche's words about women and explores the web of imagery that locates 'truth' and 'woman' in male fantasies. Derrideans – and sometimes even Derrida himself – present Nietzsche as a kind of sexual revolutionary: 'The discourses of Nietzsche, [James] Joyce and the women's movement . . . epitomize a profound and unprecedented transformation of the man-woman relationship' [Derrida, 1984, p.121]. Politically outraged by a Ph.D. thesis [Barnard, 1984] that argued in this manner, I asked two eminent British deconstructionists (both male) if I should infer from this that any true deconstructionist is also a feminist. Although I would have thought that any such answer proves itself false, both assured me that such a conclusion is sound.

A useful corrective to such a view of Nietzsche – and to the supposedly revolutionary implications of this deconstructive mode of 'feminism' – comes from situating Nietzsche's remarks on women, culture and the '*Übermensch*' (the 'overman' or 'superman') within the late nineteenth-century debate about the relationship between degeneracy, genius and women. The psychologists had defined the 'degenerate' in evolutionary terms as one who is a throwback to an earlier (more primitive, and inferior) stage of human development. Nietzsche, by contrast, mocked the Darwinian notion that human beings become more perfect over time. In the case of human beings, he claimed, simple evolutionary laws do not apply. This is because morality (in particular Christian morality) has enabled weak individuals to gang up against the strong, and has obstructed the development of a higher form of consciousness of the type that would characterise the élite *Übermensch*.

Nietzsche pointed out that the last human being to exist is by no means the same as the best human being, and is certainly not to be identified with the *Übermensch*. Such an 'overman' would be as far above the level of ordinary humanity as man himself is above the animals. He would be a 'creator', who would construct a new reality out of the focused energies of his will-to-power. Nietzsche gives the *Übermensch* most of the

Gender and Genius

characteristics of the Romantic genius-personality; but he refuses to accept that such superhuman beings might be sickly or degenerate ('*degeneriert*'). It is only the sickness of *our* culture that represents the *Übermensch* in this way. Indeed, to counter the whole idea of degeneracy, Nietzsche introduced the concept of the 'decadent' ('*die Décadence*'), of a society (or a self) that is moribund. Like all things that are dying, the decadent group or individual is breaking down into a collection of component parts which act separately, instead of together. The decadent organism is a weak organism, because its energies are dispersed and it is unable to resist the external forces that threaten its capacity for unified activity. Since the time of Socrates and Plato, Nietzsche argued, human beings have been becoming *less* strong: Greek metaphysics and the Judaeo-Christian tradition have stunted human growth. If the *Übermensch* is in some ways a throwback, it is to an older, more perfect, healthier mode of human existence. It is the normal European male (and the society in which he thrives) that is decadent, not the *Übermensch* as such.

Up to this point, Nietzsche's theories sound promising enough from a feminist point of view. The 'objective facts' that had been used to rank civilised European males above degenerate females fragment into subjective value-judgements. But there is also another side to Nietzsche! Although Nietzsche's *Übermensch* belongs to a trans-historical élite and is thus not restricted to membership of any particular culture, race or historical epoch, the *Übermensch* is still always represented as a male. Nietzsche does indeed suggest that the whole notion of a 'self' is a fiction; but his imagery still always bonds the strong and healthy will-to-power of the highest and healthiest life-forms to *male* sexual energies. Nietzsche's women might be useful to breed overmen and to provide 'recreation' for overmen; but they can't themselves be overmen [1883–5, p.178]. Nor can they be great artists. The art-work has its genesis in 'the cerebral system bursting with sexual energy', and this is quite definitely *male* sexual energy, 'Physiologically: the creative instinct of the artist and the distribution of semen in his blood' [1883–8, §805, p.424]. Nietzsche claims that women have contributed nothing to culture, and that it is against women's nature to be psychic creators. Asking 'Would any link at all be missing in the chain of art and science if woman, if the works of women were missing?', he concludes there would be no gap:

Admitting exceptions — they prove the rule — woman attains perfection in everything that is not a work: in letters, in memoirs, even in the most delicate handiwork, in short in everything that is not a métier *. . . [ibid., §817, pp.432–3)*

The cultural professions remain within the male domain.

Nietzsche makes woman's task biological reproduction; cultural production involves sublimated virility. Moreover, since artistic creation is envisaged as an organic process, Nietzsche appropriates language associated with human gestation for the cultural tasks of the males. Creators are 'male mothers', caught up in 'spiritual pregnancy', 'pleased to

A Degenerate Breed

submit' and to give birth [1882, §72, p.129]. Just as the healthy woman must be always ready to conceive (physically); the highest kind of man has to keep himself ready to conceive (spiritually). A male who fails to create has failed in his psychic task of becoming 'a "mother" type in the grand sense', utterly absorbed in 'the pregnancies and deliveries of his spirit' [ibid., §369, p.326].

Compared to a genius – that is, to one who either begets or gives birth, taking both terms in their most elevated sense – the scholar, the scientific average man, always rather resembles an old maid: like her he is not conversant with the two most valuable functions of man. [1886, §206, p.125]

Nietzsche's similes thus place him quite securely amongst the throng of late nineteenth-century writers who commandeered for male creators and a male cultural élite those aspects of 'femininity' that had come to be prized during the agricultural, industrial and gender revolutions of the previous century. From his first text to his last, Nietzsche maintained that the greatest art is born out of an openness to Dionysus: the god that Greek and Roman myth presented as male, virile, and also as 'feminine'. Significantly, as Nietzsche himself lapsed into the literary silence of (syphilitic?) madness, he identified completely with this god of male femininity. However, like Schopenhauer (a major influence), Nietzsche combined an admiration of a third (supermale) sex, with the phraseology of a sexual bully:

When a woman has scholarly inclinations there is usually something wrong with her sexually. Sterility itself disposes one toward a certain masculinity of taste; for man is, if I may so so, 'the sterile animal'. [ibid., §144, p.89]

Verbally, at least, Nietzsche took the advice of the 'little old woman' who advised his hero, Zarathustra: "'You are going to women? Do not forget the whip!'" [1883–5, p.179]

It is not as if Nietzsche's women are powerless or psychically lacking in energy. Far from it. But Nietzsche takes great care to delimit the proper outlets for this energy so as not to overlap with male labour. For Nietzsche, women and men are necessarily and eternally involved in a power struggle – a struggle that favours woman, as long as she does not seek to fight man with his own weapons and on his own ground. In the sphere of culture (and even of speech) women must lose out. It was 'man's thoughtfulness and consideration for woman' that forbade women to speak in church, demanded their silence in matters of politics, and then insisted that women should be silent about woman [1886, §232, p.164]. The woman that is Nietzsche's contemporary 'dabbles in writing, she dabbles in art, she is losing her instincts' [1883–8, §817, p.433]. Nietzsche even attacks the 'imbecilic friends and corrupters of woman' who 'defeminize' women by advising them of the advantages of education, 'probably even of reading the newspapers and talking about politics' [1886, §239, p.169]. Nietzsche's woman – like his genius/overman – is not born a 'degenerate', nor even a 'decadent'. But woman – unlike the overman – *becomes* decadent as soon as she writes, reads, becomes educated, or turns from reproductive to productive activity.

Gender and Genius

We should ask whether such comments really contribute to 'a profound and unprecedented transformation of the man-woman relationship', as Derrida claimed? Nietzsche might have rhapsodically embraced the 'feminine' element within the male psyche. He might have undermined male truths, male values and male identities. But he retains membership of the Virility School of Creativity. Ironically, the deconstructionist interpretation of Nietzsche does, to my mind, make his philosophical position even more misogynistic. For, if Nietzsche is to be read as saying that all 'reality' is a language-generated fiction, then we should ask why he is so abusive of women who add their voices (and their pens) to those of the males? Nietzsche asks us to listen to him with a 'third ear': one that is tuned into the pauses between the music of reality. He situates 'woman' in those pauses, and aims to write *like* a woman. But he does not write *as* a woman. Nor will he even allow women to write *as women*. We should ask whether it is *at all* revolutionary to locate feminine 'strength' (and Otherness) in the (pregnant) pauses between the words and sentences of the *logos spermatikos*?

It is true that Nietzsche's 'woman' is permitted an indirect role in the shaping of culture, since the silences between the sounds also delimit and thus indirectly shape the male-constructed language. But the voices of real-life women are erased from history in a blanket of (white) male noise, and the female sounds that still intrude are disguised as a choir of *castrati*, as 'defeminized' voices. For Nietzsche truth is perspectival: different linguistic cultures produce different truths. Even 'historical facts' are cultural constructs produced by those who write and speak. But since Nietzsche refused to hear what actual women say, those born female are disenfranchised from power over both past and future realities. This is not 'feminism' . . . only 'femin*in*ism'. And since it was not the 'feminine' that was consistently downgraded in the nineteenth century, but rather the 'female', there is nothing 'unprecedented' about Nietzsche's simultaneous revaluation of the feminine and his attempt to exclude females from power. Indeed, present-day deconstructionists who depoliticise the term 'feminist' and appropriate it for their own anti-metaphysical metaphysics conserve (via Nietzsche) the patrilineal traditions of Romanticism – which reassigned the vocabulary of female power to *males*, thereby increasing the difficulties facing feminist women.

A Degenerate Breed

13
Scientific Facts and Aesthetic Values

Nietzsche argued that there is no such thing as truth, and that all 'facts' are no more than projections of male values. It is not, however, necessary to adopt such a radical mode of scepticism to recognise the evaluative element in our present-day notions of genius and of creativity. Analytic philosophers standardly make a distinction between factual and evaluative judgements. A factual judgement describes a state of affairs, and is either true or false. Evaluative judgements are, by contrast, normative: they guide or prescribe actions and opinions. To call somebody a 'genius' seems merely descriptive: to identify a property of a person's mind or output. But it is not. It is a complex value-judgement: which involves invoking norms of cultural achievement and, simultaneously, ranking the *oeuvre* of the 'genius' against those norms. The classification of an art-work as a 'work of genius' does not simply record one's own (or even other people's) reactions to what the 'genius' has produced. There is an element of prescription – of telling others (and oneself) what the response to that work *ought* to be – whether or not that response is forthcoming.

Because value-judgements are not straightforwardly objective, it is often supposed that they are 'merely' subjective expressions of personal taste. But judging that an artist is a genius is not the same as deciding that you like his or her art-work. It makes perfect sense in English to say, 'Alfred Hitchcock is a genius, but I don't like *Psycho*, and indeed I can't say that I really enjoy any of his films.' This is because being recognised as a 'genius' involves being perceived as a part of a tradition – in this case, Hollywood cinema, horror films, melodrama, etc. – and as marking that tradition in some significant way. The 'genius' provides a new standard of excellence in terms of which other artists can be judged. This is what Kant meant when he wrote that the genius 'gives the rule to art' [1790; and see Chapter 8 above].

The genius disrupts the tradition of which s/he is a part. Sometimes this disruption is so radical that we think of the genius as starting the new tradition from scratch, and forget to think about the previous artistic media which s/he adapted or threw aside. But without a historical background against which to situate the artist, the Romantic emphasis on the *originality* of genius makes no real sense. Not everything that is new is original. We describe as original only those forms of innovation that we judge to be valuable or significant, and this again involves situating the artist in terms of a tradition and *prescribing* to other people (and to oneself) how they *ought* to see, how they *ought* to react, and how

Gender and Genius

they *ought* to bring their reactions in line with those of an ideal observer.
Artists who come to be counted as geniuses are those placed by the critics on the boundaries of an established tradition, and as being on that point on the boundary that is the cutting edge of change. Artists who are not located in terms of chains of influence, have no chance of ever being classified as geniuses. But the lines and chains of influence can be re-drawn again and again to suit subsequent historical perspectives and value-systems. This is shown by such examples as Van Gogh, William Blake or Richard Dadd, whose work was reassessed after their deaths, and who were retrospectively assimilated into the contours of progress.

To call somebody a genius seems to imply a social consensus or, at least, recognition by some persons whose opinions have weight in terms of the history of culture. Being a genius is never simply a matter of projecting oneself as one. Nor can it be one insignificant person deciding that one of their friends is a genius. However, confusingly, one of your friends *might* eventually be counted as a genius, and you might be the only person who has as yet recognised this fact. The objective/subjective dichotomy is misleading . . . for aesthetic value-judgements are essentially inter-subjective. Feminists, more than others, are likely to be aware of the consensual *resistance* built into the notion of 'genius'. Henry Miller, D. H. Lawrence, Rousseau and Schopenhauer remain 'geniuses' – or, in more fashionably euphemistic terms, 'great, innovative writers' – despite the narrowness of their sexual vision. This may not always be the case, since their status as geniuses depends on critical consensus and is not some immutable fact. (Not everyone who is influential artistically is counted as a 'genius'!) It is through aesthetic value-judgements that an individual registers the existence of group-values, and her assent to (or dissent from) those values. Also – and this is why a feminist aesthetics must be central to an overall feminist project – it is through such value-judgements that individuals group themselves into alternative collectives that (together) re-shape the past and the future of the society in which they live.

In general, scientists (including social scientists) and psychologists who have gone in for an 'empirical' study of genius, originality and creativity have tried to play down the evaluative element in such judgements. In a sense this is not surprising, since the methodology of the natural sciences encourages its practitioners to practise objectivity, and to screen out all individual value-judgements. Even so, the naïvety of the statistical methods used in much of this research is shocking, as is the degree of gender-blindness (disguised as gender-indifference) concealed by the statistics. In order to be able to measure 'genius' statistically, it has been re-defined by scientists working within these disciplines. Unfortunately, it is *then* supposed that these (in any case dubious) conclusions reached about the re-defined types of 'genius' establish *facts* about human beings' capacity (and hence female versus male capacities) for creative achievement. Statistics have been used to confirm cultural (and gender) prejudices in a most *un*scientific fashion.

Scientific Facts and Aesthetic Values

The 'father' of such 'scientific' approaches to genius was Francis Galton
whose *Hereditary Genius* [1869] was all the vogue in the 1890s. Galton is
commonly described as being the first person to introduce 'empirical'
methods into the study of higher mental functioning. He believed in
'*measurement* as one of the basic necessities' for the study of humans, and
he tried to study 'genius' using statistical methods [Wiseman, 1967,
p.19]. One of his fundamental concerns was to increase the amount of
genius available in a population, and his work had far reaching
influence on eugenics and on those who wished to know how to *breed*
genius. He also influenced those concerned with *training* genius, and
was the inspiration behind the development of standardised measure-
ments of intelligence, such as the IQ tests, and other tests that were
used to 'stream' children into different schools and different ability
groups.

Using probability theory, Galton tried to prove that where there is one
genius in a family there is a high likelihood of there being another, and
that this probability increases with the degree of closeness of the relationship. Although Galton focused almost exclusively on *male* achievement and the relationships between *males* within families, women did
creep into his statistics here and there. Thus, for example, his chapter
on 'Literary Men' instances four women 'geniuses'; and the names of
talented women who were related to male geniuses are scattered
through the rest of his text. Women are sometimes part of his database,
and sometimes not.[1] The word 'men' is occasionally used in an all-
embracing sense – more often it is not. This did not bother Galton,
since he saw 'genius' as primarily a male attribute. Galton, incidentally,
was Charles Darwin's younger cousin and Erasmus Darwin's grandson
which, he was anxious to demonstrate, made him likely to be a genius
himself!

Galton (simplistically) used social eminence in the male professions as
an indicator of 'genius': he included talented judges, commanders,
clergymen, oarsmen and wrestlers – as well as poets and musicians –
amongst his 'geniuses'. It is thus clear that by 'genius' Galton meant
something like 'that inheritable factor which provides the potential for
eminence'. Clearly Galton was not measuring Romantic genius – the
type of (very exceptional) cultural creator who marks and changes the
course of human development. And in the second edition he had the
grace to admit that 'genius' was a confusing word to have used. But it
was, nevertheless, apt! Originally, in Latin, *genius* had meant that aspect
of the male that is passed from a father to his male offspring. And this is
basically what Galton was interested in recording.

Galton called the factors that father and son have in common 'stirps'
[Barron, 1969, pp.117–18]. The stirp was the genetic stream that finds
its outlet through the individual – but so was *genius* in the original Latin.
The stirps were long-lasting; individuals are born and die. Galton's
composite photographs (a series of photographs blended together so as
to obtain a single condensed image) were attempts to capture on paper
the 'stirp' or 'genius' of a family. Families (male bondings, with females

Gender and Genius

as the glue) would involve combinations of various 'stirps'. Galton was writing prior to Mendel; but the 'stirp' resembled a gene. 'Gene' and 'genius'. Both have the same root and take their inspiration from an old, old idea. Galton's re-working of this Roman notion of genius – and the composite photographs that he took of it – influenced Freud amongst many others [Spector, 1972].

Present-day Anglo-American psychologists working in the empirical sciences take from Galton the notion that 'genius' is a kind of 'potential for eminence'. They also take from him the idea that such potential can be statistically measured, although most have (thankfully!) shied away from his techniques of measurement. Instead, an idea that Galton himself proposed – but failed to develop successfully – has been adopted. Questionnaires have been devised which attempt to assess a child's potential in isolation from his or her family or environment. Indeed, the IQ questionnaires which are so fundamental to our modern (limited) conceptions of intelligence were devised as techniques of assessing 'genius'. The Frenchman, Alfred Binet (who devised the tests) might have been working independently; but Cyril Burt and L. M. Terman (who adapted the tests for general application in Britain and the US), were both admirers of Galton (although not necessarily of eugenics). It is true that in England the first educational use of intelligence-testing procedure was to identify the subnormal – rather than the supernormal – group of school-children; but this was primarily a result of institutional pressures [Sutherland, 1984]. In the United States, where bureaucratic pressures were less, matters took a different turn. From the start Terman used a standardised version of Binet's tests to try and identify a group of supernormal children with the genetic potential for 'genius'.

By 1922 Terman had tested and identified a group of 1,000 Californian children with an IQ above 135 whose progress was to be followed throughout their lives. Later 528 extra cases were added: making a total of 857 males and 671 females. The first results of this study were published in a series of volumes called *Genetic Studies of Genius* (1925, and still ongoing). Terman believed that by using his modified IQ test he could identify a group of eminent 'geniuses' (in Galton's sense) who would demonstrate their gifts via their achievements. Feldman comments that it was only in 1954, after several follow-up studies, that Terman finally concluded that those of his subjects who had an IQ of 150 or more could not justifiably be described as 'geniuses' [Feldman, 1979, p.336]. In the literature, 'gifted' became the preferred word for this group of high scorers, but 'gifted' started out as a synonym for 'genius'.

Although the substitution of the term 'gifted' for 'genius' in the majority of contemporary Anglo-American educational and psychological texts might be thought to signal a decisive break with older traditions of thinking about 'genius', this is largely an illusion. In Chapter 11, I praised the scientific literature for having moved beyond the Romantic notion that ties creative genius to a particular (supermale) type of

Scientific Facts and Aesthetic Values

personality . . . a male so 'feminine' and so exceptional as to appear mad. On the surface, these scientific texts are utterly anti-Romantic: 'genius' and 'giftedness' are bound (Enlightenment-style) to talent and skill, rather than to a kind of personality-type or mode of creative process. But, as we will see, the scientific literature is muddled. 'Genius' and 'giftedness' are still associated with the qualities admired by the Romantics – self-expression, originality, sensitivity, imagination and strong emotions – but it is now supposed that it is possible to isolate such 'gifted persons' and grade such qualities (even the 'femininity' and 'masculinity' of the gifted) on the basis of questionnaires. Many of the scientists do not seem to have recognised that very different notions of 'genius' and of 'giftedness' are being employed. Although it is probably possible to measure 'talent' and manual and mental dexterity by such crude means, the Romantic notion of genius involves a projection of values. It is not a psychic property of a person: or a 'fact' about his or her potential. 'Creativity' and 'originality' are inappropriate subjects for measuring and quantifying.

What is the relationship between general levels of intelligence and creativity? Cyril Burt, who standardised the first IQ test for general use in Britain, claimed that unless we have a test that accurately measures creative intelligence, we can't be said to have developed a satisfactory measure of intelligence at all. He even suggested that creativity was one of the factors measured by his own version of the IQ test [1975, pp.143, 164ff.]. Other researchers have reached different conclusions. They have denied that IQ-type tests measure creative thought, while allowing that they are useful predictors of intellectual attainment. These researchers define 'gifted' children not simply in terms of intelligence, but as having a variety of talents – some of which might be talents for creative or productive achievement. Indeed, a variety of special 'creativity' tests have been devised in order to measure the potential to be culturally productive.

There is, however, no consistency in the way that the new jargon is used. As an educationalist remarked in 1985:

During the past twenty years, few topics have received as much attention in research, textbooks, and popular educational magazines as has creativity . . .

It would seem that with all the interest the topic has aroused, we would by now have clearer notions as to what it is, how it is encouraged, and how it is maintained. But such is not the case. Creativity remains an elusive concept, the focus of a great deal of debate as to its origins, characteristics, prevalence, processes, and its place in education. [Parke, 1985, p.377]

Reviewing the literature, it is tempting to put forward an operational definition: creativity is what creativity tests test [see Swassing, 1985, p.31].

There is not even any agreement as to what 'giftedness', 'talent' and 'creativity' are – let alone whether they are inborn characteristics of a child, or best thought of as potentials requiring the right environment to unfold. And once we focus on the question of gender the picture

Gender and Genius

[1967] described Galton as the 'father of experimental educational psychology', he described him well . . . given the way that recent research continues to be biased towards the statistics of *male* potential. Young children are tested at school, and a small group of them is identified as creatively gifted. The tests then need themselves to be validated, by checking the future career successes of these children against the norm. If a good percentage become judges, lawyers, artists, successful architects and the like, it is argued that the test has proved its efficacy. Checking the boys is relatively (if suspiciously) easy. But where girls are used in the tests, how can the tests be validated? A good number of them do not fulfil the potential that the test predicted. They marry, have children and the like. Are the hobbies of these women, the stability of their marriages, or when and whom they marry, a guide to success? Terman's team does, at least, follow up the group of girls identified, and thus has endeavoured to tackle these problems head-on . . . however dubious the criteria employed to measure attainment [see Sears, 1979].

Nor are these the only problems relating to gender in such 'scientific' studies. Thus, for example, Terman's tests were not gender-balanced: more boys than girls were identified as 'gifted'. But this seems largely to have been a consequence of the methods used for selecting potential high-achievers. Because Terman lacked the financial resources to test a random sample of the American population, he relied on teachers to nominate bright pupils suitable for testing. As programmes to help gifted under-achievers show, however, teachers are more likely to pick out boys as potentially bright than to pick out similar girl students [Whitmore, 1980, pp.87,89]. In addition, some children volunteered themselves to be tested, and it has also been established that girls are more likely than boys to underestimate their abilities [Maccoby and Jacklin, 1974, p.117]. In 1954 Terman himself pointed out this metho-dological drawback to his procedure; but this study (still ongoing) remains the most thorough effort to follow up the career of 'gifted' children, and has consequently been used frequently to buttress conclu-sions about sex differences amongst the gifted.

The Terman tests were not gender-neutral. But at least his researchers always tell us how many women there are in the statistics, so that we can examine their tests and inferences for concealed (or not so concealed!) sex bias. In much of the rest of the scientific literature, women seem to be a problematic variable. Sometimes, somewhere girls are there in the database, and occasionally a pronoun or recorded deviation gives this fact away. But often it takes the eye of a determined detective to figure out where. A volume of articles that appeared in 1975, which attempted to summarise the previous twenty-five years' work on the topic of creativity, neatly illustrates the problem. If I turn to the index of Taylor and Getzels' *Perspectives in Creativity* and look up 'Creative persons: sex differences', I find only one page number. 'Women, creative' yields one extra location. The first reference is to an article by Donald W. MacKin-non; the second to an article by Frank Barron, one of his colleagues at

Scientific Facts and Aesthetic Values

the Institute of Personality Assessment and Research at Berkeley, University of California. Neither article is primarily about sex differences or women creators: instead, both authors make passing reference to a series of articles by yet another colleague, Ravenna Helson, who is not represented in the volume, but who researches these areas.

Helson herself is quite careful in the conclusions she reaches on the basis of her statistical work, despite her reliance on the psychoanalytic hypotheses of Erich Neumann and Otto Rank – both of whom take male genius as the norm and make female creativity a puzzling anomaly. In her work on mathematicians, for example, Helson concludes that although creative males score highly on measures of feminine orientation and interest, creative female mathematicians do not score highly on measures of 'masculinity', at least where masculinity is taken to imply 'dominance, assertiveness, or analytical ability' [1971, p.245]. When Helson's work is appealed to by MacKinnon, however, its implications seem less clear. In the 1975 article MacKinnon introduces Helson's work via his own research which uses the 'femininity' of male scientists to support the Jungian hypothesis that creative 'persons' reconcile within themselves opposed personality types . . . even though Jung himself insisted that only *males* are culturally creative, and that 'masculine' women are useful creatively only in so far as they inspire the men [MacKinnon, 1975, p.76; and see Chapter 1 above].

Nor are the credentials of MacKinnon's team for undertaking such research exactly reassuring. In the early sixties MacKinnon questioned three groups of architects as part of a research programme into the nature and nurture of creative talent. They wanted to discover some of the personality coordinates of 'creative persons'. The groups were matched for age and geographical location; but there is no mention of the sexual composition of the three groups, nor of gender matching. Indeed, the 1962 summary of this research suggests that 'Architects I', supposedly the 'most creative' subjects, was probably an all-male group. I can only guess this, however, from a passing mention of 'father-son' relations and from MacKinnon's easy transition from the high 'femininity' score of the male creative architects to the conclusion that 'the more creative a person is' the more 'feminine' he is [1962, pp.492,488]. There is nothing more explicit either here or in his other summary of the research [1965] about the sex of the subjects used as a base to develop general conclusions about the nature and needs of creative 'persons'.

Given the way that MacKinnon's team selected the group of most creative architects, it would be unsurprising if it was all-male. They asked five professors of architecture their opinions as to who were the most creative architects in the United States; and then checked the names provided by appealing to the editors of eleven architectural journals and the nominated architects themselves. 'Creativeness' was defined as involving originality (or at the least statistically infrequent novelty); as entailing a full development of the initial insight; and as yielding a product well adapted to some particular end, goal or

Gender and Genius

purpose. The stress on originality indicates that MacKinnon's team was working with a modification of the Romantic notion of genius. But, of course, this method of selection meant that those who were picked out were the darlings of the academic establishment, rather than those disruptive of established cultural traditions, as the fully developed notion of Romantic genius demands. Since the two control groups of less creative architects were (a) architects who had worked with the first group for at least two years, and (b) ones who had never overlapped professionally with the first group, it is possible that women were included here. MacKinnon does not let on. Neither does his fellow team-member, Frank Barron, in his *Creative Person and Creative Process* [1969], a book that rehearses the main details and conclusions of MacKinnon's study of architects. These writers carry on the traditions of Galton, who sometimes included women in the statistics and sometimes excluded them.

This early work carried out by MacKinnon's team is generally represented as 'typical' of research into personality differences between 'extraordinarily creative' and 'more ordinary' artists [Winner, 1982, p.23]. Was it then 'typically' assumed that the most creative persons would be males? Was the omission of data about women a careless oversight? It is unlikely that these researchers supposed that general conclusions about types of creative personality are gender-indifferent, since Barron can be found justifying his own theories about the femininity of male creators with the assertion that:

The creative act is a kind of giving birth, and it is noteworthy that as an historical fact intellectual creativity has been conspicuously lacking in women, whose products are their children. At the risk of making too much of a linguistic parallel, it might be said that nature has literally arranged a division of labor. Men bring forth ideas, paintings, literary and musical compositions, organizations of states, inventions, new material structures, and the like, while women bring forth the new generation. [Barron, 1968, p.221]

In this passage – appalling in its naïvety about historical 'fact' – we can see how thoroughly the hypotheses and research programmes of the 'empirical' sciences have been contaminated by a Romantic view of genius and of artistic productivity. The exceptional creator is *like* a woman who procreates . . . but is *not* a woman who procreates. Although Barron goes on to suggest that the 'masculinity' of creative women should be confirmed or disconfirmed by statistical methods, this passage should make us worried that culturally relative notions of 'femininity' and 'masculinity' are to be embodied in the tests as universal personality-types.

Indeed, we can observe this happening if we look at MacKinnon's remarks – made seven years later – on the need for a research programme that would 'for the first time' investigate the personality traits of female creators as thoroughly as their male equivalents [1975, p.80]. MacKinnon proposes to fill out Jung's theories of psychic bisexuality – which were, as we have seen, already biased against creative women – with the division made by Erich Neumann (another Jungian analyst)

Scientific Facts and Aesthetic Values

132   between 'patriarchal' and 'matriarchal' consciousness-types. MacKinnon's team has tested (statistically!) for 'matriarchal' and 'patriarchal' modes of thinking. The latter are 'purposeful, assertive, objective, and analytical, concerned with mechanical or logical causation'. 'Matriarchal' thought, by contrast, takes as its model organic growth: 'the psyche is filled with an emotional content over which it "broods" until an organic growth is "realized"' [loc. cit.]. The 'matriarchal' is, in other words, passive, thing-like and irrational; the 'patriarchal' is active, purposive and rational. Although it is not suggested that this matriarchal/patriarchal division corresponds to a male/female division, this is nevertheless still a constraining view for a programme of semi-empirical research.

It is constraining because Erich Neumann's theory – which is needed to buttress the (otherwise absurd) matriarchal/patriarchal dichotomy – actually *excluded* female creators. Neumann himself openly admitted that creative women were a puzzle to him [1959, p.182]. And this is not surprising, given that he continued to take the psychic processes of the *male* as both norm and perfection. Neumann argued that all children and primitive cultures associate power with a first androgynous 'Great Mother', and that all creation comes from a strong ego positioning itself with regard to this fantasy. For the normal man (= male) in Western culture it is psychically unhealthy to identify with passivity, femininity and the promptings of a primitive/infantile unconscious. By contrast 'The Great Individual' has the strength to be bisexual without going mad. A creative individual is a 'Hero', who confronts psychic 'Dragons' in the service either of the patriarchal order or the matriarchal order. The patriarchal hero tries to prove his identity with his 'Spirit Father' to his Spirit Mother. By contrast, the matriarchal hero remains the 'son' and 'lover' of the 'Great Mother' throughout his life [ibid., pp.20ff.]. Neumann's metaphors thus make the 'Great Individual' a male individual . . . and the 'bisexuality' of creators is thus *still* the femininity of some exceptional males.

The language might mystify; but one thing should be clear: we are back to Romantic notions of a supermale genius-personality who is permitted a 'primitive' (= feminine) mode of consciousness. What is characterised as 'matriarchal' thought is thus no such thing. Female creators are (once again) at best freaks or anomalies. It seems a sad state of affairs for MacKinnon to propose an empirical research project into real-life women creators using such a template. Neumann's model can cope much more easily with 'the eternal feminine' than with flesh and blood women. If this is genuinely the 'first' systematic research programme into sex differences amongst creative people, women creators have every right to feel depressed. The scientists have attempted to draw lessons from the history of culture to guide their research programmes. But they draw the *wrong* lessons. Instead of simply applying notions like 'matriarchy' and 'patriarchy', or 'femininity' and 'masculinity', to grade the creative subjects that they test, they would be better thinking through the relationships between 'scientific facts' and patriarchal values. Or, if this is deemed too abstract, they would be better

Gender and Genius

investigating the social obstacles that have been placed in the way of girls who wish to create, and the psychic obstacles that have prevented women's creations being categorised as works of 'genius'.

14
The Margins Within

Psychoanalytic hypotheses have been incorporated into the framework of research programmes in the empirical sciences. But all the classical psychoanalytical models made normal creativity an abnormal (but not pernicious) variety of maleness. Classical psychoanalysis thus, in effect, recycled the Romantics' account of the relationship between male sexual energies and cultural creation. The most influential of these models was, of course, that of Freud himself. For Freud artistic creativity involved sublimated sexual energy ('libido'). Although Freud did not make the maleness of the libido an inevitable law of nature, 'Nevertheless the juxtaposition "feminine libido" is without any justification' [Freud, 1932, p.131]. According to Freud, women are not *born* inferior, but they are socially conditioned into becoming intellectual, moral and cre.tive subordinates. The adult woman's inferiority is not a *natural* deficiency, but is a *normal* consequence of the way that the young girl resolves the Oedipal drama – the triangle of jealousy and desire (Mummy/Daddy/Infant) – which Freud placed at the centre of family life. The only women to escape this fate are the 'masculine' women. [See Kofman, 1980, for a brilliant account of the details of the story.]

For Freud's 'feminine' woman the crisis of puberty that forces her to suppress her curiosity about the nature of her own sexuality also leads to the abandonment of her intellectual precocity. She is envious of the penis, but represses knowledge of this. Without sexual curiosity there is no intellectual or creative curiosity. The 'feminine' woman sublimates her desire for a penis into a desire for a child (as penis-substitute) [Kofman, p.203]. Normal femininity, neurosis and creativity comprise a three-dimensional figure. Normal femininity differs from neurosis only in virtue of the way and degree to which childhood sexuality is repressed. But the same is true of creativity:

An artist is once more in rudiments an introvert, not far removed from neurosis. He is oppressed by excessively powerful instinctual needs. He desires to win honour, power, wealth, fame and the love of women (sic.)*; but he lacks the means of achieving these satisfactions. Consequently, like any other unsatisfied man, he turns away from reality and transfers all his interest, and his libido too, to the wishful constructions of his life of phantasy, whence the path might lead to neurosis. [Freud, 1916–17, p.376]*

How boringly familiar! Freud rationalises the schemata of Romantic aesthetics. Madness and 'genius' (a word often used) are once again twin brothers. To be creative a male genius has to avoid one false path that seems at first sight almost identical to the path of genius: neurotic madness. A woman can only be creative by avoiding this route and also the 'feminine' route to her own development into mature sexuality. To what extent Freud believes 'femininity' to be not only *normal* for women, but *proper* for women, is a much-disputed question. What is clear, however, is that a woman can *either* be a truly feminine female *or* be a creative genius – she can't be both.

In recent years Freud has been re-read and re-interpreted by Jacques Lacan, and by feminists influenced by Lacanian ideas. Lacan disturbed the conventional understanding of Freudian theory and, in the process, undermined the idea that psychoanalysts should aim at establishing a strong, healthy (and paradigmatically male) ego. Despite this, it seems in some ways as if Lacan's theories are just another variation on an old Romantic theme. We are back with the great patriarchal 'I am' that underlies the space-time reality within which we exist, except now it is not just an individual male psyche that creates our culture's conceptual scheme. Instead, this construction is (as with Nietzsche) the action of a masculine collective. Once again it is suggested that what we think of as 'reality' is a function of a language and a culture that privileges the male. But Lacan reached this conclusion not through a reading of Nietzsche, but by a *mélange* of Freud, surrealism and phenomenological and linguistic theory. He made the 'I am' – and the very notion of a self that persists through time – a construct of the unconscious, but then added that the unconscious is structured like a language, and that all language-systems express the divisions and hierarchies of the patriarchy.

According to Lacan, a child enters the (patriarchal) world of language reality as soon as s/he learns the difference between 'I' and 'you'. When a child is very tiny it is unaware of the boundaries of its self: the Other/ the Mother is not really conceptualised as a separate being. The child and the universe are, in a sense, one. Gradually, the child loses this initial completeness of being which then haunts it all its life: the adult desires to be re-united with the (M)other – a desire that can be read in human agency and products. In a way highly reminiscent of Plato (and the myth of the androgyne) and de Meun (and the quest for the rose), Lacan made all desire an expression of hunger for an originary completeness of being. Except that in Lacan's world the individual no longer exists: 'I is another'. There is not a *self* that is looking for a complementary self; but a nexus of desires and wants reaching out to compensate for what is lacked. Language overlays this desire and directs it from 'subjects' towards 'objects', via 'causes' – all fictions of the patriarchal language-system.

Lacan posited three levels of psychic significance that cannot be mapped on to each other. These levels are explained in terms of the binary opposition: *'masculin'/'féminin'*. Lacan claimed – with Nietzsche – that 'woman' is but a fiction of a patriarchal language. But, since the French term *'féminin'* encompasses both the English words 'female' (a biological given) and 'feminine' (the culturally acquired characteristics

The Margins Within

associated with womanhood), there are biologistic overtones to the
vocabulary that Lacan employs.[1] The linguistic (or 'symbolic') order is
the masculine domain that children enter as they use words to differen-
tiate self from not-self. By 'language' Lacan means all systems of symbolic representation. Music, painting, mathematics: all are languages and
all embody 'The Law of the Father' that governs possible relations
between separate entities. In this world, the phallus symbolises both
separation from the (M)other, and the desire to re-unite with the
(M)other. Lacan thus makes the phallus the transcendental signifier –
the paradigm 'I am'. Thus, despite Lacan's refusal to equate the 'phallus' with anything as mundane as a simple penis, 'The Law of the
Father' turns out to be that hoary (and not very venerable) grandfather
of European philosophy – the *logos spermatikos*.

The tedium of recognition increases as we examine Lacan's second
order of psychic significance, that of the pre-linguistic (or 'imaginary')
which is associated with the *féminin*. In this realm of the imaginary there
are no fully-formed concepts, but images that originated prior to language in the pre-Oedipal stage of human development. The baby
started out with the illusion that s/he was co-extensive with the universe.
However, Lacan claims it was in the gaze of the (M)other's eyes that the
child received the first inklings of the limits to its autonomy. The infant
then constructed a false body *image* (the mirror image) to compensate
for the disintegration of that original completeness. In Lacan's metaphysics, the *féminin* thus continues to be allied – as it was during the
Renaissance – with seeing the world via the clouded mirror of a distorting consciousness. (See Chapter 3 above.) And, since Lacan explains
psychosis by reference to entrapment in this pre-symbolic universe, he
also carries on the tradition of gendering madness. Neurosis (seen by
Freud as near to 'genius') is associated with dysfunction with regard to
the masculine order of symbols. Psychosis, by contrast, is allied to a
féminin form of consciousness, and the failure to develop the fiction of
an autonomous ego which marks entry to the symbolic realm.

Lacan's 'imaginary' realm is thus by no means an area of potential
psychic freedom, (as it would become for feminists such as Hélène
Cixous, Julia Kristeva or Toril Moi who adapted, or relayed, the Lacanian system in ways that would privilege the pre-linguistic or pre-
symbolic '*féminin*'). According to Lacan himself, human development
can only occur by breaking free of the illusions of the imaginary and
into those of the symbolic. There is, however, also a positive side to
femininity in Lacan's system. Indeed, he describes his own texts in
terms of *jouissance*: the extremes of feminine (sexual and mystical)
ecstasy that disrupt and expose the conceits of the male ego. This is
Lacan's third order: that of 'the real'. And, as Jardine puts it,

*In Lacanian literature, the 'Real' designates that which is categorically unrepre-
sentable, nonhuman, at the limits of the known; it is emptiness, the scream, the
zero point of death, the proximity of jouissance. [1985, pp.122–3]*

In orgasm the self fragments into pleasure-centres: the boundaries
between self and not-self collapse in ways reminiscent of the time when

Gender and Genius

self and (M)other were one. This 'real' is revealed by language; but it is unrepresentable *by* language or *by* consciousness. To approach it at all, consciousness (and even unconsciousness) have to be caught off-guard: something that Lacan's (unorthodox) techniques of lecturing, writing and treating patients were designed to do. To this end Lacan acted out the part of a *féminin* psychotic. He turned himself into a mouthpiece for the not-self as a way of breaking down the (illusory) sense of self of his audience and/or analysand.

In the 1970s Lacan became one of France's most popular cultural heroes. In *The Lives and Legends of Jacques Lacan* [1981], Catherine Clément describes his power as that of a 'shaman' who has allowed himself to be used as a mouthpiece for the unconscious. She even refers to him as a *'génie'*, a prophet, and as a male who had assumed *féminin* madness [pp.49, 78ff., 85, 108ff.]. In other words, Lacan was represented (and represented himself) in terms of the old stereotype of the Romantic genius-personality. And it seems to me that it is more than a simple irony of history that the man who denied the ego should have so promoted his own ego. [And see Turkle, 1978.] Lacan's techniques of *seeming* to let language (and hence the unconscious) speak through him – while manipulating it and his audience in a very deliberate way – should alert us to the sexual conservatism implicit in his stance.

Ecstatic surrender to that which is outside self; the Mother; Otherness; egolessness; hysteria; the *féminin* – these are concepts that cluster together in Lacanian thought, as they did in other post-Romantic philosophers such as Schopenhauer and Nietzsche. Through his practice, Lacan glorified a form of hysterical babble and of psychotic madness that has rendered women victims. Lacan could (safely) ally himself with a specifically *féminin* form of ecstasy, because he was perceived as a strong (male) ego that would not really fragment into psychosis (or get locked up in asylums) for parading his incoherence in public. Women who act like Lacan will have difficulty in being perceived in the same way as Lacan. For speaking *like a woman* is not at all the same thing as speaking *as a woman* . . . Lacan relied on the values of a patriarchal culture for his classification as a psychic hero who has embraced madness and femininity *and remained sane*.

Lacan's psychoanalytic theory has, nevertheless, appealed to a number of feminists and women influenced by feminism.[2] It seemed that the pre-symbolic *féminin* order of the imaginary and the 'real' offered a means of eluding the privilege allotted to the male in the language of the unconscious. The British artist Mary Kelly, for example, glosses the theory behind her work with a document that invokes the 'feminine' as 'the unnameable, the unsaid', adding that 'in so far as the feminine is said, or articulated in language, it is profoundly subversive' [1977, p.310]. But, to my mind, Kelly is mistaken in supposing that a Lacanian 'feminine' can offer real-life women creators the theoretical back-up for their attempts to undermine the values of patriarchal culture. If the 'feminine' is genuinely excluded from language and all symbolic representation, how can it be subversive? If language is 'coincident with the

The Margins Within

patriarchy' (as Kelly claims) why isn't the notion of the 'feminine' simply a fiction of the patriarchy? And why is she so anxious to prove herself 'feminine'? One thing that the history of the concept of 'genius' reveals is that being a woman and being 'feminine' are radically different things. It is *women* who have been excluded from culture; not the 'feminine'. And women won't progress by embracing the mythology of the patriarchy that turns *female* Otherness into some kind of metaphysical metaphor for that which eludes consciousness and language.

If Lacan were correct about the relationship between patriarchy and culture, it seems to me that feminist creators might as well simply give up the political struggle and relax into *jouissance*. But *are* we as passive with respect to language as Lacanians make out? Is the feminist art historian, Griselda Pollock, right to claim that 'Learning to speak is learning to be spoken by the culture to which one is accessed by language' [1987, p.92]? Although advertisers and image-makers work on the assumption that a person is just a collection of desires, drives and impulses, this myth of modern capitalism is as dangerous to women as the old myths that defined identity in terms of male individuality. Indeed, since in advanced industrial societies women are more important as consumers (as the targets of advertising campaigns) than as breeders or a class of domestics, I feel we should be doubly suspicious of any new theory of the self that suggests a special connection between the *féminin* and a bundle of free-floating desires. Otherwise, like the Romantic women, we may find ourselves humming just another variation on the old theme: female=egoless=manipulable=audience=non-producer.

To understand more fully why a feminist aesthetics cannot rest on Lacanian attempts to undermine the very notion of ego and individuality, it is necessary to make a distinction between two different kinds of marginality:

i *Others* – those who, because of our racist and sexist paradigms of normal humanity, get viewed as not-quite-human;

ii *Outsiders* – those who are viewed as fully-human but not-quite-normal. Under this category come 'feminine' males, genius males, crazy males, degenerate males, shamanistic males . . . even pseudo-males (cf. Lombroso's 'the women of genius are men').

Of course, we no longer believe that the greatest cultural creators are feminine 'degenerates'; but in popular culture the great creators are still Outsider-figures. As Tom Gretton comments despairingly:

Over the last century and a half concepts such as that of Bohemia have been much more successful in constituting the public persona 'artist' than the earnest attempts of a large number of painters and so forth over the same period to live 'bourgeois' lives, and to convince the world of the respectability, of the ordinariness of the profession. Painters and so forth are stereotyped as special people, as 'artists'. [1986, p.66]

But the bohemian artist-figure is categorised as such in so far as he is outside the norms of the *male* personality. Some women might be treated as pseudo-males; but most are concealed by 'Otherness'. Thus, as we will see, this notion of the artist as the great Outsider serves to camouflage the achievements of creative women.

In *The Outsider* [1956] Colin Wilson traced the figure of the Outsider through modern literature, Romantic theory and existentialist philosophy. Wilson's book was an overnight success: the anti-hero observed so sharply by Dostoyevsky in the 1860s became the hero of the mid-twentieth century. The Outsider is a personality-type: one who sees himself as unlike other people, as estranged from conventional wisdom, morality and lifestyles, as misunderstood, alone and suffering. The Outsider feels forced to behave in ways that his own conscious mind finds irrational and evil. Beneath the skin and face of the normal human being, the Outsider discovers the mind of a wolf or a monster – a self which most men mask by a patina of civilised behaviour. His morality is to be true to himself (the Wolf in himself) – whatever the costs to other people. So secretly he enjoys his suffering, his loneliness; and part of him finds the face of the monster that of perfect beauty.

We all know the type. It has been celebrated and explored in the lyrics of countless pop songs. But this Outsider is paradigmatically male, as Wilson's opening paragraphs make clear. Wilson uses Henri Barbusse's novel *L'Enfer (Inferno)* to establish the character of the Outsider. Wilson describes Barbusse's 'hole-in-corner man' who ventures out of his anonymous hotel room to loaf down city streets, stirred by 'desires' that 'separate him sharply from other people'. Barbusse's '"pale and heavy-eyed"' hero explains, '"It is not a woman I want – it is *all* women, and I seek for them in those around me one by one . . ."' Wilson makes sure we don't dismiss these male desires as simply banal. Barbusse's nameless hero follows women in the street, propositions them, and has sordid and casual sex with them. This is not 'animal' need, but a metaphysical quest. The hero is not really a monster – certainly not an Other – he is a fully-human (= fully-male) individual with wolf's eyes that help him see ' *"too deep and too much"* ' [Wilson, 1956, p.21].

Wilson might have adopted a semi-ironic tone in describing the Outsider, but he was not ironic enough. The perverted male sexuality of this 'type' receives no comment in his 1956 study. Instead, the Outsider is presented as a compelling figure: a stage on the modern individual's way to becoming a truly fulfilled person. Although Barbusse's anti-hero had '"no genius, no mission to fulfil, no remarkable feelings to bestow"', his mentality had been shaped by the Romantic traditions of writing about the genius and the (male) artist [ibid., p.22]. The tragedy of Wilson's Outsider is that he would like to be able to express himself and have the vivid perceptions of the artist; but he can neither do this, nor become balanced and normal [pp.214–15].

Wilson's *The Outsider* has (deservedly) declined in popularity in comparison with those perennial favourites of sixth-formers and undergraduates that it sought to describe: Camus' *The Outsider (L'Étranger)*; Sartre's *Nausea*; and Hermann Hesse's *Steppenwolf*. But the Outsider

The Margins Within

140   figures that they portray are very like Wilson's archetype. The obscure
desires that drive these anti-heroes to be at odds with bourgeois society
include male sexual urges. In all of them woman is Other, rather than
Outsider. And this remains true of *The Misfits: A Study of Sexual Outsiders*, Wilson's 1988 follow-up to his study of the 'Outsider'. Here
Wilson does comment (with pornographic relish) on the relationship
between 'genius', the 'outsider' and sexual perversion. And although
Wilson purports to develop a theory that will explain the psychic
mechanisms driving both men and women, there *are* no women in his
study. The theories of 'Dr Charlotte Bach' on the psychic bisexuality of
cultural creators are considered in detail. But – despite being referred
to as 'she' throughout Wilson's book – 'Charlotte' turns out to be a
transvestite male. Other females are sexual objects, disqualified by
Wilson's account of 'human' sexuality from counting as 'human beings'
at all – let alone successful human beings ('geniuses') or sexual perverts
('outsiders').

'Genius' is represented as the flip-side of sexual perversion: great art is
made possible because 'The human (*sic*) sexual impulse has ceased to be
a response to the smell of the female on heat' [p.110]. Human evolution
occurred not because women ceased to be purely instinctual animals
(who come 'on heat'); but because

Human beings have ceased to be dependent on the smell of oestrum (sic) *to
trigger sexual desire; it has been replaced by visual stimuli* and imagination . . .

*Yet this is what all sexual perversion amounts to. Barbusse's 'outsider' is . . .
attempting to achieve erection – not just of the penis, but of the reality function –
through a kind of play-acting. [pp. 112–13]*

Pornography (= male replacement of real sexual objects by fantasised
sexual objects) shows how men (= males) have evolved above the
animals. It is the imagination that makes man (= males) capable of the
greatest – or most perverse – acts. Significantly, the metaphors for this
greatness of 'human' imagination are as sexed as the account of 'human'
sexuality itself:

*In sexual excitement, it is as if the spirit itself becomes erect, and becomes capable
of penetrating the meaning of life. Normal consciousness is limp and flaccid; its
attitude towards reality is defensive. [p.45]*

Women might feel relieved to find themselves excluded from this
account of the origins of human art; but Wilson's soft-core mysticism is
more than merely distasteful. It reveals how the personality (and sex
drives) of the abnormal – and supernormal – male continues to blinker
male vision . . . and reduce *women* to the status of Others. Less-than-
fully-individual; less-than-fully-human: women are (smelly) absences
. . . holes in the history of culture.

The Misfits evidently represents more than one kind of abyss in the still-
popular notion that the genius-personality is a variant of the Outsider-
personality! Even in less philistine art criticism, however, there is a
significant difference between the way male and female artists are

Gender and Genius

described in terms of the Outsider/Other dichotomy. We can see an example of this if we look at the 1984 edition of John Rothenstein's *Modern English Painters, Hennell to Hockney*. Rothenstein's biographies of important recent artists include a married couple: Catherine Dean (1904–83) and Albert Houthuesen (1903–79). None of Dean's paintings are reproduced in the book, and only two locations are given for originals, so I find myself unable to form an independent judgement of her talents. My comments are not, therefore, ones about the quality of Dean's work as compared to Houthuesen's. Nor am I critical of Rothenstein's intentions – he obviously intends his chapter as a homage to a dead friend who is also a neglected woman artist. What I am arguing is that, even when art critics are struggling hard to be fair to women artists, 'Otherness' is a norm for female artists and 'Outsiderness' the norm for male artists. As a consequence, the relationship between individuality and tradition is constructed in very different ways on either side of the artistic gender divide. And this is a major factor in obscuring the presence of important women in the history of the arts.

Dean is presented almost entirely as a supplement to Houthuesen. Of the twelve pages on Dean, one is introductory (how her paintings came to Rothenstein's attention when he was visiting Houthuesen); seven are mainly about her engagement or marriage; and one a conclusion. Her most remarkable achievement

is negative, namely that her art was in no way affected by the intimate association of more than fifty years with an artist of rare and highly individual talent, and one whose work she always so deeply revered. Yet at no time was her own painting influenced by his. Her Entombment *(1928) . . . does, indeed, closely resemble the treatment of the same subject in certain of Albert's, but anticipates it by a number of years; not that Catherine's painting ever remotely influenced Albert's . . . [p.92]*

We hear in passing about her frail health, her cancer, and a life devoted to managing Houthuesen's professional and business affairs during his long bouts of serious illnesses. We hear very little about her artistic influences, nothing about her philosophy of art, or even about the psychological set that led her to devote her own life to her family.

By itself, the biographical sketch of Catherine Dean would not be very surprising. After all, this might be the appropriate way of summing up a life of sacrifice. What is so extraordinary is the contrast in treatment to that of her husband. Houthuesen has the same amount of space devoted to him, but out of this there seem to be only four sentences on his marriage and engagement – including one that tells us that 'Life after leaving the College, in spite of the happiness of his marriage, was something of an anticlimax' [p.60]. We learn about the dramas of his tragic childhood, his artistic father (murdered by his mother?), his artistic influences, his membership of artistic groups and his philosophy of art. Despite his fifty years of marriage to a woman painter who 'revered' his work, despite his links with artistic contemporaries and predecessors, Rothenstein concludes:

The Margins Within

The painters who figure in these pages are, as painters, mostly solitaries, but none as solitary as Albert Houthuesen was: never a member of any group, or a participant in any 'movement', deeply grateful for what other artists taught him yet the disciple of none, going his own way, against the way of the world, the complex of ideas that dominated it. [p.68]

If the male artist does not set himself up as the isolated and lonely Outsider, the art critic is likely to do it for him. The husband here is a fully developed individual, and can therefore be isolated and ignored even when supported by a devoted wife and situated in the context of artistic masters. The wife, who seems artistically the more estranged from tradition (in that it is barely mentioned with regard to her work), lives her life as a half-person, and can never therefore be an Outsider. Only an Other. She is presented as outside artistic traditions: not influenced, and without the power to influence even the man she lived with for more than half a century. If this is really all there is to say about Dean, Rothenstein should have chosen someone else to eulogise. As I explained in the last chapter, to deserve the label 'significant' an artist has to be located in terms of a tradition. To be 'great' or a 'genius', the artist must be positioned by the critics at a point within that tradition that is viewed as the boundary between the old and the new ways. Artists like Catherine Dean have no chance of ever being viewed as 'geniuses' . . . or even as artistically important. She is not even represented as a fully-developed individual, let alone located within the (patrilineal) chains of influence and inheritance out of which 'culture' is constructed.

It is notable how many of the works and names of women painters and sculptors that have survived are of those who were married (or otherwise related) to male artists. Art critics have seemed unconcerned with adequately identifying the women who have shaped the contours of culture. Furthermore, the achievements of the women who *have* been identified are frequently underestimated, because their 'Otherness' means that they have been wrongly located in terms of *patrilineal* traditions of art and successions and groupings of *male* artists. From such a perspective a number of extremely important women seem mere hangers-on . . . and (eventually) disappear into invisibility. In *How to Suppress Women's Writings* [1983] Joanna Russ has shown how this process works with regard to the literary genres. But the situation is even more extreme in the fine arts.

To take one of many possible examples, Hannah Höch (1889–1978) is generally seen – if she is seen at all – as simply working in the field of collage and photomontage . . . although she was also a sculptor, a painter and a print- and doll-maker. Höch is also generally represented simply as a 'Dadaist' . . . although she firmly rejected this label as in any way adequate to characterise the last *fifty* years of her working life. Höch has been frozen into a static moment in history (Berlin *c.* 1916–24): a caption to a face in a photo of an era that is dead. Although her works have obvious affinities with the later surrealists, the expressionists and the constructivists, some critics have looked and seen only

Gender and Genius

stasis: unchanging Dada and photomontage. An alternative group of critics have looked and seen no constancy: only a kaleidoscope of changing allegiances.

These critics have failed to find in Hannah Höch's work a unified *oeuvre* which has developed and matured in the same way as would that of a Picasso or an Ernst. Except for a few (mostly feminist) critics, Höch remains an Other: a fragmented egoless phenomenon. And, since the very concept of an *oeuvre* implies full individuality (*unity through change*), Otherness makes her disintegrate into insignificance. Her name is (still) standardly excluded from the summary histories of modern art − despite her role in inventing and developing the techniques of photomontage and collage. She is even (frequently) absent from the surveys of Dadaism itself − despite being one of the founder members of the Berlin group. It is, therefore, unsurprising that Höch is also missing in a number of the best-known of the English-language histories of women artists.

For an artist's achievements to be recognised, her work has to be read generously, as an expression of the psychic richness and unique individuality of a fully-human self. Even though, in Höch's case, there is enough information to be sure that we are dealing with a person whose contributions to art were neither insignificant nor sporadic, Höch has been treated as an Other, not as an Outsider. Her life's work has been diminished into uni-dimensional fragments. Höch's case is symptomatic of the problems facing women artists. To recognise the uniqueness of Höch's artistic achievement, we need to understand her own individual project for her life (a project that she might never have recognised herself). We need a narrative that can bind her output together into an *oeuvre*, and that narrative must be anchored by contextualising the artist's work adequately in terms of tradition and genre. And it is here that the difficulty lies for Hannah Höch, as for all the greatest female artists.

In order to make sense of the paradoxes of her art, Höch has to be fitted into a *female* tradition of art-production that cuts across patrilineal traditions of art and undermines them. This is symbolised by Höch's most famous collage: 'Cut with the Cake-Knife DADA through the last Weimar Beer Belly Cultural Epoch of Germany' (1919/20). At its centre is the head of Käthe Kollwitz (the famous woman painter) balanced on the body of Niddi Impekoven (the celebrated woman dancer). The distorted images of other well-known personages and technological 'inventions' erupt in paradoxical shifts of scale from a centre that focuses on the *female* contribution to art and anti-art. The dominating image in this collage might be that of Einstein − that *other* Other, the Jewish 'genius' − but the irreverent mockery of Höch's gaze has at its reference-point a *matrilineal* tradition of image-making that skews the whole concept of German '*Kultur*'.

I believe Höch knew how radical was her vision. In her writings and words she theorised the importance of presenting alternative sub-human and semi-human perspectives on reality. Her change of forename from Johanne to the more Jewish-sounding Hannah signals her allegiance with all Others within the German State. Symbolic also was the way Höch survived the Second World War: in a watchman's house on an abandoned air-strip in a remote suburb of Berlin. Much that now remains to us of Dada comes to us courtesy of Höch. Concealed in the cupboards of her house, and buried in her garden, was a treasure-trove of documents and art condemned by the Nazis as 'degenerate'. Although her name was on the Gestapo's blacklist of 'cultural bolshevists', and although (after reports from her neighbours) she was questioned and her house searched by the Nazis, the authorities did not know how to look – or how to listen to her voice. Not an 'Outsider' – only an 'Other' that disrupts *Kultur* from *the margins within* – she seemed insignificant. Neither Jew nor genius, this female Otherness allowed her to merge into the scenery . . . in much the same way as she later blended into the background in the histories of art.

Around 1915 (already in her mid-twenties and shortly before becoming a Dadaist) Hannah Höch immersed herself in reading philosophy and psychoanalytic theory. From that time on, her paintings and collages (and her weird marionette-dolls and half-human sculptures) would engage in a kind of mocking debate with the metaphysics of Romanticism that made the 'sublime' a saturnine (and melancholic) male and left the female a beautiful and monstrous Other. 'The Melancholic'; 'Alien Beauty' ('*Fremde Schönheit*'); 'Grotesque'; 'Woman and Saturn': the titles of her creations confirm the metaphysical (the anti-metaphysical) motives. Like the other Dadaists Höch was anti-Art; but even her attack on art could not altogether coincide with the males' rejection of the patrilineal traditions of art. (Hence the representation of Höch as somehow peripheral, or an insignificant presence in the Dadaist group.) Although not identifying herself as a feminist, her ironical gaze is always *female* . . . it accepts, and rejects, the 'Otherness' of women that has served to mask her own achievements. 'The Eternal Feminine' (1967) is a picture of a display-dummy in a fashion-factory . . . and in the earliest photos of Höch with her Dada-dolls (1918) she poses in the same costume as the machine-like wooden puppets that she manufactured herself. The dummies and other grotesques enact her own treatment by the art historians, who could not register her as a fully individual artist because she bent the apparently straight lines of patrilineal art-tradition. Not an Other – but also not a brother – Höch demands reassessment in terms of those matrilineal zigzags that complicate the tracks of art and anti-art.

The fact that I (a non-specialist) know of the existence of Hannah Höch, and can begin to position her in terms of a *female* tradition of art, means, of course, that the complex task of re-thinking women's relation to culture is well under way.[3] But the practice of feminist art critics has been inadequately theorised. In recent years many Anglo-American feminists (both inside and outside the academies) have looked to the notion of an *écriture féminine* to provide a grounding for a 'woman-centred' perspective on art, literature and cultural history. This idea of a kind of feminine/female writing typical of feminine/female consciousness is taken from the texts of a number of key French female theoreticians who have developed out of the Lacanian and Derridean debates that marked psychoanalysis, linguistics, philosophy – and indeed feminism itself – during the 1970s.[4]

It might be thought that such a notion would offer the 'female tradition' in terms of which the words and works of women creators can be heard and appreciated. It is notable, however, that the examples given of *l'écriture féminine* are generally examples of *male* authors (James Joyce, Nietzsche, etc.) who are psychically *féminin*. Indeed, in *Writing Differences* [1988] Hélène Cixous complains that, with the notable exception of the Brazilian novelist, Clarice Lispector, in the past *female* authors have been too *masculin* [p.25]. And this should not surprise us. What Cixous prizes as *féminin* is a type of self-projection that undermines the fiction of a stable and unitary ego.

Cixous values that which is resistant to conscious analysis, ecstatic, fluid, egoless, apparently incoherent and 'hysterical'. But an aesthetics based on this kind of 'femininity' actually discriminates against women in the histories of the arts. To be thought of as a great author exposing or *fictionalising* her fake ego, a woman must first be represented as a creator who has a body of work (an *oeuvre*) that is worth analysing. And this implies seeing the author or artist in terms of an ego. It also involves situating that artist's work in terms of traditions and genres, and registering her as individual but not unique; exceptional but not isolated, strange, freakish or simply crazy. Sadly, the mythologies of female Otherness still make it extremely difficult for critics (and women themselves) to see women in such ways. A male creator credited with an *oeuvre* that is *féminin* might retain his cultural significance while celebrating non-entity; but a female viewed as hysterical and ecstatic has to fight off a much more mundane kind of cultural nonentity. As the concept of genius has demonstrated, it is only in *great individuals* that madness has been valued . . . and women have been denied the same full individuality as genius-males.

Women creators still have to struggle (both socially and inwardly) against dispersing into the kind of Otherness now endorsed as 'feminine' by many of those who look to *l'écriture féminine*. To be seen as an individual – with an *oeuvre* that persists (coherently) through the (apparently incoherent) fragments that make it up – a woman creator has to be positioned within male *and* female traditions of art. But female traditions of art will not emerge via a revaluation of supposedly 'feminine' characteristics of mind or of body. Indeed, such traditions will remain concealed by those whose language (and textual practices) blur the distinctions between writing *like a woman* and writing *as a woman*. Being female involves not some collection of innate (or acquired) psychological or biological qualities. It is rather a matter of being consigned – on the basis of the way one's body is perceived – to a (non-privileged) position in a social nexus of power.

The Margins Within

15
Post-modernism and the Female Author

Post-modernists have proclaimed the death of the author. But for an author to die, he must first have lived. In the last chapter I argued that female authors and artists have disappeared from the histories of culture precisely because they were not granted the same kind of life — the same kind of individuality — as their brother artists. Although in theory post-modernism divorces a text from its author and should be gender-free, in practice post-modernism is parasitic on the canons of 'great texts' and 'great authors' established by Modernism (which was simply a development of Romanticism). Established authors and *oeuvres* are dismembered and decentred via a process of re-reading, reinterpretation and parody that fractures both *oeuvre* and tradition into discontinuity. The emphasis on debunking the subjective authority of an author, as well as all objective standards of artistic 'truth' or 'greatness', means that new authors and new traditions cannot get established. Thus, in practice, post-modernist artists and critics carry on the patrilineal lines of tradition, which record only the occasional female presence.

We can see a confirmation of this in Richard Kearney's *The Wake of Imagination* [1988]. There are no female authors, artists or film-makers amongst the post-modernists analysed by Kearney in this text. Furthermore, even the definitions that Kearney provides of post-modernist art marginalise women's art — especially feminist art. Apparently, post-modernists have left behind such old-fashioned (Modernist) ideas as 'artistic progress' and 'innovation and change'. Not for the post-modernists the notion that an artist could be 'a precursor, a prophet of the future, a harbinger of new and better things to come' [pp.21, 23]. Kearney carries on:

What, if any, is the role of the creative imagination in a postmodern age apparently devoid of a project of emancipation? If the only future is one we look back to, what can we look forward to? Has the artist or intellectual any positive contribution to make to society? Has history anywhere to turn but inside out? Has art any role apart from self-parody? And where does all this leave imagination? [p.25]

From a feminist perspective, this series of questions is extraordinarily interesting. The rhetoric suggests that political apathy (or at least paralysis) is integral to the 'post-modern age'. Could one guess from this description of art during the 1970s and '80s the influence that second-wave feminism has exerted (and continues to exert) on women in the arts? The very notion of a feminist art is represented as out of

Gender and Genius

step with the times. To dream of changing society via the arts is an anachronism; even an awareness of a 'project of emancipation' jars with the mood of a male-dominated élite.

Kearney is himself critical of post-modernism. He wants to move on past post-modernism: to inject a political dimension back into aesthetic theory and practice. An extraordinary footnote describes his project as 'post-patriarchal' as well as 'post-centrist', 'post-egological', and 'post-logocentric' [pp.460–61]. He will adopt 'a feminist-allied praxis attentive to the hitherto suppressed dimensions of alterity, difference, marginality' [loc. cit.]. Kearney, in other words, places himself on the side of the Other/ the 'feminine'. He sees the way forward for art (post-post-modernism) to be through the re-writing of history, and showing the 'others' that history has excluded: 'the remembrance of things past may become "a motive power in the struggle for changing the world"' [p.394]. Despite the footnote, however, it is notable that Kearney does not really appreciate what is involved in re-thinking *female* 'Otherness'. Indeed, his example of such an 'other' kind of history is limited to learning 'to appreciate what "other", non-Western cultures have to offer' [p.392].

Kearney might think of himself as 'feminist-allied', but his own book continues to erase women from culture. The index of *The Wake of Imagination* contains the names of about eight women (counting 'The Nolan Sisters' as one), none of whom figure in his narrative in any significant way. Kearney does not even register that his 'new' type of history is precisely what feminist critics, historians and artists have been struggling to produce for the last two decades. Feminist scholarship does not impinge on his gaze, blinkered as it is by 'post-modernist' concerns. He provides us with a history of thinking and writing about creativity that is utterly blind to the way that imagination has been gendered in the history of Western thought. Since Kearney will found his new politics of the imagination on the historical analysis provided in this study, this omission is serious. Lacan's attack on the imaginary appears to Kearney, for example, to be breaking new ground. Whereas, from a feminist perspective, Lacan's refusal to celebrate the imagination of a 'feminine' subject fits into a long tradition of thinking biased towards the male.

In the gulf between Kearney's theory (open to feminine Otherness) and his practice (ignoring female Otherness) we can detect a process similar to that which occurred as Romanticism got under way. As the industrial society was born during the closing years of the eighteenth century, aspects of mind previously downgraded as 'feminine' were revalued and re-assigned to the psyche of the genius-male. A similar process is occurring now as the industrial fades into the post-industrial age. 'Otherness', 'fragmentation', 'babble', 'marginality' have been revalued. The term 'feminist' itself has been depoliticised and appropriated within male (and female) fantasies that privilege the male even as the way forward is described in terms of a *post-patriarchal* culture. As the term 'post-patriarchal' suggests, post-modernism (and post-post-

Post-modernism and the Female Author

modernism) remains within the ambit of the patriarchal mythology that would retain all power, language and culture within the masculine domain. A feminist aesthetics should not be *post*-patriarchal; it should be *anti*-patriarchal. A feminist aesthetics cannot simply be an openness to Otherness; feminists have to concern themselves with what is involved in writing or creating *as a female* – as a subject positioned within the social and historical networks of power. It is, therefore, premature to announce the death of the female author.

There are two critical enterprises that are dangerously close to each other. One is the feminist task of exposing the fractures that must mark the selves and *oeuvres* of all female creators in our culture. The other critical exercise is the post-modern task: of fragmenting selves and *oeuvres* completely. The two critical activities need to be carefully distinguished. The post-modernist is a 'femin*in*ist' – concerned with psychic bisexuality . . . and with what it is to be a male (or pseudo-male) who writes *like a woman*. The *feminist* critic, by contrast, examines what is involved in writing *as a woman*: as a person confronting the paradigms of male individuality and female Otherness, defining herself in terms of those paradigms . . . and resisting them. In order to create at all, women have had to adopt a double perspective on themselves. But this fissured ego is by no means the same as the egolessness celebrated (in different, but disturbingly similar ways) by the later Romantics, the Lacanians and by other post-modernists.

We can see this *doubleness* of female vision in the present-day projects of Cixous, Irigaray and Kristeva (who both accept and reject the psychoanalytic perspective that represents the female as lacking in respect to the male). But, although Cixous claims that 'Until now women were not speaking out loud, were not writing, not creating their tongues – plural' – we can also see this doubleness of perspective (and of voice) in the writings of women in the past [Cixous, 1975, p.137]. Mary Elizabeth Coleridge (1861–1907) is a useful example, since her poem 'In Dispraise of the Moon' (1896) barely disguises its author's distaste for her own femininity. The moon acts as a transparent metaphoric substitution for woman, with the sun standing for the male. From this point of view, woman lacks her own ego, energy and reason. She reflects male glories in a passive and dead kind of way:

I would not be the Moon, the sickly thing,
To summon owls and bats upon the wing;
For when the noble Sun is gone away,
She turns his night into a pallid day.

She hath no air, no radiance of her own,
That world unmusical of earth and stone.
She wakes her dim, uncoloured, voiceless hosts,
Ghost of the Sun, herself the sun of ghosts.

The mortal eyes that gaze too long on her
Of Reason's piercing ray defrauded are.
Light in itself doth feed the living brain;

[Poems, 1954, p.189]

Mary Elizabeth was only distantly related to Samuel Taylor Coleridge: her father's grandfather was Samuel Taylor's brother. But Mary's own poetic ambitions were utterly deadened by these patrilineal links. Although she published her novels and prose works without any kind of fuss, she refused to defile her surname by publishing her poetry (the part of her output that she most valued) under the name of 'Coleridge'. Indeed, her friends had to use Robert Bridges (later Poet Laureate) to trick and bully her into publishing any of her poems. Even then her verses only ever appeared during her lifetime under the male pseudonym 'Anodos' ('Wanderer'). If we detach this information and 'In Dispraise of the Moon' from the rest of her life and *oeuvre*, Mary is likely to seem the embodiment of a female who has completely internalised the perspective of lack.

We can only really work out the multiplicity of fractures within Coleridge's sense of self by reading her poetry again in the light of her novels, her short stories and the fragments of her notebooks and letters that have survived. We are likely to read 'In Dispraise of the Moon' differently, for example, when we know that she also wrote:

I am a different person every twelve hours. I go to bed as feminine as Ophelia, fiery, enthusiastic, ready to go to the stake for some righteous cause. I get up the very next morning, almost as masculine as Falstaff, grumbling at Family Prayers. [1910, p.221]

Here (intriguingly) Mary lines up 'femininity' with positive values (fire, enthusiasm, courage) and 'masculinity' with 'grumbling' negative values. Despite going on (almost immediately) to refer to herself as 'Anodos' – and 'he' – Mary Coleridge retains a woman-centred perspective that sees femininity as both norm and ideal, and which judges masculinity a distortion (deficient or excessive). From seeming to occupy a central position in Mary's sense of self, 'In Dispraise of the Moon' shifts to become just one of a kaleidoscope of moods about being a female in a male-dominated world.

Until we recognise women's double perspective on themselves, we might be surprised that this poet – who seems so obviously contemptuous of female powers – should also have written 'The White Women' (1900). For this is a poem about an apparently matriarchal race of women. These women are also pale; but they are not described in terms of the conventional symbols of feminine moon circling male sun. These women are not pallid, sickly, or voiceless. They have never submitted to any kind of slavery, and are more powerful than the tiger, the falcon or the eagle – those conventional symbols of masculine daring.

Where dwell the lovely, wildwhite womenfolk,
  Mortal to man?
They never bowed their heads beneath the yoke,
They dwelt alone when the first morning broke
  And Time began.

Post-modernism and the Female Author

Taller are they than man, and very fair,
  Their cheeks are pale,
At sight of them the tiger in his lair,
The falcon hanging in the azure air,
  The eagles quail.

The deadly shafts their nervous hands let fly
Are stronger than our strongest – in their form
Larger, more beauteous, carved amazingly,
And when they fight, the wild women cry
  The war-cry of the storm.

Their words are not as ours. If man might go
Among the waves of Ocean when they break
And hear them – hear the language of the snow
Falling on torrents – he might also know
  The tongue they speak.

Pure are they as the light; they never sinned,
  But when the rays of the eternal fire
Kindle the West, their tresses they unbind
And fling their girdles to the Western wind,
  Swept by desire.

Lo, maidens to the maidens then are born,
Strong children of the maidens and the breeze,
Dreams are not – in the glory of the morn,
Seen through the gates of ivory and horn –
  More fair than these.

And none may find their dwelling. In the shade
  Primeval of the forest oaks they hide.
One of our race, lost in an awful glade,
Saw with his human eyes a wild white maid,
  And gazing, died.

[1954, pp.212–13]

For not a few of her contemporaries Mary Coleridge embodied the ideal woman poet: 'a feminine of Blake more incandescent than burning' [Sichel, 1918, p.135; and see Bridges, 1907, who compares her with Heine, as well as Blake]. Despite this, Mary has been reduced by patrilineal lines of tradition to the nerveless, voiceless, ineffectual female that she so dreaded . . . a pallid pre-Raphaelite wraith who has drifted out of all but a small percentage of works of feminist criticism.[1] But Coleridge's output demands reappraisal (and re-publication). Her *oeuvre* needs to be situated within the matrilineal traditions of writing. Walter de la Mare [1907] might have written of her, 'Once sure this heart beat beneath a man's cloak; and of how brilliant and youthful and Mercutio-like a man!'; but it's not clear that Mary would have liked this as an obituary. The poet of female lack refused to disown her sense of being distinctively female: 'If we do not retain sex I don't see how we can retain identity. Male and female we were created; and it is of the very essence of our nature' [1910, pp.233–4].

Gender and Genius

In her novel *The Shadow on the Wall* [1904] Mary tried to work through the problems that face women who 'care most' for other women [p.70], and who are also caught up with the values of the pre-Raphaelite 'brotherhood' of art:

'Genius is the best thing a man can have,' . . .
'It is what beautiful eyes are to a girl.'
'But if she knows she has beautiful eyes, at least, if she lets anyone see that she knows, that spoils it all directly.' [1904, p.75]

Unsurprisingly, Mary's narrative fractures into complexity. It is the images that survive and haunt, not the ending. Alone, beneath the moon, her heroine dances, like some character in a (then unwritten) D. H. Lawrence novel. The hidden male watcher laughs out his shock at her 'animal' (and implicitly sexual) excess of energy [p.91]. It was not only in an isolated poem that this unmarried spinster conjured up images of women 'Swept by desire'.

A man is allowed genius – and a great ego that knows its own genius – but a woman is not. Mary Coleridge's characters suggest (with irony) that to retain her power over a man a woman has to disguise her energy . . . and even learn to deceive herself every time she peers into her looking-glass. But although this seems to fit with de Beauvoir's claim in *The Second Sex* that a woman lives in bad faith, and is Other even to herself, Mary Coleridge also *resists* such a negative account of the female condition. This resistance is sited along the fracture-lines that the critic must use to unify her literary output into a distinctively female *oeuvre*.

A woman is presented with film-like images of herself (her Otherness) which are inconsistent and which therefore resist synthesis. Since a woman in our culture has to construct her self out of fragments, the work that she produces is likely to seem incoherent unless we fit it together into an overarching unity. This unity will not be seamless or monolithic. But we should not infer from this that we are not dealing with an *oeuvre*, or with a person who is not fully *individual*. It is disturbing that, at the historical moment that second-wave feminism has brought to the surface a rich hidden history of female authors and artists, the very concepts of 'individuality' and 'authorship' have come under attack by an élite group of critics who draw on recent French theories of writing and language. Here again, feminists have to keep separate two lines of argument that have become blurred. On the one hand, there is the track taken by Roland Barthes, who would seem to want to kill off authors and eliminate selves and individuality completely [see Barthes, 1968, for example]. On the other hand, there are the theories of Jacques Derrida and (more importantly) Michel Foucault who do not prove – as some seem to suppose – that there is no such thing as a self or an author. They only show that these categories are by no means as simple and straightforward as they look. [See Derrida, 1984, p.125; and Foucault, 1969.]

It is this latter position that is both more plausible and of more use to feminists seeking a basis for an aesthetics. The existence of fragments

Post-modernism and the Female Author

or fractures within a self or an *oeuvre* does not imply that there is no way of representing the pieces as a part of a whole. Indeed – as for the pathologist who must reconstruct a dead body after a crime – the existence of fracture-lines might be an important clue in assembling a model of the missing person. The analogy is useful since, as for Foucault's analysis of authorship shows, an 'author' is not simply a flesh-and-blood person who scribbles, paints, sculpts, etc. We credit an author with an *oeuvre*; but it is the readers or art-consumers who decide what belongs in that *oeuvre*, and what should be cast aside as worthless. Thus, for example, an *oeuvre* often includes first-drafts, sketches and even letters; but it generally excludes doodles, memos and laundry lists. The face of an *individual* gradually emerges out of a jumble of fragments; but it is the audience that (collectively) creates the 'author' or 'artist' out of the facts at its disposal.

Imagine a child constructing a picture of a face out of a range of cut-out pieces. The child has first to decide whether she wants to construct a clown-face, a policeman-face or some other kind of face. Her choice will be determined by the game she happens to be playing, or the context that she finds herself in. Once this choice has been made, certain features will be selected as appropriate, and others discarded as inappropriate to her tastes and to her purposes. It would be odd to stick a big smiling, painted mouth on the neck of a policeman . . . unless, of course, the child's purpose was to surprise or joke. It is 'tradition' that provides the context or 'game' within which the individual art critic sets out to construct the features of the artist. This analogy is not exact, since critics don't play these 'games' of tradition alone. Indeed, our knowledge of traditions is part of our cultural inheritance; and the 'traditions' are defined in part by the faces that fit into them. Furthermore, some of the fragments of 'facts' have been irretrievably destroyed, or temporarily mislaid by previous critics, biographers and historians working on the pieces. Nevertheless, the 'personality' of the author or artist that emerges out of this collective enterprise represents the values and projects of the audience in much the same way as does the face formed by the child.

Since the woman artist does not stand in the same relation to tradition as the male, her face can only emerge clearly by playing two separate games. She has to be positioned in two different, but overlapping patterns: the matrilineal and patrilineal lines of influence and response that swirl through (and across) the intricate network of relationships out of which we shape our past. A female creator needs to be slotted into the context of male traditions. But to understand what that artist is doing, and the merits or demerits of her work, she will also have to be located in a separate female pattern that, so to speak, runs through the first in a kind of contrapuntal way. Feminist cultural history offers us tricks of perspective as disturbing as those in a painting by Escher. Women are not just outside cultural traditions. They structure the spaces that lie between the bold lines picked out by previous generations of art critics and literary critics. Now after a lengthy period of sustained effort by feminist historians and critics, we are at last learning

Gender and Genius

to see the depth of these spaces. We are gradually adopting the switch in perspective that allows us to appreciate the artistic achievements of many more women in the past. We cannot let post-modernist attacks on the notions of authorship, historical continuity and tradition deflect us from this task.

16
Forward via
the Female Past

To talk about great female authors or artists is to talk about the values and tastes of *readers* and *critics*. And, since female consumers stand in a different relation to culture than male consumers, feminists have also to concern themselves with developing a notion of 'female' – not 'feminine' – values. This does not mean that we should drop the important distinction between 'gender' and 'sex'. An emphasis on the question of the sex of authors and artists need not be (must not be) a return to some kind of essentialism. What makes a woman special is not her biology, but the way society categorises her and treats her because of her biology. A person brought up as a woman can never occupy the same social or artistic space as one reared as a man. However superficially similar, her words, works and perceptions will never be the same as those of a man, and are likely (whether she knows it or not) to have features in common with those of other women.

Feminist aesthetics can only move forward if we look further at what women in our society need from art, and whether or not the records of artistic achievement fairly reflect women's tastes and values. We are right to be concerned by such issues as what percentage of books written *by women* feature on the pages of reviews of newspapers, or what proportion of paintings *by women* are stuffed away in museum basements . . . or never even acquired by galleries. I think there is even more reason for concern about what proportion of reviewers or gallery-selectors are women. The evidence collected by 'Women in Publishing' and presented in *Reviewing the Reviews* suggests that the UK in 1985 was still a very long way from allowing the tastes of women equal weight with those of men. The daily newspaper then most highly regarded by the liberal establishment, the *Guardian*, boasted 91 per cent of male reviewers and 9 per cent female reviewers. In 1987 there was not a solitary woman picking the Christmas list for the *Guardian*. And yet (at least for the ordinary reader) these lists are the most important selections of the year. It's not being biologistic to care about this.

From some perspectives, feminism has already made such a difference to women's status in the arts that the development of a feminist aesthetics is simply not needed. It is supposed that the gradual liberalisation of the art establishment makes theoretical adjustments unnecessary. As Rothenstein put it,

The recognition that Frink's work, however original, and her personality, however fiercely independent, now receives, provides an illuminating comment

Gender and Genius

The trouble with such optimism is that, since the eighteenth century at least, there have been original and important women artists whose work has been recognised and celebrated in their own times as atypical of 'feminine' talents. What matters to future generations of women is not primarily what contemporaries recognise, but what gets recorded in the annals of the summary histories of art. And it is when I go through one of those survey-books on the state of twentieth-century literature, art, or music that pessimism gets the upper hand.

How could Robson's *A Prologue to English Literature* [1986] find the space to mention such minor writers as David Storey or Malcolm Bradbury, but not a word about Jean Rhys or Doris Lessing . . . or even (if, despite T. S. Eliot, foreign birth is used as an excuse) women as indisputably English as Dorothy Richardson or Rebecca West? The 'quiet domestic novels' of Barbara Pym get a cautious nod of approval, as do the 'pretty, half-nonsensical verbal tunes' of Edith Sitwell [pp.234, 213]. Women writers are there; but selected and described in terms of outmoded categories which damn them with faint praise. If we look at Edward Lucie-Smith's *Movements in Art since 1945* [1984 ed.] we find a similar thing. Where is Frink in this story? Not even mentioned. Hardly any women artists are indexed at all – except in the final Chapter 10, which functions as a kind of appendix, updating the main text.

Unlike Robson (whose final page includes four querulous sentences on feminist theory), Lucie-Smith has tried to adjust his perceptions. He ends on a note of high rhetoric about feminist art. But Judy Chicago's 'The Dinner Party' is linked with ethnic art and 'group identity' rather than with the individualism, style, and the formalistic values that his book as a whole promotes [p.276]. Indeed, Lucie-Smith seems quite unable to escape the old stereotypes of femininity. This is most obvious when he is discussing male artists' portrayals of women. The most stunning example is his comment on a super-realist 'sculpture' of a teenager by John de Andrea (1974). The rather ordinary, quite pretty young woman sculpted has a figure of the type fashionable amongst dummies in shop-windows, and (except for the body hair) is con-structed in a manner reminiscent of a dummy. But the sculpture is judged by Lucie-Smith as if the woman portrayed were genuinely dummylike. De Andrea's sculptures of 'apparently fresh and innocent co-eds' reveal 'milk-fed mindlessness and complacency . . . despite the physical beauty the sculptor depicts'. His works thus illustrate 'the nullity and despair to be found in large areas of urban society' [p.258].

The body of de Andrea's model could (once) have (almost) been mine! How depressing this reaction from a critic who thinks he is being fair to feminist art by praising (as a postscript) 'The Dinner Party' and its painted china ('a skilled craft hobby which has long been popular with American women') decorated with 'the vagina and the butterfly' [p.275]. Butterflies were hardly amongst the most striking parts of Chicago's imagery! Craft; decorative butterfly motifs; an art moulded

Forward via the Female Past

by women's reproductive organs; no individual creators, only a group of semi-individuals. We are being presented with a more explicit version of the way in which the Victorians saw women's art. I feel my despair at such reactions is far more appropriate than Lucie-Smith's existential *angst*.

Men like Lucie-Smith and Richard Kearney are trying to be sympathetic to the feminist aim of re-writing cultural history. But they don't seem to have grasped that allying with feminism requires more than an appendix or a footnote. Until male (and female) critics learn to *see* women not as Others nor as animated dummies, but as fully-human individuals, feminist aesthetics will have to use all the resources at its disposal to help the males adjust their vision. And that will require appropriating the vocabulary of genius for feminist ends. Since we can't stop journalists or popular historians from using the word 'genius' – or from recycling the concept through fuzzy notions of 'creativity', 'originality' or simply artistic 'greatness' – we have to join in, and project our own artistic values by picking out female 'geniuses'. I am aware, of course, that exploiting the language of 'genius' for feminist ends is awkward and (even) dangerous. To use the term 'genius' at all, feminists need to understand the history of the concept, and must also distinguish the separate notions of genius that have become muddled in the course of that history.

There are five separate strands in our modern usage of the term 'genius' . . . only *one* of which can be utilised for feminist ends. The first idea of genius that must be rejected comes to us from Romanticism and represents 'genius' in terms of a personality-type (an outsider, near-to-madness, degenerate, shamanistic, etc.). A second (related) idea of 'genius' comes to us from the pre-Romantics – who explained it as a specific mode of consciousness: variously (and conflictingly) described as passion, imagination, instinct, intuition, the unconscious, reason. A third strand (again related, and again slightly different) describes 'genius' in terms of energy (usually, sublimated sexual energy). These first three senses of genius are utterly contaminated by past usage, and by the way that the male (still) provides the paradigm for both the normal and supernormal personality-types, consciousness-types and energy-types. As such, they are useless for building a feminist aesthetics.

The fourth notion of genius is the one that was predominant in the early eighteenth century, and which survives in modern scientific (and pseudo-scientific) theories that seek to quantify talent and creativity via tests and statistical surveys. Genius is treated as a kind of 'potential for eminence'; a potential which is then glossed in terms of skill or talent. Here also, as we saw in Chapter 13, the standards of achievement and of talent have been devised with males in mind. This fourth sense of genius is also fundamentally flawed by a naïvety about the relationship between facts and values. It is thus only the fifth sense of genius that feminists can appropriate for the purposes of transforming cultural history. This fifth sense of genius is a much more pragmatic notion. A

Gender and Genius

person's cultural achievement is evaluated and assessed against an appropriate background of artistic genres and traditions. The genius is the person whose work (a) marks the boundary between the old ways and the new within the tradition, and (b) has lasting value and significance.

For a feminist, a female 'genius' is not some kind of élite being, different from other (ordinary) women, nor one with a greater 'potential for eminence'. A female 'genius' is, instead, a woman who is judged to occupy a strategic position in the matrilineal and patrilineal patterns of tradition that make up culture. Her work must be seen to have a worth and importance that extends beyond mere popularity or influence on other artists. In so far as we use the word 'genius' for feminist ends, we have to be clear that we are not describing a personality-type or any kind of psychic process or energy. Indeed, we're not *describing* at all, although our evaluations have always to be grounded in fact. That an artist is influential is a fact that is relevant – though never by itself enough – for allocating 'genius'. And, since women have been excluded from the academies and have found it difficult to have their art-products taken seriously, we should expect (even today) that there will remain fewer female than male 'geniuses'. Indeed, in subjects such as philosophy – in which degree of influence is disproportionately important in getting counted as significant – we might expect to find very few women whose work can be seen to have the kind of cultural 'momentousness' that is requisite for 'genius'. Even here, however, women are not such an absence as is generally supposed.

The use of the 'genius' vocabulary in a feminist context does not entail that we are mythologising the act of creation . . . nor that we are wrenching the individual artist out of the historical and social context within which her art was produced. The historical dimension is a necessary part of understanding what is involved in creating *as a woman*. Since the rationalisations of male superiority have changed radically through the course of history, appreciation of a woman's acceptance of and resistance to 'Otherness' will involve exploring the social and historical background against which her self – and her *oeuvre* – was constructed. Thus the emphasis on the achievements of *individual* women in no way denies the importance of *collectives*. On the contrary, I am arguing that to see the significance of an individual woman creator it is necessary to situate her within a collective (or rather series of collectives) of tradition. Furthermore, it is only by a collective enterprise of feminist critics – working perhaps individually, but sharing common values and ends – that the matrilineal traditions of art can creep into the history books and transform the general understanding of what was (and therefore is and will be) possible for women.

Feminist criticism is a *collective* enterprise. But feminist literary and art criticism is currently in a state of crisis. At present there is no way forward for a feminist aesthetics that does not confront the debate between the historically-minded feminists (who remain within the

Forward via the Female Past

dominant traditions of Anglo-American empiricism) and those post-structuralists who believe themselves to have moved beyond empiricism and beyond mere history, into the fragmentary world of 'feminine' texts. This is, in a sense, a false dichotomy, because it omits those who (like me) think post-structuralist insights can enrich investigation into historical traditions. But this is how the debate has been presented by the francophile Toril Moi in her (influential) *Sexual/Textual Politics* [1985] . . . and see Janet Todd's *Feminist Literary History: A Defence* [1988] for a critical account of the current state of play in the literature departments of the British and American academies. Both in these circles and amongst the avant-garde critics of film and the visual arts, post-structuralists seem at present to have gained the upper hand. This is, in part, because of the sheer complexity of the vocabulary and syntax that they employ – always a good technique for disabling opponents! But it is also because – at least in English – we have lacked an alternative overview of the history of Western thought that attacks the view that Cixous (and Derrida and Lacan) have put forward:

. . . the history of philosophy . . . is marked by an absolute constant which orders values and which is precisely this opposition, activity/passivity.

Moreover, woman is always associated with passivity in philosophy. [Cixous, 1975, p.64]

In the course of this long trek back into some of the most obscure reaches of history, mysticism and sexology to find the origins of the language, resonant with male sexuality, that we still use to describe great art and creativity, I have discovered that Cixous's 'constant' is really a complex. Males, too, have prided themselves on their passivity, on their surrender of ego, on their passion, on their ability to respond to intuition and instinct.Women have been accused of being active: of having a rampant sexual desire or a lust for power that has to be severely checked. Although 'femininity' seems always to have been associated with passivity, femaleness has not. Males can be feminine and be superior; passivity and egolessness are only failings in semi-human and sub-human types.

Structuralists and post-structuralists have debated the question of whether 'male' is to 'female' as 'culture' is to 'nature' [see Ortner, 1974]. I do not see how we can answer this equation until we have decided whether 'male' is to 'masculine' as 'female' is to 'feminine'. My reading of the history of philosophy would suggest that this question does not go through. To be a 'real woman' is to be seen as having certain biological characteristics; to be a 'real man' is not just to have body characteristics, but to have maturity, independence, courage, virility and the like. 'Maleness' might refer in the first instance to biological facts; but there are also behavioural ideals associated with these 'facts'. In this respect, the category of the 'male' is more like that of the 'feminine' than that of the 'female'. And, since these distinctions are not easy to make in the French language, perhaps this is where Cixous's analysis of the history of philosophy goes wrong. Since both the 'feminine' and the 'female' run foul of the norms for male personality-types and characters (the 'masculine'), it is supposed that they are also excluded from our notion of the supernormal male. But this seems to be a false assumption.

This book has (inevitably) involved itself – in a fairly preliminary way – with the task of re-writing the history of culture with these distinctions to the fore. 'Genius' was one of the key terms that the males employed to give their (supposed) physical superiority a metaphysical dimension. 'Genius' was linked with 'maleness': its apparent openness to feminine passivity and egolessness masked a refusal to conceptualise spiritual power in female terms. Because of this, we still lack an accepted vocabulary for describing female productivity in a non-reductive way. It is hard to translate into non-gendered language passages that praise art-works as 'seminal', artists as 'virile', authors as 'masterly'. It seems at first sight that we require a new dictionary before women creators can resist the *logos spermatikos*. But the future for feminist aesthetics would be grim if it were necessary to invent a new 'positive' vocabulary to describe female strengths, virtues and relationships. History also suggests that any such dictionary can be swallowed whole by males insecure enough or greedy enough to demand sexual superiority.

As we have seen, from the Stoics to the Romantics, vocabularies used to describes specifically female strengths have been appropriated to laud the perfect male. Jupiter was *Genius*. As the father of the universe, he was also (sometimes) its mother. But Juno (the mother) was never the father. When Weininger wrote about 'genius', he meant something quite different. The relationship between 'male' and 'female' remained the same, however. In a ludicrous reversal of biology, Weininger insisted that the complete male includes the female within himself, but the perfect female is only a fragment of a greater whole. I have suggested that Lacan's appropriation of the language of Otherness to describe what is at the heart of patriarchal language repeats this act of swallowing female strengths.

Continuing the traditions of Romanticism, Lacan represented 'egos' and 'culture' as a part of the masculine domain. The title of Susan Griffin's book, *Woman and Nature: The Roaring Inside Her* [1978], evokes nature inside every woman, roaring a message opposed to male culture. Griffin's voice is powerful and poetic . . . but it is not the voice of nature. 'Nature' must play a part in the lyricism of her anger; but after centuries of male mystification of 'woman' and 'nature' it is impossible to tell how much, or what part. Griffin seems to have accepted as a (partial) truth the fiction that would make the culture within which we live monolithically male. But Griffin's is not a solitary voice. Her words join those of other women. Within Western culture (past and present) are the voices of women which roar and subvert that culture from within. The roar is many different messages being shouted at once, as individual women confront the various and devious means by which men have sought to limit female power, to tame women, and confine them to subsidiary roles . . . as consumers, companions and helpers for the (supposedly) metaphysically superior males. I will be happy if this

Forward via the Female Past

exploration of the concepts of genius and of artistic creativity will help women and men to disentangle individual, compelling voices from amongst the roar that might otherwise seem a jumble of background noise.

I am not claiming that the only voices worth listening to in the past are the voices of these individual women. The revaluation of stereotypically 'female' arts – embroidery, pottery, musical ballads and the rest – are valuable feminist enterprises that should coexist with that of picking out great female creators in the traditions of high and popular culture. Nor am I condemning all women who find it strategically valuable to ally themselves with nature, 'Otherness', motherhood and 'feminine' values. If we listen to the voices of women coming from the past we will hear many of them crying that this is what they had to do to enable them to create. Women can adopt this as a device to increase their powers, as long as the strategem does not make them deaf to the roar of their grandmothers' and great-grandmothers' voices. Men would not have needed to make silence a virtue for women unless women talked – and unless men were afraid that women would be heard. Men would not have insisted that creativity is a male prerogative unless women created – and unless men were afraid that women's creations would be taken seriously.

We can only reinstate women creators in cultural history when we pay them the compliment of treating their works with the care and respect that we accord to the individuality of (white) males. And we cannot do this if we negate the fact that they were writing *as women* who emerge from a female situation (which needs to be explicated), and who fit into the patterns of patrilineal and matrilineal continuity (whose links have to be exposed). One way to make these hidden *female* traditions emerge is, of course, to focus on the continuities (and absurdities) of the male cultural traditions that have served to obscure them. But this is not the only way forward. Feminists haven't been mealy-mouthed about saying that (from our point of view) some male geniuses deserve to be crossed out of the history books, and awarded the faint praise so often meted out to women. So why should we be shy of pointing to great female artists as we trace new patterns of inheritance? The fact that much feminist art is, and always will be, a collective enterprise shouldn't obscure individual women creators.

To talk of a great woman author, artist or composer need not involve re-vamping Romanticism. We can praise and rank women artists while, at the same time, denying that the 'great' work of art is produced in some special psychological state or by some special class of person. Great art is not a matter of inspiration, or of being in tune with one's unconscious. Far from being a return to Romanticism, what I am recommending is a form of pragmatism. My concern is with the effectiveness of *a body of work* in terms of promoting feminist ends. Some works have more potential than others for undermining the damaging stereotypes of female excellence that have served to limit female ambition in the arts. To call a woman a 'genius' is to say

Gender and Genius

something about what matters to us as feminist readers or spectators. It is to construct a new tradition that enables us to remove the gag (or the veil) that covers the features of the women buried in the past and the present. A female genius is a construct created as we, the feminist consumers and critics, look back at the past, create a new tradition, and project ourselves and our values towards the future.

Forward via the Female Past

Notes

Abbreviations: *corr.* = corrected translation (the reference given is to the English translation, but I have corrected it against the original).

Dates in square brackets refer to the first appearance, publication or relevant edition of the work, not to the date of the text consulted. Where square brackets are used in the footnotes or in the body of the text, full details of the work referred to and the edition used can be found in the bibliography.

Chapter 1

1 Parker and Pollock do recognise that the surrealists praised the femininity of male creators [1981, pp.137ff.]. But Surrealism is treated as atypical of Romantic and modernist conceptions of genius. As Pollock sums up their conclusions in the basically unchanged perspective of 'Feminism and Modernism' [1987]: 'a division was established by the late eighteenth century between representations of the artist as a Man of Reason and of Woman as a beautiful object' [Parker and Pollock, 1987, p.86]. But by this time – indeed as soon as creativity became an admired feature of men of genius – masculine reason was no longer always the distinguishing characteristic of great male artists.

Chapter 2

1 The description of Lord Byron is provided by Lady Caroline Lamb, the most notorious of his many mistresses. Byron (bisexual, promiscuous, and rich in vice) is the archetypal Romantic literary genius. But the archetype for the sciences is provided by the fictional Dr Frankenstein. It is surely no accident that *Frankenstein* [1818] was dreamed up by Mary Shelley during some months spent in Switzerland in 1816 with Byron, Claire Clairmont and Percy Bysshe Shelley – Mary Wollstonecraft Godwin's husband-to-be. See Chapter 4, below.

Chapter 3

1 Some of the witch-hunters denied women the capacity for melancholy altogether: arguing with Jean Bodin (1580) that the coldness and wetness of women is proof that their fantasies come from the devil, and not from melancholia. But others, such as Johan Wier (1563), explained the fact that women were more likely than men to be witches in terms of their greater tendency to the vicious forms of melancholy – which

Gender and Genius

weakened resistance to the devil. Since both forms of reasoning were used to justify the torture and slaughter of countless women, this was a desperate double-bind. Sydney Anglo gives the facts in his 'Melancholia and Witchcraft' [1973], although the gender-context – and, therefore, the logic of Bodin's argument – does not seem to be fully understood.

Chapter 4

1 For the diary entries of Dr Polidori and Claire Clairmont (Mary's step-sister, as well as Byron's mistress), see Cameron [1974], pp. 92, 586. In her own 'Introduction' to *Frankenstein*, written for the 1831 edition, Mary denies that she was ever in competition with Byron and her (dead) husband [1817, p.53]. This has been interpreted by Poovey as a part of Mary's unwillingness to measure herself against her two intimidating male companions, and as an indication of her 'wholehearted acceptance of an essentially subordinate and passive role' [1984, pp.141, 142]. But such a reading is suspect. We know that Percy Bysshe Shelley invented several details of the occasion: that the writing was an exclusively night-time activity, and that it involved only the three authors. Why should we accept his account of the rest of the story? By refusing to slot herself into her dead husband's mythologising of authorial competition – a mythologising that, in Mary's words, shows the two men downgrading 'the platitude of prose' – Mary resisted the males' claim to superiority of vision. As Poovey shows, Mary did herself internalise the social denigration of female authorship; but this does not make her a thoroughgoing conservative . . . even in later life. [See also Chapter 10, below.]

2 It is not just in his fiction that John Fowles associates great art with maleness. In one of his critical pieces, 'Hardy and the Hag' (1977), psychoanalytic theory is employed to rationalise the gendering of creativity. See Bruce Woodcock [1984], p.21.

Chapter 5

1 For Nin's later views see her 'Diary versus Fiction', from her *The Novel of the Future* (1968), in Webber and Grumman [1978], pp. 39–45.

Chapter 7

1 Plato compares the soul's journey through life to a chariot pulled by two horses. The horse on the right is reason (the white and noble steed); the black and unruly horse on the left represents base passions. Only the man who controls the chariot and lets his life be guided by reason can ever reach the truth. Reason should govern every aspect of a man's life, including his sexual habits and the way he seeks to seduce another (through rhetoric). The Pythagoreans had associated the right hand with masculinity; the left hand with femininity. Plato is not much interested in femininity here: the ideal love is assumed to be that of (chaste) male homosexuality. But the left hand is still 'sinister'. Alain makes extensive use of this vocabulary: the chariot images; the (good) right-hand rhetoric of one who has seen the truth and experienced noble love; the (bad) left-hand rhetoric of the one guided by mere

appetite. But for Alain all homosexual tastes – however controlled – would be put down to leftish (effeminate) lusts.

2 Although I am very much indebted to Wetherbee's [1973] translation and notes to *Cosmographia*, he has tidied up and interpreted the (very imperfect and obscure) Latin text, rather than given a literal rendering of it. But modern scholarship has not provided all the background information that would enable us successfully to gloss the passages on *Genius* in the text. I am, therefore, enormously grateful to my colleague, Dr D.C. Barrett, for many hours spent patiently checking key passages in Wetherbee's translation against the Latin text and English summary provided by Peter Dronke [1978] and against the fragments of a translation provided by Stock [1972]. The sometimes ungrammatical and (in every sense) crude English deliberately mirrors the eccentric (but powerful) Latin. For the benefit of readers without Latin I have kept references to Wetherbee's translation as in-text references; but where *corr.* is marked there are minor or (in the case of the closing pages of *Cosmographia*) major deviations from Wetherbee's version.

3 It never seems to have occurred to the experts on Bernardus, or to Nitzsche (the expert on *Genius* in the Middle Ages) to identify the twin *Genii* as Gemini. A variety of other candidates have been suggested: the tutelary spirits of marriage; the early *genius* and *juno* of generation and marriage; the masculine and feminine aspects of creativity; aspects of man's procreative instincts. But there are too many clues pointing to Gemini for any other reading to be plausible. See also note 2 on the translation of this passage.

Chapter 9

1 In vol. i. of *Male Fantasies* [1977], Klaus Theweleit suggests that there had been a successive desexualisation of the female body since the Middle Ages, and that by the middle of the seventeenth century, 'Only the image of the noblewoman (an unattainable woman) had been sexualised in any fundamental sense' [p.332]. But this is odd, since he recognises that the mass execution and torture of witches was an attack on the sexuality of lower-class women [p.299]. And this '*gynocide*' worsened during the fifteenth to seventeenth centuries: reaching a grisly climax during the years 1600–1650. [See Mary Daly, *Gyn/Ecology*, 1978.]

Theweleit analyses the change that happened in the eighteenth century in terms of a conflict between aristocratic and middle-class values, with the bourgeois women appropriating the '"freer" sexuality' (!) of the noblewomen [p.334]. Against this, I suggest that the Enlightenment saw a *new* anti-aristocratic ideal of marriage, which yoked together lust, romantic love and monogamy into patterns of feeling alien to the old land-based societies. Before this it was women who transcended the category of 'wives' who were likely to be perceived in a sexualised way. Thus, it was unmarried women and widows who were most likely to end up on the witches' bonfires. And – despite Theweleit's analysis of medieval courtly love in terms of a monogamous ideal of a 'one-and-

only' (lusted after) Beloved [p.295] – it was *adulterous* relationships that
the troubadours celebrated in their poetry.

Theweleit's historical analysis is suspect; but it is, none the less, a welcome effort at charting this neglected area of social history. Foucaultnotwithstanding, we still await a comprehensive history of sexuality that focuses on the construction and control of *female* lusts, and not simply on changes in the patterning of *male* lust and/or female sexual pleasure. Indeed, we should ask why Foucault has erased the transitions from witches' bonfires to mental asylums and prisons from his histories of madness, of sexuality, and even of punishment.

Chapter 11

1 In-text references have been provided by H.M. Parshley's translation of *The Second Sex* (Harmondsworth: Penguin, 1972) for the benefit of readers without French. But *corr.* indicates I have corrected the passage referenced. Parshley's own training as a zoologist leaves him unfamiliar with key issues in the history of culture. Thus, the only English translation of this classic text is unreliable throughout, especially with regard to de Beauvoir's philosophical (and existentialist) terminology. To make matters worse, Parshley has also shortened the text by condensing passages in which de Beauvoir provided details of the words and deeds of women in history. For this ref. see *Le Deuxième Sexe* (Éditions Gallimard, p.b. ed., 1968) ii, p.472. Although it doesn't announce itself as such, this French paperback version is also incomplete, although in different ways.

2 Both quotes from Jung are taken from interviews with him. The first was from a report in the *Observer* (London: 18 October 1936). The second was published first in *Hearst's International-Cosmopolitan* (January 1939; based on an interview with H.R. Knickerbocker, October 1938). Reprinted in *C.G. Jung Speaking*, pp.103, 126.

Chapter 13

1 Since the feminist social historians Davidoff and Hall provide a genealogy of one of Galton's families (the Taylors) in *Family Fortunes* [1987], it is possible to see which women have been omitted from Galton's database at this point. Although not designed as such, Davidoff and Hall's social history of Galton's *own* family is also an effective refutation of his theories.

Chapter 14

1 There is a French term *'femelle'*; but, since it is generally reserved for animals and plants, it has different connotations than the English-language 'female'. This word is, consequently, avoided in most analyses of human sexuality. See Chapter 16 below for some consequences of the fact that the French language tends to conflate the 'female' and the 'feminine' under the *'féminin'*, and for a complication to the apparently straightforward distinction between biological sex (male/female) and

cultural norms (masculine/feminine) in the English language.

2 There are terminological difficulties in describing those French women– like Hélène Cixous or Julia Kristeva – who have been so influential on feminist theory in Britain and the United States, but who shrug off (or loudly denounce) the label of 'feminist'. For a (somewhat partial) account of Cixous's celebrated distinction between the women's move-ment – a good thing (she supposes) – and feminism – a bad thing, in that feminists struggle for equal power and rights within a patriar-chal world – see Toril Moi's *Sexual/Textual Politics* [1985], pp.103ff.

3 For my acquaintance with the work of Hannah Höch I am indebted to an Exhibition – 'Hannah Höch 1889–1978: Collages' – that toured the UK in 1988, under the auspices of the Institute of Foreign Cultural Relations, Stuttgart. Deborah Sugg from the National Art Library, Victoria and Albert Museum, gave an outstanding lecture in conjunc-tion with that tour, and has since been generous with her time; with help in locating secondary material; and with her own (mostly unpub-lished) material on Höch. Sugg, like a number of the German feminist critics, treats Höch as a fully individual artist with an *oeuvre* that deve-lops and matures. The same cannot be said of all the articles in the catalogue that accompanied the touring exhibition. However, I found Karin Thomas [1980] helpful . . . also an article by Dech [1980] – left out of the English catalogue, but included in that of the (much larger) German exhibition which provided the basis for the English catalogue.

4 Annie Leclerc seems to have triggered the initial interest in *l'écriture féminine*. But in America and Britain it is generally the work of Hélène Cixous, Luce Irigaray and (sometimes/some of) Julia Kristeva that is grouped together under this heading. Their stances are quite different; but for an introductory account of the underlying similarities see Ann Rosalind Jones [1981]. A much more detailed English-language over-view (and summary) of the multifarious positions and debates within French feminism is in Gelfand and Hules [1985]: a text which gives an excellent feel for the sharp theoretical disagreements that have been engendered inside France around the concept of *l'écriture féminine*.

Chapter 15

1 It was in Gilbert and Gubar [1979] that I first encountered a poem by Coleridge. 'The Other Side of the Mirror' is quoted in full as 'central to the feminist aesthetics' constructed in *Madwoman in the Attic* [pp.15–16]. On reading it, I stopped in surprise. It is so strong. Wondering why I had never heard of her (and thinking that it was, perhaps, her only good poem), I went off to the library to look up her work. I found – to my astonishment – a richness of poetic vision, plus several novels, short stories and a biography (of Holman Hunt). Although individual poems by Coleridge have been reclaimed for feminist ends, her *oeuvre* has not. *Collected Poems* was last published in 1954, and most of the prose has yet to be reprinted. I could find no recent monographs on her work. Indeed, she is at present so obscure that her name is even missing from surveys of turn-of-the-century poetry in Britain.

Gender and Genius

Bibliography

Dates in square brackets refer to the first appearance, publication or relevant edition of the work, not to the date of the text consulted.

A Ableman, Paul, *The Doomed Rebellion*, London: Zomba, Bee in Bonnet Book, 1983.

Abrahamsen, David, *The Mind and Death of a Genius*, Columbia University Press, 1946.

Aers, David, 'Blake: Sex, Society and Ideology', in *Romanticism and Ideology: Studies in English Writing 1765–1830*, eds. D. Aers, J. Cook and D. Punter, London: Routledge, 1981.

Alain de Lille (Alanus de Insulis, d. 1202), *De Planctu Naturae*, trans. by Douglas M. Moffat as *The Complaint of Nature*, New York: Yale Studies in English, no. 36, 1908.

Alaya, Flavia, 'Victorian Science and the "Genius" of Woman', *Journal of the History of Ideas* 38 [1977], pp. 261–80.

Allen, Prudence, *The Concept of Woman: The Aristotelian Revolution 750 BC–AD 1250*, Montreal; London: Eden Press, 1985.

Altheim, Franz, *A History of Roman Religion*, trans. Harold Mattingly, London: Methuen, 1938.

Altman, Leslie, 'Christine de Pisan: First Professional Woman of Letters', in *Female Scholars: A Tradition of Learned Women before 1800*, ed. J.R. Brink, Montreal: Eden Press, 1980.

Anderson, Perry, *Passages from Antiquity to Feudalism* [1974], London: NLB, 1975.

Anglo, Sydney, 'Melancholia and Witchcraft: The Debate between Wier, Bodin, and Scot' [1973], in *Folie et Déraison à la Renaissance*, Université Libre de Bruxelles: Travaux de l'Institut pour l'Étude de la Renaissance et de l'Humanisme, no. 5, 1976, pp.209–28.

Augustine of Hippo (Saint), *Concerning the City of God Against the Pagans* [413–26], trans. Henry Bettenson, ed. David Knowles, Harmondsworth: Penguin, 1972.

B Babb, Lawrence, *The Elizabethan Malady: A Study of Melancholia in English Literature from 1580–1642*, Michigan State College Press, 1951.

Bailey, Cyril, *Phases in the Religion of Ancient Rome*, University of California Press, 1932.

Balsdon, J.P.V.D., *Roman Women: Their History and Habits*, London: Bodley Head, 1962.

Barnard, Malcolm, 'Economy and Strategy: Deconstruction as Feminism', Dissertation: University of Warwick, 1984.

Barrett, Elizabeth, *see* Browning, Elizabeth Barrett.

Barron, Frank [1968], *Creativity and Personal Freedom*, Princeton; London: D. Van Nostrand Co., 1968.

— [1969], *Creative Person and Creative Process*, New York; London: Holt, Rinehart and Winston, 1969.

Barry, Joseph (ed. and trans.), *George Sand in her Own Words*, New York: Anchor, 1979.

Barthes, Roland, 'The Death of the Author' [1968], trans. in *Image/Music/Text*, ed. Stephen Heath, London: Fontana, 1977, pp.142–8.

Battersby, Christine, 'An Enquiry concerning the Humean Woman', *Philosophy* 56 [1981], pp.303–12.

Beauvoir, Simone de [1949], *The Second Sex*, trans. H.M. Parshley [1953], Harmondsworth: Penguin, 1972.

— [1966] 'Women and Creativity', in *French Feminist Thought*, ed. Toril Moi, Oxford: Blackwell, 1987.

Becker, George, *The Mad Genius Controversy: A Study in the Sociology of Deviance*, Beverly Hills; London: Sage, 1978.

Bernardus Silvestris, *Cosmographia* [*c.* 1147–48], ed. Peter Dronke with Introduction and Notes, Leiden: E.J. Brill, 1978. And see Wetherbee, Winthrop [1973], for annotated English translation.

Biographium *Faemineum. The Female Worthies: or Memoirs of the most Illustrious Ladies of all Ages and Nations*, London: Crowder, 1766.

Blake, William [1790–93], 'The Marriage of Heaven and Hell', in Blake [1972].

— [1810], 'A Vision of The Last Judgment', in Blake [1972].

— [1820], 'The Laocoön', in Blake [1972].

— [1972], *Complete Writings*, ed. Geoffrey Keynes, Oxford University Press, 1972 ed.

Bridges, Robert, 'The Poems of Mary Coleridge' [1907], reprinted in vol. vi of *Collected Essays, Papers, etc.*, Oxford University Press: 1931.

Browning, Elizabeth Barrett [1844], 'To George Sand: A Recognition', in *Aurora Leigh and Other Poems*, Introduction by Cora Kaplan, London: The Women's Press, 1978.

— [1954], *Elizabeth Barrett to Miss Mitford*, ed. Betty Miller. London:
John Murray, 1954.

— [1969], *The Letters of Robert Browning and Elizabeth Barrett Browning, 1845–46*, ed. Elvan Kintner, 2 vols., Harvard University Press, 1969.

Burgess, Anthony, *Homage to Qwert Yuiop: Selected Journalism 1978–85* [1986], London: Abacus, Sphere, 1987.

Burke, Edmund [1757], *A Philosophical Enquiry into the Origin of Our Ideas of the Sublime and Beautiful*, ed. James T. Boulton, Oxford: Blackwell, 1987.

— [1790], *Reflections on the Revolution in France*, Cambridge: W.P. Grant, 1836.

Burt, Cyril, *The Gifted Child*, London: Hodder and Stoughton, 1975.

C **Cahn**, Walter, *Masterpieces: Chapters on the History of an Idea*, Princeton University Press, 1979.

Cameron, Kenneth Neill, *Shelley: The Golden Years*, Harvard University Press, 1974.

Carlyle, Thomas, *On Heroes and Hero-Worship* [1840], Introduction by Edmund Gosse, London: Ward, Lock; The World Library ed., n.d.

Cheyne, George, *The English Malady, or A Treatise of Nervous Diseases of All Kinds*, London: Strahan, 1733.

Citron, Marcia J., 'Women and the Lied, 1775–1850', in *Women Making Music: The Western Art Tradition, 1150–1950*, eds. Jane Bowers and Judith Tick, London: Macmillan, 1986, pp.224–48.

Cixous, Hélène [1975], with Catherine Clément, *The Newly Born Woman*, trans. Betsy Wing, Manchester University Press, 1986.

— [1988], *Writing Differences: Readings from the Seminar of Hélène Cixous*, ed. Susan Sellers, Open University Press, 1988.

Clément, Catherine [1975], *see* Cixous [1975].

— [1981], *The Lives and Legends of Jacques Lacan*, trans. Arthur Goldhammer, Columbia University Press, 1983.

Coleridge, Mary Elizabeth [1904], *The Shadow on the Wall*, London: Edward Arnold, 1904.

— [1910], *Gathered Leaves from the Prose of Mary E. Coleridge, with a Memoir by Edith Sichel*, London: Constable, 1910.

— [1954], *Collected Poems*, ed. Theresa Whistler, London: Hart-Davis, 1954.

Coleridge, Samuel Taylor, *Biographia Literaria* [1817], Introduction by Arthur Symons, London: Dent, Everyman ed., n.d.

D **Daly**, Mary, *Gyn/Ecology: The Metaethics of Radical Feminism* [1978], London: The Women's Press, 1979.

170   **Damon**, S. Foster, *A Blake Dictionary*, Brown University Press, 1965.

Darwin, Charles, *The Descent of Man, and Selection in Relation to Sex* [1871], reprinted from 2nd 1874 ed., London: John Murray, 1901.

Davidoff, Leonore and Hall, Catherine, *Family Fortunes: Men and Women of the English Middle Class, 1780–1850*, London: Hutchinson, 1987.

Davies, Russell, 'Spots of Time', *Listener*, 4 December 1986, pp.23–4.

Dech, Jula, '*Marionette und Modepuppe, Maske und Maquillage – Beobachtungen am Frauenbild von Hannah Höch*', in Catalogue: *Hannah Höch: Fotomontagen, Gemälde, Aquarelle. (Exhibition in Tübingen)*, ed. Götz Adriani, Cologne: DuMont Buchverlag, 1980, pp.79–94.

De la Mare, Walter, J., 'M.E. Coleridge: An Appreciation', British Library pamphlet, reprinted from the *Guardian*, 1907.

Derrida, Jacques [1976], *Spurs/Éperons: Nietzsche's Styles*, trans. Barbara Harlow, University of Chicago Press, 1979.

— [1984], 'Deconstruction and the Other', in Kearney [1984].

Dijkstra, Bram, *Idols of Perversity: Fantasies of Feminine Evil in Fin-de-Siècle Culture*, Oxford University Press, 1986.

Dronke, Peter [1978], *see* Bernardus [*c.* 1147–48].

Duff, William [1767], *An Essay on Original Genius: and its Various Modes of Exertion in Philosophy and the Fine Arts, particularly in Poetry*, Gainesville, Florida: Scholars' Facsimiles, 1964.

— [1770], *Critical Observations on the Writings of the most celebrated Original Geniuses in Poetry*, London: T. Becket and P.A. de Hondt, 1770.

— [1807], *Letters on the Intellectual and Moral Character of Women*, reprinted with an Introduction by Gina Luria, New York and London: Garland, 1974.

Dumézil, Georges, *Archaic Roman Religion* [1966], trans. Philip Krapp, 2 vols., University of Chicago Press, 1970.

Duncombe, John, *The Feminead: Or, Female Genius. A Poem* [1754, subtitle added 1757], University of California: The Augustan Reprint Society, no. 207, 1981.

E Ecker, Gisela (ed.), *Feminist Aesthetics*, trans. Harriet Anderson, London: The Women's Press, 1985.

Eliot, T.S., 'Tradition and the Individual Talent' [1919], in Lodge [1972].

Engell, James, *The Creative Imagination: Enlightenment to Romanticism*, Harvard University Press, 1981.

F Feldman, David, 'The Mysterious Case of Extreme Giftedness', in Passow [1979], pp.335–51.

Gender and Genius

Foucault, Michel, 'What is an author?' [1969], trans. in *The Foucault Reader*, ed. Paul Rabinow, Harmondsworth: Peregrine, 1986.

Fowles, John [1969], *The French Lieutenant's Woman*, London: Pan, 1987.

— [1974], 'The Ebony Tower', in *The Ebony Tower*, London; New York: Panther, 1975.

Freud, Sigmund [1916–17], 'Introductory Lectures on Psychoanalysis: Part III', in vol. xvi of *The Standard Edition of the Complete Psychological Works*, ed. James Strachey, London: Hogarth Press, 24 vols., 1953–73.

— [1932], 'Femininity', in *New Introductory Lectures on Psychoanalysis*, vol. xxii in *The Standard Edition*.

Fritz, Paul and Morton, Richard (eds.), *Woman in the Eighteenth Century and Other Essays*, Toronto: Hakkert, 1976.

G Galton, Francis, *Hereditary Genius: An Inquiry into its Laws and Consequences* [1869], ed. C.D. Darlington, reprinted from 2nd (1892) ed., Gloucester, Mass.: Peter Smith, 1972.

Gelfand, Elissa D. and Hules, Virginia T. (eds.), *French Feminist Criticism: Women, Language and Literature, an Annotated Bibliography*, London; New York: Garland, 1985.

Gemant, Andrew, *The Nature of the Genius*, Springfield, Illinois: Charles C. Thomas, Publisher, 1961.

Gilbert, Sandra M. and Gubar, Susan, *The Madwoman in the Attic: The Woman Writer and the Nineteenth-Century Literary Imagination*, Yale University Press, 1979.

Gimpel, Jean, *The Cult of Art: Against Art and Artists* [1968], trans. Jean Gimpel, London: Weidenfield and Nicolson, 1969.

Godwin, William, *Memoirs* [1798], *see* Wollstonecraft [1796].

Gombrich, E.H., *The Story of Art* [1950], London: Book Club Associates, 12th ed., 1972.

Goulianos, Joan (ed.), *By a Woman Writt: Literature from Six Centuries by and about Women* [1973], London: New English Library, 1974.

Grant, Michael, *Roman Myths*, London: Weidenfeld and Nicolson, 1971.

— and Hazel, John, *Who's Who in Classical Mythology* [1973], New York: Teach Yourself Books, 1979.

Gretton, Tom, 'New Lamps for Old', in *The New Art History*, ed. A.L. Rees and Frances Borzello, London: Camden Press, 1986.

Griffin, Susan, *Woman and Nature: The Roaring Inside Her* [1978], London: The Women's Press, 1984.

Gutwirth, Madelyn, *Madame de Staël, Novelist: The Emergence of the Artist as Woman*, University of Illinois Press, 1978.

172 **H Hahm**, David E., *The Origins of Stoic Cosmology*, Ohio State University Press, 1977.

Halsband, Robert, 'Women and Literature in Eighteenth Century England', in Fritz and Morton [1976], pp.55–71.

Hayter, Aletha, *Mrs Browning: A Poet's Work and its Setting*, London: Faber, 1962.

Helsinger, Elizabeth K., with Sheets, R.L. and Veeder, W. (eds.), *The Woman Question: Literary Issues*, vol. iii of *The Woman Question: Society and Literature in Britain and America, 1837–83*, Manchester University Press, 1983.

Helson, Ravenna, 'Women and Creativity' [1971], in Rothenberg and Hausman [1976], pp.242–50.

Hirsch, William, *Genius and Degeneration: A Psychological Study*, trans. London: Heinemann, 1897.

Hollingdale, R.J. [1970], *see* Schopenhauer [1970].

Huarte, Juan, *Examen de Ingenios* [1575], trans. as *The Examination of Mens Wits* [1594] by Richard Carew from M. Camillo Camilli's Italian trans., reprinted Gainesville, Florida: Scholars' Facsimiles, 1959.

Huyssen, Andreas, *After the Great Divide: Modernism, Mass Culture, Postmodernism*, Indiana University Press, 1986.

J Jardine, Alice A., *Gynesis: Configurations of Woman and Modernity*, Cornell University Press, 1985.

Jones, Ann Rosalind, 'Writing the Body: Toward an Understanding of *l'Écriture féminine*' [1981], reprinted in *The New Feminist Criticism: Essays on Women, Literature and Theory*, ed. Elaine Showalter, London: Virago, 1986, pp.361–77.

Jones, Edmund D. [1916] (ed.), *English Critical Essays: XIX Century*, Oxford University Press; World's Classics ed., 1916.

— [1947] (ed.), *English Critical Essays: XVI–XVIII Centuries*, Oxford University Press: The World's Classics, 1947.

Jung, Carl Gustav [1945 ed.], 'The Relations between the Ego and the Unconscious', trans. R.F.C. Hull in vol. vii of Collected Works, eds. H. Read, M. Fordham and G. Adler, London: Routledge, 1953.

— [1957 ed.], 'Commentary on "The Secret of the Golden Flower"', vol. xiii in *Collected Works*, 1967.

— [1977], *C.G. Jung Speaking: Interviews and Encounters*, eds. William McGuire and R.F.C. Hull, London: Picador, 1980.

K Kant, Immanuel [1764], *Observations on the Feeling of the Beautiful and Sublime*, trans. John T. Goldthwait, University of California Press, 1960.

— [1790], *The Critique of Judgement*, trans. J. H. Bernard, New York: Hafner, 1951.

Gender and Genius

— [1798], *Anthropology from a Pragmatic Point of View*, trans. Mary J. Gregor, The Hague: Nijhoff, 1974.

Kearney, Richard [1984], *Dialogues with Contemporary Continental Thinkers: The Phenomenological Heritage*, Manchester University Press, 1984.

— [1988], *The Wake of Imagination: Ideas of Creativity in Western Culture*, London: Hutchinson, 1988.

Kelly, Mary, 'On sexual politics and art' [1977], reprinted in Parker and Pollock [1987], pp.303–12.

Klibansky, R., with Panofsky, E., and Saxl, F., *Saturn and Melancholy: Studies in the History of Natural Philosophy, Religion and Art*, London: Nelson, 1964.

Kofman, Sarah, *The Enigma of Woman: Woman in Freud's Writings* [1980], trans. Catherine Porter, Cornell University Press, 1985.

L Lavater, John Caspar, *Essays on Physiognomy* [4 vols., 1775–78], trans. of abridged ed. by Thomas Holcroft, London: Ward, Lock. 18th ed., n.d.

Lefkowitz, Mary R., and Fant, Maureen B. (eds.), *Women's Life in Greece and Rome*, London: Duckworth, 1982.

Lewis, C.S., *The Allegory of Love: A Study in Medieval Tradition* [1936], Oxford University Press, 1977.

Lock, F.P., 'Astraea's "Vacant Throne": The Successors of Aphra Behn', in Fritz and Morton [1976], pp.25–36.

Lodge, David (ed.), *Twentieth Century Literary Criticism: A Reader*, London: Longman, 1972.

Lombroso, Cesare [1863], *The Man of Genius*, trans. from revised ed., London: Scott, 1891.

— [1893], with William (Guglielmo) Ferrero, *The Female Offender*, trans., London: T. Fisher-Unwin, 1895.

Lombroso-Ferrero, Gina, *The Soul of Woman: Reflections on Life*, trans., London: Cape, 1924.

Lorris, Guillaume de, *Le Roman de la Rose*, *see* Meun, Jean de.

Lucie-Smith, Edward, *Movements in Art since 1945* [1969, with revisions 1975 and 1984], London: Thames and Hudson, 3rd. ed., 1984.

M Maccoby, Eleanor E., and Jacklin, Carol N., *The Psychology of Sex Differences* [1974], Oxford University Press, 1975.

MacKinnon, Donald W. [1962], 'The Nature and Nurture of Creative Talent', *American Psychologist* 17 (1962), pp. 484–95.

— [1965], 'Architects, personality types and creativity', in Rothenberg and Hausman [1976], pp.175–89.

— [1975], 'IPAR's contribution to the conceptualization and study of creativity', in Taylor and Getzels [1975], pp.60–89.

Maclean, Ian, *The Renaissance Notion of Woman: A Study in the Fortunes of Scholasticism and Medical Science in European Intellectual Life*, Cambridge University Press, 1980.

McNiece, Gerald, *Shelley and the Revolutionary Idea*, Harvard University Press, 1969.

Mailer, Norman, *Advertisements For Myself* [1961], London: Panther, 1968.

Mann, Thomas, *Doctor Faustus* [1947], trans. H.T. Lowe-Porter, Harmondsworth: Penguin, 1968.

Meun, Jean de and Lorris, Guillaume de, *The Romance of the Rose* [*c*. 1225/1277], trans. Harry W. Robbins, New York: Dutton, 1962.

Mill, J.S., *The Subjection of Women* [1869], reprinted in Wollstonecraft [1792].

Moers, Ellen, *Literary Women* [1976], London: The Women's Press, 1978.

Moi, Toril, *Sexual/Textual Politics: Feminist Literary Theory*, London; New York: Methuen, 1985.

N *The Nag Hammadi Library in English* [1977], ed. James M. Robinson, trans. Coptic Gospel Library Project, Leiden: Brill, 2nd ed., 1984.

Neuls-Bates, Carol (ed.), *Women in Music: An Anthology of Source Readings From the Middle Ages to the Present*, New York; Cambridge: Harper and Row, 1982.

Neumann, Erich, *Art and the Creative Unconscious: Four Essays*, trans. Ralph Manheim [1959], Princeton University Press, 2nd rev. ed., 1969.

Newman, Barbara, *Sister of Wisdom: St Hildegard's Theology of the Feminine*, London: Scolar; University of California Press, 1987.

Nietzsche, Friedrich [1882], *The Gay Science*, trans. from 2nd. (1887) ed. by Walter Kaufmann, New York: Vintage, 1974.

— [1883–5], *Thus Spoke Zarathustra*, in Nietzsche [1954].

— [1883–8], *The Will to Power*, ed. Walter Kaufmann, trans. Kaufmann and R.J. Hollingdale. New York: Vintage, 1968.

— [1886], *Beyond Good and Evil*, trans. Walter Kaufmann, New York: Vintage, 1966.

— [1889], *The Twilight of the Idols*, in Nietzsche [1954].

— [1954], *The Portable Nietzsche*, ed. and trans. Walter Kaufmann, New York: Viking, 1968.

Nin, Anaïs, *The Journals of Anaïs Nin*, ed. Gunther Stuhlmann, 6 vols., London: Peter Owen, 1966–76.

Nitzsche, Jane Chance, *The Genius Figure in Antiquity and the Middle Ages*, Columbia University Press, 1975.

Nussbaum, Felicity, 'Heteroclites: The Gender of Character in the Scandalous Memoirs', in *The New Eighteenth Century*, eds. Nussbaum and Laura Brown, London; New York: Methuen, 1987.

O **O'Hara**, Frank, *Jackson Pollock*, New York: George Braziller, Great American Artists Series, 1959.

Onians, Richard Broxton, *The Origins of European Thought about the Body, the Mind, the Soul, The World, Time, and Fate* [1951], reprinted New York: Arno, 1973.

Ortner, Sherry B., 'Is Female to Male as Nature is to Culture?', in *Woman, Culture, and Society*, eds. Michelle Z. Rosaldo and Louise Lamphere, Stanford University Press, 1974, pp.67–87.

P **Pagels**, Elaine, *The Gnostic Gospels* [1980], Harmondsworth: Penguin, 1982.

Parke, Beverly N., 'Methods of Developing Creativity', in Swassing [1985], pp.376–401.

Parker, Rozsika and Griselda Pollock [1981], *Old Mistresses: Women, Art and Ideology*, London: Routledge, 1981.

— [1987], *Framing Feminism: Art and the Women's Movement 1970–85*, London; New York: Pandora, 1987.

Passow, A. Harry (ed.), *The Gifted and the Talented: Their Education and Development*, Yearbook for the National Society for the Study of Education, no. 78, pt.1., University of Chicago Press, 1979.

Pizan, Christine de, *The Book of the City of Ladies* [1405–], trans. Earl Jeffrey Richards [1982], Forward by Marina Warner, London: Picador, 1983.

Plato, *Phaedrus* [*c.* 370 BC], trans. R. Hackforth, Cambridge University Press, 1952.

Plimpton, George [1963] (ed.), *Writers at Work: The Paris Review Interviews*, Harmondsworth: Penguin, 2nd series, 1977.

— [1967], *Writers at Work: The Paris Review Interviews*, Harmondsworth: Penguin, 3rd series, 1977.

Pollock, Griselda [1982], *see* Parker, Rozsika.

— [1987], 'Feminism and Modernism', in Parker and Pollock [1987], pp. 79–122.

Poovey, Mary, *The Proper Lady and the Woman Writer: Ideology as Style in the Works of Mary Wollstonecraft, Mary Shelley, and Jane Austen* [1984], University of Chicago Press, p.b. ed., 1985.

Purcell, John, *A Treatise of Vapours, or, Hysterick Fits*, London: Newman, 1702.

176 R **Reich**, Nancy B., *Clara Schumann: The Artist and the Woman*, London: Gollancz, 1985.

Rendall, Jane, *The Origins of the Scottish Enlightenment, 1707–76*, London: Macmillan, 1978.

Ripa, Cesare, *Iconologia: or Moral Emblems* [1602; 1st ed. 1593]. Reprint of 1709 trans., printed with Michel de Marolles' *Tableaux du Temple des Muses* (1655), New York, London: Garland, 1976.

Robson, W.W., *A Prologue to English Literature*, London: Batsford, 1986.

Rothenberg, Albert and Hausman, Carl R. (eds.), *The Creativity Question*, Duke University Press, 1976.

Rothenstein, John, *Modern English Painters*, vol. iii, *Hennell to Hockney* [1952, with revisions 1976, 1984], London: Macdonald, 3rd. ed., 1984.

Rousseau, Jean-Jacques, *The Confessions* [1781], trans. J.M. Cohen, Harmondsworth: Penguin, 1953.

Rowley, William, *A Treatise on Female, Nervous, Hysterical, Hypochondriacal, Bilious, Convulsive Diseases; Apoplexy and Palsy; with Thoughts on Madness, Suicide etc.*, London: Nourse, 1788.

Russ, Joanna, *How to Suppress Women's Writings* [1983], London: The Women's Press, 1984.

S **Schopenhauer**, Arthur [1818; with supplements and revisions, 1844], *The World as Will and Idea*, trans. R.B. Haldane and J. Kemp, 3 vols., London: Routledge, 1883.

— [1851], 'On Genius' and 'On Women' from *Parerga and Paralipomena*, trans. in *The Essential Schopenhauer*, London: Allen and Unwin, 1962.

— [1970], *Essays and Aphorisms*, introduced and translated by R.J. Hollingdale, Harmondsworth: Penguin, 1970.

Schwenger, Peter, *Phallic Critiques: Masculinity and Twentieth-Century Literature*, London: Routledge, 1984.

Scott, Mary, *The Female Advocate: A Poem* [1774], University of California: The Augustan Reprint Society, no. 224, 1984.

Sears, Pauline Snedden, 'The Terman Genetic Studies of Genius, 1922–72', in Passow [1979], pp.75–96.

Shaftesbury, Anthony Ashley Cooper, Third Earl of, *Characteristics of Men, Manners, Opinions, Times* [1711], ed. John M. Robertson, Indianapolis: Bobbs-Merrill, 1964.

Shelley, Mary [1818], *Frankenstein; or, The Modern Prometheus*, containing P.B. Shelley's 1818 'Preface' and the author's 1831 'Introduction', ed. Maurice Hindle. Harmondsworth: Penguin, 1985.

— [1826], *The Last Man*, London: Hogarth Press, 1985.

Shelley, Percy Bysshe, 'Preface' to *Frankenstein* [1818], in Shelley, Mary [1818].

Showalter, Elaine, *The Female Malady: Women, Madness and English Culture, 1830–1980*, London: Virago, 1987.

Sichel, Edith [1910], *see* Coleridge, Mary E. [1910].

— [1918], *Letters, Verses and Other Writings*, ed. Emily Marion Ritchie, London: printed privately for friends, 1918.

The *Spectator* [1711–14], ed. Henry Morley, London: Routledge, n.d. c. 1876.

Spector, Jack J., *The Aesthetics of Freud: A Study in Psychoanalysis and Art*, London: Allen Lane, 1972.

Staël, Madame de (Anne Louise Germaine), *Corinne, or Italy* [1807], trans. Avriel H. Goldberger, Rutgers University Press, 1987.

Stevens, Wallace, 'The Figure of the Youth as Virile Poet' [1943], reprinted in his *The Necessary Angel: Essays on Reality and the Imagination*, New York: Alfred A. Knopf Inc., Vintage ed. 1951.

Stock, Brian, *Myth and Science in the Twelfth Century: A Study of Bernard Silvester*, Princeton University Press, 1972.

Storr, Anthony, *The Dynamics of Creation*, London: Secker and Warburg, 1972.

Sutherland , Gillian, *Ability, Merit and Measurement: Mental Testing and English Education 1880–1940*, Oxford University Press, 1984.

Swassing, Raymond H., *Teaching Gifted Children and Adolescents*, Columbus, Ohio; London: Charles E. Merrill, 1985.

T **Tatarkiewicz**, Wladyslaw, *A History of Six Ideas: An Essay in Aesthetics*, trans. C. Kasparek, The Hague; Boston; London: Nijhoff, 1980.

Taylor, Irving A., and Getzels, J.W. (eds.), *Perspectives in Creativity*, Chicago: Aldine Publishing, 1975.

Taylor, Lily Ross, *The Divinity of the Roman Emperor*, Middletown, Conn.: American Philological Association, 1931.

Tennyson, Alfred (Lord), *The Poems of Tennyson*, ed. Christopher Ricks, London: Longmans, 1969.

Tervarent, Guy de, *Attributs et Symboles dans l'Art Profane, 1450–1600: Dictionnaire d'un Langage Perdu*, Geneva: Droz, 1958.

Theweleit, Klaus, *Male Fantasies*, vol. i, *Women, Floods, Bodies, History* [1977], trans. Stephen Conway *et al.*, Cambridge: Polity Press, 1987.

Thomas, Karin, 'Hannah Höch – the "good girl who works hard": The Feminist Question-Mark' [1980], trans. in Catalogue: *Hannah Höch 1889–1978: Collages. (Exhibition organised by the Institute of Foreign Cultural Relations, Stuttgart)*, Stuttgart: Dr Cantz'sche Druckerei, 1985, pp.70–83.

Bibliography

Tissot, S.A., 'On the Diseases of Literary and Sedentary Persons' [Lausanne, 1766] and 'An Essay on Onanism, or A Treatise upon the disorders produced by Masturbation' [1760], trans. in *Three Essays*, Dublin: James Williams, 1772.

Todd, Janet, *Feminist Literary History: A Defence*, Cambridge: Polity Press, 1988.

Tomalin, Claire, *The Life and Death of Mary Wollstonecraft* [1974], Harmondsworth: Penguin, 1985.

Turkle, Sherry, *Psychoanalytic Politics: Freud's French Revolution* [1978], London: Deutsch, Burnett Books, 1979.

V Vasari, Giorgio, *The Lives of the Artists* [1550 and 1568], selection trans. George Bull, Harmondsworth: Penguin, 1965.

Veith, Ilza, *Hysteria: The History of a Disease*, University of Chicago Press, 1965.

W Webber, Jeannette L. and Grumman, Joan, *Woman as Writer*, Boston: Houghton Mifflin, 1978.

Weininger, Otto, *Sex and Character* [1903], trans. from 6th German ed., London: Heinemann; New York, Putnam, 1906.

Wellek, René, *A History of Modern Criticism*, vol. i, *The Later Eighteenth Century*, London: Cape, 1955.

Wetherbee, Winthrop, *The Cosmographia of Bernardus Silvestris*, trans. with Introduction and Notes, Columbia University Press, 1973.

White, Barbara Ehrlich, 'Renoir's Sensuous Women' [1972], in *Woman as Sex Object*, eds. Thomas B. Hess and Linda Nochlin, London: Allen Lane, 1973, pp.166–81.

Whitmore, Joanne Rand, *Giftedness, Conflict, and Underachievement*, Boston, Mass.; London: Allyn and Bacon, 1980.

Wilson, Colin [1956], *The Outsider*, London: Picador, 2nd ed., 1978.

— [1988], *The Misfits: A Study of Sexual Outsiders*, London: Grafton Books, 1988.

Winner, Ellen, *Invented Worlds: The Psychology of the Arts*, Harvard University Press, 1982.

Wiseman, Stephen (ed. and introd.), *Intelligence and Ability*, Harmondsworth: Penguin, 1967.

Wittkower, Rudolf and Margot, *Born under Saturn: The Character and Conduct of Artists*, London: Weidenfeld and Nicolson, 1963.

Wollstonecraft, Mary [1787], 'The Cave of Fancy', in vol. iv of *Posthumous Works of the Author of A Vindication of the Rights of Woman* [1798], reprinted as vol. ii, Clifton, N.J.: Augustus M. Kelley, 1972.

— [1788], *Mary*, reprinted with *The Wrongs of Woman: or, Maria. A Fragment*, Oxford University Press: The World's Classics ed., 1980.

— [1789], *The Female Reader: or Miscellaneous Pieces, in Prose and Verse . . . for the Improvement of Young Women*, by Mr Cresswick (pseudonym), London: Joseph Johnson, 1789.

— [1792], *A Vindication of the Rights of Woman*, printed with John Stuart Mill, *The Subjection of Women* [1869], London: Dent; New York, Dutton, Everyman ed., 1929.

— [1796], *A Short Residence in Sweden, Norway and Denmark*, printed with William Godwin, *Memoirs of the Author of 'The Rights of Woman'* [1798], Harmondsworth: Penguin, 1987.

— [1979], *Collected Letters of Mary Wollstonecraft*, ed. Ralph M. Wardle. Cornell University Press: 1979.

Women in Publishing, *Reviewing the Reviews: A Woman's Place on the Book Page*, London: Journeyman Press, 1987.

Woodcock, Bruce, *Male Mythologies, John Fowles and Masculinity*, Brighton: Harvester; New Jersey: Barnes and Noble, 1984.

Woolf, Virginia [1929], *A Room of One's Own*, New York: Harcourt Brace, 1929.

— [1931], 'Professions for Women', in Woolf [1979].

— [1979], *Women and Writing*, London: The Women's Press, 1979.

Wordsworth, William, Preface to 2nd ed. *Lyrical Ballads* [1800], in Edmund D. Jones [1916].

Y Young, Edward, 'Conjectures on Original Composition' [1759], in Edmund D. Jones [1947].

Index

181

Index